Theodor Fontane

# DELUSIONS, CONFUSIONS
## and
# THE POGGENPUHL FAMILY

# The German Library: Volume 47
### Volkmar Sander, General Editor

Theodor Fontane

# DELUSIONS, CONFUSIONS
and
# THE POGGENPUHL FAMILY

Edited by Peter Demetz

Foreword by J. P. Stern

Introduction by William L. Zwiebel

CONTINUUM · NEW YORK

PT
1863
.I6
E5
1989

The Continuum Publishing Company
370 Lexington Avenue, New York, NY 10017

The German Library
is published in cooperation with Deutsches Haus,
New York University.
This volume has been supported by a grant
from the funds of Stifterverband
for the Deutsche Wissenschaft.

Printed in the United States of America

*Library of Congress Cataloging-in-Publication Data*

Fontane, Theodor, 1819–1898.
[Irrungen, Wirrungen. English]
Delusions, confusions ; and, The Poggenpuhl family / Theodor
Fontane ; edited by Peter Demetz ; foreword by J.P. Stern ;
introduction by William L. Zwiebel.
p.    cm. — (The German library ; v. 47)
Translation of: Irrungen, Wirrungen and Die Poggenpuhls.
ISBN 0-8264-0325-5  —  ISBN 0-8264-0326-3 (pbk.)
I. Demetz, Peter, 1922–    . II. Fontane, Theodor, 1819–1898.
Poggenpuhls. English. 1989.  III. Title.  IV. Series.
PT1863.I6E5   1989
833′.8—dc20                                                89-7740
                                                              CIP

Acknowledgments will be found on page 283, which constitutes an extension of the copyright page.

# Contents

# Foreword

More than a century and a half before the politicians of Europe made their first effective moves toward a European community, the novelists of European realism were fashioning a community of themes and attitudes to the world. It would be absurd to claim that what these writers were intent on conveying was a single mode of experience cast in a single style. Yet there are family likenesses: one and the same family album contains the portraits of Sir Walter Scott, Tolstoy, and the early Thomas Mann, of George Sand, Jane Austen and George Eliot, Dickens and Balzac, Mazzini and Stendhal, Flaubert and Fontane, Eça de Queiròs, Pérez Galdós and Jan Neruda; and a uniquely rich time-space continuum stretches between nineteenth-century Moscow, Madrid, and Lisbon, between London, Edinburgh, Paris, Berlin, and Prague. Indeed, for the first time since the Middle Ages *Europe* has something like a single "literature" with recognizably similar cultural and spiritual concerns, and her two notorious outsiders, Great Britain and Russia, too, are seen for what they have always been: inseparable partners in Europe's spiritual and cultural heritage. The German contribution to this family album of realist novelists comes a little later than do the others, but the distinction it attains in the work of Theodor Fontane makes up for the delay.

The fact that "realism" eludes definition is something it shares with every term in our cultural vocabulary that is worth thinking about. But if this *ism* cannot be defined, it can certainly be described; and when we find that the portraits in the family album are composed of different parts of realism's overall inventory, that again is what we should expect from a terminology that has proved indispensable not only in literary criticism but outside literature too, in the sphere of morality and practical conduct.

Talking about "realistic" doctors and politicians in the same breath as about literary realists, Fontane himself was fully aware of the connection. If (in common parlance) "being realistic about something" means having an eye for the main chance, gauging correctly what is possible and what is not, and asserting the hunches of common sense against the will-o'-the-wisp of illusion and every kind of fanaticism—if *that* is what "being a realist" means, then no writer deserves that designation more fully than he. And if tolerance (hardly a typical Prussian quality), and especially tolerance ironically coded, is recognized as the moral attitude which, more than any other, clips the wings of any fanatical conviction, then again realism is its most appropriate literary mode, and Fontane among its most accomplished practitioners.

What are the attributes of Fontane's literary realism? To start with its most obvious aspect: he writes as one who is unconcerned with "models of reality," and trusts the world to be one and of a piece (as we all do, day in, day out), to be unblemished by ontological cracks. About the philosophical questions of Being, of Appearance, and Reality, he remains incurious. He trusts language, written and spoken, to communicate a stable meaning from one character to another, from author or narrator to reader and, unlike the fictional tradition of *Don Quixote,* his novels and novellas never play with epistemological dubieties. His narrators are usually omniscient, though they do occasionally engage in easy and familiar discourse with the reader. Sometimes Fontane adds an extra dimension to his fiction by confessing, briefly and without fuss, that it is indeed *fiction,* but a radical challenge to the novelist's métier, such as we find in *Tristram Shandy* and its offspring among the *nouveaux romanciers,* does not belong to the literary conventions he follows.

Chief among these conventions is the narrator's practice of keeping his language identical with the conversational language of his characters. There is, in this sober, easy and accurate prose, not even a Dickensian or Zoalesque opening on the language experiments of modernism, not a whiff of Jamesian finicking or finesse. Fontane has a perfect ear for the tone and lexical range of every character he portrays: no German novelist, from his day to ours, has as fine a grasp of the nuances of dialogue that can take its antagonistic partners to the very limits of a shared civility. There is irony and mild satire in some of his conversation scenes, but his reproduction of conversational clichés is not merely superbly accurate, it is also quite uncensorious: when (as occasionally happens) such clichés are shown to hide true emotions, these emotions may or may not be base. His characters resort to contingent, occasionally tedious patter, but as often as not the reasons for that are morally neutral, "symbolical" of nothing beyond the meaning of the conversation itself, indicating simply a lack of verbal fastidiousness.

What he—in true realist fashion—challenges are not the verbal but the moral conventions of the society he shows; which, at his most successful, is the Prussian and German society he knew. He does what all realists do: with the utmost confidence in its reliability he creates a world in which life depends on, and takes place in, institutions: family and clan, regiment or civil service, municipality or castle, royal court or market gardening, *Ferienkolonie* (holiday camp) or genteel convent, aristocratic dinner table, *haut bourgeois* restaurant or grocer's shop. These institutions—the nonverbal equivalents of conversational clichés—are never apologized for. They may be very far from perfect, their tyranny is clearly shown for the soulless, destructive thing it is, but social institutions are the only thing that stands between us and another kind of tyranny, that of arbitrariness, and Fontane acknowledges them as such. For social outsiders with a literary passion the imagination provides the only domicile: since Fontane's imagination is entirely at home in the society of his time, from the lowest middle class to the Junkers and the courtly entourage of Berlin, he knows intimately what penalties have to be paid by those who transgress its conventions. His sympathy with the men and women who challenge the social institutions in which they live their incomplete, often stunted lives is deep and generous and almost unlimited, but it is always the kind of sympathy that can see the other side of the social argument, too.

Radicalism of any kind, whether political or aesthetic, social or religious, is never the mode of his own writing, though it is often an object of his criticism, and that criticism is by no means always ironical. He does not believe in belief. On the contrary: he often shows how the intensity with which a belief is held corrupts its content, how fanaticism destroys its own good cause. Such an attitude may seem old-fashioned to us, in fact it is only out of tune with our own attitudinizing; oddly enough, it was Nietzsche who took the trouble to formulate it.

Fontane has often been criticized for his conservatism, and it is certainly true that the few working-class characters he portrays tend not only to aspire to the ethos of the middle classes, but to practice that ethos rather more forthrightly than do their social betters. Yet his conservatism never leads him to portray the social order either as providential or God-given, and any claim made for it as the "natural" order of things is invariably refuted—not explicitly, but by the drift of narrative sympathies. Unlike the writers of the German Romantic tradition and their heirs in our time, he portrays solitude always as a breakdown of sociability, and never as a value. In all, the realist prescription works with remarkable subtlety: the violations of moral, social, and occasionally aesthetic conventions and taboos are used to test the strength of characters and determine their fate, yet such violations also yield the negative contours of a given society—nowhere more clearly than in the portraits of Fontane's heroines. Of them it can be said, as a critic remarked apropos of *Anna Karenina,* that "their predicament [is presented] as the test of the moral and human worth of any given state of society."

Much could be said, and indeed has been said, about the *things* that make up Fontane's realism: about the meals, the furniture, the *bürgerlich* (bourgeois) apartments and aristocratic rack-rent castles, the dresses and uniforms that fill his novels, the old silver and brand-new carriages, Turkish carpets and Meissen china, the French wines and North Sea lobsters, dogs and horses, coffins and bathing machines, genre pictures, and marble statues of simpering nudes. . . . While all this bric-a-brac has an inimitable charm of its own, not all of it is informed by "deeper" or symbolical meanings. But the charm is something enjoyed by his characters and readers alike: the "things" are there to offer moments of assurance, arrests of oncoming catastrophes, reminders of times irretrievable, imperfect consolations for happiness beyond recall.

A last attribute of Fontane's realism relates to the weightiness of the represented world, its recalcitrancy to ideas and ideals, its resistance to dreams. Though this world is Christian in a formal sense only, it is a repository of values, most of them Christian: but these values are as nothing unless they are tested in this everyday, secular world. The novelist's debunking of philosophical speculation, and indeed of any abstruse reasoning, is not only a formal device in the service of *vraisemblance,* but it is also thematized as a way of underlining the solidity, resistance, and inertia of his chosen milieu. The values that are tested—faithfulness, compassion, honesty, and love—have a hard time of it; so has wisdom, which is prone to slither into complaisance; and nowhere is the weightiness of experience more clearly manifest than in the quest for happiness, in which many of his characters are engaged and which few ever attain. And decency—the one value men like Fontane sought to preserve from the debris of the Christian faith—has the hardest time of all.

Critics of German literature are prone to evaluate its products according to their "prophetic" qualities. This is a regrettable tendency, if only because it encourages bad reading habits—a reading not for what is there, but for what is to come. Happily, Fontane was an indifferent "prophet" of what the new century would bring. He didn't think it would be up to much, decline (he felt) was in the air, no abstruse "historical laws" were needed to show that change was bound to come—but it would not necessarily be change for the worse. This lack of proleptic wisdom is, I think, a price one gladly pays for the insights which his narrative genius, his accuracy of observation, and his tolerance of outlook provide for us—sympathetic insights into the human condition in a time and place somewhat different from our own, yet illuminating precisely because it is both similar and different.

J. P. STERN

# Introduction

As time intervenes between a certain era and place, and its immediacy recedes, it not infrequently falls to a single individual or artist to assume representative stature for that particular epoch and locale. In the case of imperial Germany in its initial period, Bismarck has certainly towered as the dominant political figure, but as the chronicler of everyday life at that time, especially of Berlin, the capital city of the empire, distinction has fallen in great measure to Theodor Fontane. With grace, urbanity, consummate sophistication and finesse, Fontane portrayed his Prussian countrymen, while at the same time turning a penetrating light upon their flaws and foibles. Through the prism of his novels present-day readers are able to survey a generation and social landscape now utterly remote from our own, a society which seems in some respects even more distant than that of the epoch of the French Revolution or the Napoleonic Wars, although it ended less than a century ago.

As his name suggests, Theodor Fontane's forebears were not originally German but had been of French origin, part of the wave of Huguenots emigrating to Prussia after the revocation of the Edict of Nantes in 1685. Yet, as Fontane himself pointed out, his family's immediate association with France and French culture existed more in the imagination of his parents than in reality. Both his mother's and father's forebears had lived in Prussia for over a century and had become thoroughly acculturated. The author's paternal grandfather had in fact been a drawing teacher to the children of King Frederick William II and later, private secretary to Queen Louise of Prussia, while his father, Louis Henri Fontane, had served in the Prussian army during the Napoleonic Wars. In 1819 he married Emilie Labray. Despite similar cultural backgrounds, however, Fontane's parents were not well suited to each other, and chose to live apart in later life. Yet, as is so often the case, the diverse qualities of personality that over the years undermined their marriage somehow combined harmoniously in their son and echo in his stories. The gracious urbanity and sophistication of Fontane's often frivolous father and the earnest practicality of his mother seem to have found expression, not only in the characteristics of the fictional personages who people his tales, but in the attitude of humor, skepticism, and ambiguity which infuses them in general.

Theodor Fontane was born not far from Berlin in the small Prussian town of Neuruppin on December 30, 1819. After elementary schooling in Neuruppin and Swinemünde, to which the family moved for a time, the boy was sent in 1833 to a vocational school in Berlin. Following in his father's footsteps, he began an apprenticeship in pharmacology there three years later. It became evident, however, that the young man's real interests lay elsewhere, for poetic attempts soon competed with his duties at the apothecary's bench, along with a growing disaffectation towards the repressive policies of the Prussian crown. Fontane's role in Berlin during the Revolution of 1848 is today nearly impossible to judge. In memoirs written nearly half a century later for a public having little sympathy for revolutionary fervor, he tended to trivialize his activities, describing himself on the barricades armed with a prop rifle confiscated from the warehouse of a local theater, into which in the excitement of the moment, he had poured too much powder—a mistake difficult to believe, however, considering he had several years earlier completed a required year of military service as an officer candidate in a Berlin regiment. Shortly after his failure on the barricades, he was elected as neighborhood elector for the Berlin National Assembly, in itself no small accomplishment for a budding poet and suggesting that his revolutionary involvement may have been substantially greater than he later wished to recollect. As the forces of reaction once more asserted themselves in Prussia, however, his belief in the liberal cause began to waver; although never fully abandoning essentially democratic views, the failure of the liberal movement to take advantage of its gains in a practical fashion after 1848 led Fontane to become increasingly disillusioned with its unfocused idealism and rhetoric and his political career came quietly to an end. Moreover, after more than a decade of vocational uncertainty and dissatisfaction, he abandoned pharmacology in 1849 at the age of thirty with the intent of devoting himself entirely to writing.

Unable to find a secure position that would fully employ his talents, however, and eager to establish a firm footing on which to marry his fiancée, Emilie Rouanet-Kummer, Fontane gravitated to journalism, accepting posts wherever he could find them, despite the fact that most were with Prussian government press organs whose reactionary policies were inherently at odds with his essentially liberal views. At the same time he took part in Berlin's literary scene through membership in the society *Tunnel über der Spree,* making a modest name for himself through the composition of lyrical poems and ballads, often based on historical events or characters, occasionally drawn from Scottish or English history. Fontane's interest in England, dating from his days as a pharmacist's assistant when he had prepared compounds for export, had been given further impetus during his military service, when he was given leave for a two-week visit to Britain in the company of a friend who had offered to pay all expenses. His knowledge of English and fascination with British life and culture served to gain him a post as representative of the Prussian press office in London some years later, a position involving translations from English newspapers, writing for Prussian journals concerning Anglo-Prussian affairs, as well as reporting back to Berlin on the interpretation of Prussian policy in the English press. In such a capacity he visited England several times, staying for over four years in the late 1850s. Apart from his official duties, Fontane traveled extensively throughout Britain. An important outcome of his English sojourns was a number of works describing the English and Scottish countryside and culture for German readers, published in 1860 under the title, *Aus England: Jenseits des Tweed, (Impressions from England: Beyond the Tweed).* Without question, Fontane's protracted stay in England, as well as his thorough study of English character and literature, contributed significantly to the objectivity and skepticism with which he was later able to view and portray his own countrymen and their social and cultural values.

When Fontane returned to Prussia in 1859, he reluctantly accepted a post for English affairs with the conservative daily, *Die Kreuzzeitung,* where he remained for a decade before transferring to the more liberal *Vossische Zeitung.* Besides newspaper duties, in keeping with his previous efforts devoted to the British Isles, he now occupied himself with an extensive study of the lore and legend of his homeland, ultimately published in four volumes from 1862 to 1882 as *Wanderungen durch die Mark Brandenburg (Excursions through the Brandenburg March).* During Prussia's wars with Denmark, Austria, and France, Fontane was at the front as a war correspondent, later collecting his recollections in volumes devoted to each of these conflicts. Covering the Franco-Prussian War in 1870, he was captured by the French, imprisoned for several months and nearly executed as a spy. Appeals from various quarters, including the American ambassador and one by Bismarck himself, ultimately saved his life. In 1871 these events too found their way into the book *Kriegsgefangen (Prisoner of War).*

His long journalistic career notwithstanding, it was not until 1878, nearly his sixtieth year, that Fontane published his first novel, a historical work, *Vor dem Sturm (Before the Storm),* dealing with events in Prussia during the Napoleonic Wars. With this book the floodgates of his narrative genius opened, and for the next two decades he continued to produce novels or long stories along with several volumes of memoirs. At the same time he began to make a name for himself as one of the most forward-looking theater critics in Berlin, fostering the works of new dramatists such as Ibsen and Hauptmann. Except for a period of ill health in his seventies, Fontane's productivity continued unabated until his death on September 20, 1898, at a time when he was still correcting proofs of what is considered by some the finest of his novels, *Der Stechlin (Lake Stechlin).*

*Delusions, Confusions,** whose German title *Irrungen, Wirrungen* suggests the vicissitudes and complications that often beset even the most orderly life, established its author as one of the

---

*The translation of the German title stems from the book, *The Berlin Novels of Theodor Fontane* by Henry Garland, New York, Oxford University Press, 1980.

significant voices of the age. Although its moral connotations have long since become innocuous, the work produced something of a scandal when initially serialized in the *Vossische Zeitung* during the summer of 1887. By portraying the ossifying and repressive conventions of the Prussian nobility in unvarnished fashion, along with a straightforward presentation of what was euphemistically described as a "mésalliance," Fontane managed to alienate a substantial number of readers from both the aristocracy and the middle classes, leading many to drop subscriptions to the newspaper. Nevertheless, the work enjoyed sufficient regard, especially among critics of the younger generation, to lead to publication in book form within a year of its initial appearance.

On one level the novel may be regarded as a study in the moral ambiguities inherent in late nineteenth-century Berlin society. The story is simple, almost operettalike in its latent sentimentality. An engaging young member of the Prussian aristocracy has taken up with a charming and unsophisticated girl from the lower class. Both recognize from the outset that marriage is out of the question because of the rigid caste system that prevails in their world. Despite genuine love, they accept the precepts of the social order, notwithstanding the realization that in doing so they will lose the absolute happiness promised by their love. Thus they part, each to the role that society has assigned them. But Fontane does not end the story here, showing instead the everyday reality to which each succumbs and the cost of their efforts to come to terms with the lives they have been compelled to choose.

That such relationships, whereby members of the nobility carried on liaisons with women of the lower classes for what was perceived as their mutual gain, were a commonplace in Berlin society, is made evident in several parallel episodes throughout the story. Such affairs—provided discretion was maintained, of course—were normally tolerated by much of European "polite society" at the time. Fontane's willingness to deal openly with such matters, even to the point of creating a situation in which the lovers unmistakably spend the night together, lifted the cover of tacit acceptance and offended not only the nobility but also the middle class with its rigid moral code and sanctimonious sense of propriety. A clear indication of the response the novel elicited from many members of the middle class, and one that betrayed unmistakably their general sympathies for the nobility rather than those less fortunately situated on the social scale, is the comment attributed to a family member of the publishers of the very newspaper in which the work appeared, who indignantly asked, "Will this abominable whore's story be done with soon?"

For his part, Fontane found the attitude of many of his contemporaries plainly hypocritical. In a letter to his son written soon after the work's initial appearance, he commented, "You are right that the whole world, outwardly at least, will not think as leniently with regard to Lene as do I, but as readily as I concede this, I am equally certain that in this open acknowledgment of a certain stance regarding these matters lies a tiny bit of the value and significance of the book. We are up to our ears in all sorts of conventional lies and ought to be ashamed of the hypocrisy we commit and the dishonest games we are playing. Is there really . . . any sort of cultivated and truly honest individual who gets morally indignant over the free love affair of some little seamstress? I don't know any, and to that I add, thank God that I don't."

Yet *Delusions, Confusions* is more than an exposé of the moral duplicity sometimes found in Prussian society. It is also a portrait of an epoch, offering finely drawn sketches of life in Berlin during the era immediately following the establishment of the German Empire through Bismarck's remarkably successful political pragmatism. The country forged in 1871 by unifying most of the German-speaking states under Prussian dominance, with the king of Prussia assuming the title of German Emperor, despite apparent success and quick political ascent, inherently represented an anachronism. Although essentially an industrial nation whose source of strength lay in the bourgeoisie and working classes, in its social structure the empire nevertheless sought to continue the hegemony of a long since decadent feudal order by restricting political and military power primarily to the nobility. Yet, in its early days, the period, known in German as the *Gründerzeit,* The Epoch of the Founders, an air of satisfaction and well-being generally prevailed, fostered by rapid industrial and economic expansion. Of course, even at this time some of the flaws that were ultimately to lead to the downfall of the Second Reich were already becoming apparent. Yet the extraordinary successes of its military might were for a time sufficient to mask their emergence; in place of social discontent, militarism and national pride generally succeeded in checking or at least redirecting for a generation the desire of large segments of the populace for equality and individual freedom. As a result of the German nation's rapid rise to the status of a major European power under Prussian leadership, a significant portion of its society, especially in Prussia, became increasingly chauvinistic. Berlin in the late decades of the nineteenth century, as the novel makes plain, had become more or less an armed camp, in which uniformed officers and enlisted men, firing ranges, marching battalions, and parading troops all contributed to the local color.

In documenting Prussian life in the era of Bismarck, *Delusions, Confusions* offers a rich but by no means complimentary picture of the life-style and values of the lower ranks of the nobility and junior officer class. To an extent greater than their English counterparts, Prussian aristocrats were a snobbish, highly inbred, anti-intellectual, clannish, and militaristic caste. The army was considered the only fitting occupation for young noblemen and relatives and comrades formed the building blocks of security and stepping stones to advancement within its ranks. An arrogant sense of class consciousness dominated their thinking even though some of them, including the protagonist of the novel, Baron Botho von Rienäcker, clearly recognized that the standards and conventions of the Prussian aristocracy were by no means all-embracing and eternal precepts of human existence. Nevertheless, horses, military exercises, gambling, elegant living, and witty banter, along with sexual dalliances with women of all classes, are shown to be the chief elements that filled the lives of most of these young officers. Even the thinking of their women was shaped by military values, as the chatter of Botho's wife and her friends, not to mention that of the ladies of more questionable virtue, patently reveals.

At the same time conflicts within the Prussian nobility are also suggested. Many older members of the titled class were by no means convinced that the creation of the empire at the expense of the loss of the independence of the kingdom of Prussia necessarily represented a positive step. For a variety of reasons, Bismarck had many enemies, even among the aristocracy. Thus Botho's old Junker uncle, whose apoplectic brusqueness contributes one of the work's humorous moments, indulges in a tirade against the popular hero and his high-handed treatment of the nobility, while also suggesting that the spirit of his own generation, going back to the Wars of Liberation, in its uncompromising devotion to duty and honor, had been perhaps more in keeping with that of the founders of Prussia's might and national character than the duplicity and cunning of the Iron Chancellor.

It is not merely the nobility but the lower classes as well, which are drawn with expansive detail. There can be no question that Fontane, although endowing each with characteristic limitations as individuals, had a sympathetic eye for the cabdrivers, servants, and small shopkeepers of Berlin and its surroundings. Hard work, honesty, a regard for the simple pleasures, and solicitude for one another are some of the virtues which mark them throughout his novels, finding their fullest expression, of course, in the sensitive yet down-to-earth heroine, Lene. Even the secondary characters—Lene's mother, the indomitable Frau Dörr, and the stingy old gardener Dörr—are shaped with an appreciative if sometimes condescending pen. In a similar fashion, the openhearted simplicity and honesty of the citizenry of Berlin, including their indefatigable love for outings and penchant for caustically witty remarks, contribute to the local color and charm of the work.

A host of other touches completes the picture of the newly created empire: the hostility of other Germans to Prussian dominance is briefly mentioned; at the other end of the scale, undertones of Prussian superiority, anti-Semitism, and class arrogance lie just beneath the surface of the comments made by Botho's wife regarding the rich Jewish woman she meets on her travels, as well as in the exaggeratedly mocking rendering she makes of her traveling companion's broad Viennese accent Related to this is, of course, the reaction of the traditional nobility as the nation's economic base shifted from an agricultural and feudal order to an industrial one, and an aristocracy of capital gradually displaced the landed gentry as the dominant cultural force. This change is, in fact, one of the chief motivating forces in the novel, for it is the declining fortunes of Botho's family that function as the immediate motive for his decision to renounce Lene, although it is his sense of class responsibility that is determinant in the long run.

The immutability of the structure of Prussian society and its apparent justness seem beyond question to most of the characters in the novel, and not only among the nobility. The same class consciousness found in the upper strata of Prussian society may also be discovered in those far lower on the social scale, who seem to bask in the reflected glow of distinction which they perceive in their traditional first families. Botho's gardener's daughter regards the handsome and aristocratic young officer with admiring eyes; a coachman knows him on sight; the Dörr's are obsequiously honored to share his company, despite its compromising moral implications. Lene too accepts the ultimate outcome of her relationship as an inevitability, never for a moment questioning the validity of a system that in the end blights her one opportunity for unblemished happiness and fulfillment because of an accident of birth. A brief allusion is made to Lene's mysterious origins in the novel and Frau Dörr suggests that she may even be a fairy princess, an idea to which Frau Nimptsch makes no response. Apart from implying that Lene's background is itself dubious and is very likely a consequence of the system, the episode adds another dimension to the work: Lene is indeed no fairy princess and her story no fairy tale. Moreover, in its social and moral connotations, the entire novel makes it clear that Germany in the declining decades of the nineteenth century was no magic kingdom.

A subtle interweaving of parallel situations is incorporated into the finely wrought structure of the work, essentially a two-part rising and falling action, reaching its high point in the brief idyll of the lovers' outing to Hankel's Depot. Leitmotivs skillfully varied contribute a taut unity: the word *bound,* for instance, is used in a variety of meanings, ranging from Botho's engagement to Käthe, through his love for Lene as well as his sense of obligation to tradition and caste. *Wreaths* occur with differing and ironical connotations at various points in the novel, and Botho's ride to the cemetery to place one on Frau Nimptsch's grave is almost Wagnerian in its interplay of allusions to former events and remarks.

By the same token, contrasts, both in character and in situation, abound. Especially striking is that between the two chief women in the novel, Lene and Käthe. Although she is unquestionably from the lower class, Lene's genuine feelings and unfeigned openness are able to captivate Botho precisely because she is utterly without pretense and cultivated sophistication. She is also shown to have no illusions, moral or otherwise, about her forbidden liaison; her relationship with Botho represents an opportunity to enjoy a brief fling at happiness that her social position would otherwise deny her. For this reason she is willing to accept the consequences of her actions inasmuch as they affect her alone, while accepting the exigencies of her time and place as completely as her aristocratic lover. Käthe, shallow, superficial, and empty-headed, yet not without a certain cynical insight into her function as a socialite—his doll Botho calls her—is nevertheless not really unlikable. She is content to play the role which life has assigned her—not a difficult one, to be sure—provided the great questions of human existence, which briefly trouble her, are kept safely from her door.

It is important to note that although it is class difference that keeps Botho and Lene from realizing happiness together, Fontane's novel is not explicitly a document of revolution or social protest. At its core without doubt lies a deeply felt skepticism towards the existing order, but no direct call for change. The code of values to which Botho is "bound," which sublimates personal fulfillment to the preservation of an outmoded social order under the guise of *Ordnung,* is held up for close scrutiny, and the reader is left to draw his own conclusions.

Despite its local and temporal dimensions, the work transcends time and place. Part of its timelessness lies in the implied message that there are no easy or unequivocal solutions to life's problems and that contrary to popular romantic assumptions, true love, regardless of its ardor, does not always conquer all. Similarly, the question that has for so long been central to German political thought, represented in Fontane's own life by his two chief cultural poles, England and Prussia—the rights of the individual when measured against those of the collective—is left unresolved. Nevertheless, it is not difficult to perceive where the author's deepest sympathies lie. Even though Botho attempts to convince himself that Bismarck's Berlin and the place he occupies in it represents "probably the best of all possible worlds," and although he reaffirms his decision to submit to the contingencies of his existence by ratifying the obligations of his caste during a conversation with a fellow officer, the ambiguous last words of the novel seem to suggest that he is by no means certain that the choice he has made is really the best one.

Von Rienäcker's decision is made as a member of the upper level of Prussian aristocracy for whom a life-style of wealth and indolence were still well within the realm of possibility. For the lower order of nobility, however, whose claim to eminence lay not in high position or extensive landholdings but instead in centuries of military service, even the establishment of the empire on a semifeudal basis could not avert what economic and military developments had made inevitable. In the short novel *Die Poggenpuhls* (*The Poggenpuhl Family*, 1895), Fontane gave the plight of such a clan half-comical, half-melancholy treatment. It is not a Prussian sense of duty that drives the action in this portrayal of a down-at-the-heels and impoverished officer's widow and her children, but a desperate attempt to keep up appearances and survive in an era in which historical forces have rendered them irrelevant. *The Poggenpuhl Family* takes place a full decade after the action of *Delusions, Confusions*. Although the actual chronology does not quite coincide with historical reality, it is 1888; the Second Empire is now almost two decades old, Bismarck's skillful foreign policy has created stability in Europe, and the heroic days of the petty Prussian military nobility have long since yielded in Germany to unrestrained commercialism and the growing power of both the bourgeois and lower classes. The observant reader will note that cracks have begun to appear in the tranquil social unity found in *Delusions, Confusions*. The Poggenpuhls have not only been compelled to sell off their country properties in order to make a tenuous last stand in the capital, but their very existence is dependent upon the generosity of a former trooper in the fallen major's battalion. While a sense of respect mixed with patriotic reverence for his blue-blooded tenants still inspires their landlord, the house porter, whose very name suggests the proletarian dwarfs of Wagner's *Das Rheingold,* grumbles about the preferential treatment accorded the "aristocratic gang." The precariousness of the Poggenpuhl's social predicament is unmistakably symbolized by Fontane not only in the physical surroundings in which they find themselves—a sparsely furnished and threadbare Berlin apartment with hereditary cemetery monuments visible from the front window and a gaudy advertisement for candy at the rear—but also in the trappings that they have been able to preserve of their past. Especially striking is the heroic-comical painting of the "most significant moment in the life of the family," the portrayal of an ancestor, half-undressed and barefoot, in an unsuccessful defense of a cemetery during a minor engagement of the Seven Years War, which falls from the wall at every attempt to dust it.

Each of the chief figures in the novel deals with the situation in a different fashion: Therese, the eldest daughter, is portrayed as snobbishly pretentious, grimly defending her sense of caste superiority as a last bulwark of family position, alternating between malice and pomposity in her vain attempt to keep the already tattered Poggenpuhl banner aloft. At the same time, her propensity for a rocking chair subtly assigns her to a foregone era. Manon, the youngest and thus least restrained by fossilized traditions, cheerfully ignores blue-blooded snobbery while conniving at somehow revivifying the fortunes of the Poggenpuhls by the most expedient method at hand, marrying off her brother to a rich Jewish family. Yet she knows full well that in the newly evolving social order those she has in mind no longer consider her kind as an acceptable rung on their way up the social ladder. Sophie, the middle daughter, whom the author ironically characterizes as possessing something normally not distinguishing the Poggenpuhls, practical talents, which in other times would have been disdained by a family of their superior social aspirations as beneath them, is nevertheless best prepared for the life that awaits her and her sisters with historical inevitability: that of an old-maid governess or ladies' companion.

Both of the young men of the family are officers. Wendelin, symbolically absent throughout the novel, will unquestionably be the most successful of the Poggenpuhls. Entirely devoted to the pursuit of his army career, he ignores his family's name and traditions. Tactics, strategy, firing-pin rifles, military scholarship, and the esteem of influential superiors are the determinants of his workaday existence; the cannon-fodder heroics of another era mean nothing to him. Despite his familial background he, more than his siblings, has come to terms with the realities of his age; clever, sober-minded, and ambitious, Wendelin has thrown off the outmoded sense of caste superiority and is well on the way to becoming something Fontane inherently disdained, a member of the calculating and materialistic bourgeoisie. Yet precisely in the shadowy character of Wendelin we are able to recognize the author's ability to endow even peripheral figures with individual touches that raise them far above the merely one-dimensional; in his readiness to see his brother's presence at their mother's birthday celebration he exhibits a selflessness totally out of keeping with what might otherwise be expected of him.

His brother Leo, the darling of the family, is almost a stereotype of the amiably dashing and irresponsible aristocratic officer, with two duels behind and mounting debts before him. His conversation with his mother serves to present the profound contrast between the middle-class ethos of reward on the basis of merit and the traditional optimism of those to the manor born, who hold fast to a belief that fate will somehow single them out in keeping with their preferred social position. It is a pathetic comment on the family's hopes that they even jokingly envision Leo regaining their lost glory in a battle of a sort long since rendered obsolete by the Wendelins and Moltkes of their era.

Yet Leo is not without moments of insight into his situation; behind his flippant comments that he believes "atheism and all the other disagreeable phenomena of our times . . . on the way out," and that "the poor aristocracy will go to the very top," lies a bitter sense of hopelessness. The Poggenpuhls, he tells his sister, are nothing but a one-place number in a society which recognizes only four and five-place figures. Similarly, he characterizes the loss of refinement and grandeur in the world in which the family must make its way as he explains that new names, associated with money-grubbing, commerce, and manufactured goods, have completely displaced those of the first families, artists and heroes of a previous and more genteel era. Like Manon, he too toys with the idea of tying his coattails to the fortunes of the rising Jewish bankers, although his facetious remarks on the matter no longer have the humorous ring they might once have had.

Through the figure of Leo and even more so in that of General Eberhard von Poggenpuhl, Fontane captures some of the characteristics which he admired most in the old Prussian aristocracy. Less desperate than his nephew, the older man exhibits qualities of self-reliance, candid straightforwardness, and geniality that enable him to take the world entirely as it is. He too is able to recognize that the glory days of the old Prussian families survive now only in presentations such as Ernst von Wildenbruch's patriotic drama *Die Quitzows*. At the same time, he is loath to see the old values mocked in a stage parody, even though his sense of the inevitable demise of the old order enables him to find the apostasy of a former comrade of Leo's, who has given up the officer's sword for the actor's makeup kit, amusing rather than scandalous. Perceiving that all of them have been reduced to historical extras in what has become for the lower Prussian aristocracy essentially the last act of a bad play, he is resigned and fatalistic about the outcome. Nevertheless, a true aristocrat, he is not given to troubling himself with bourgeois matters such as money; he presents his nephew with a hundred-mark note to pay a modest bill for an evening's entertainment and refuses to consider the change. Indeed, his truly cavalier attitude in financial affairs leads both Therese and Leo—in whom want has inspired a far more realistic attitude—to believe him niggardly in what they consider his duty toward their upkeep. Yet he is in fact not much better off than they and is supported by the holdings of his wife's first husband's family, so that in fact he has little to give to his poor relations. His death and funeral represent a final ceremonial act for the Poggenpuhls, for with him they lay to rest the last representative of the family's greater glory and its aristocratic independence.

Yet Fontane clearly suggests that with the passing of the old order, the aristocratic sense of gentility has not been rendered extinct. Indeed, if nobility of soul is the criterion, it is not so much the surviving younger Poggenpuhls, but the Frau Majorin and Frau Generalin, both of whom are from nonaristocratic families, who display greatness of spirit, the former in her understanding of the loyalty of the servant woman Friederike and of the forces that have shaped her own life, and the latter in her generosity when at the end she employs her own resources to keep her late husband's poor relations afloat. Although Therese's last remark would indicate that she has finally begun to recognize her mother's worth as a human being, and that there are other standards in life than the degree of one's lineage, nevertheless whether any of the younger generation, including Therese, have seriously deepened as individuals is doubtful. Their future, as the novel comes to an end, is a bleak one and it is not by chance that it is the up-and-coming Bartensteins who in effect have the last word.

General agreement prevails that *Delusions, Confusions* represents Fontane at his finest. Regarding *The Poggenpuhl Family,* however, critical unanimity has been lacking. More than one critic has felt the work to be a substantial indication of the author's declining powers. Others, in contrast, have viewed it as a splendid forerunner of Fontane's final effort, *Der Stechlin,* a novel also devoted to the passing of the old nobility and its values.

Very little happens in both novels. For *The Poggenpuhl Family* the lack of external action itself may be regarded as symbolic, for just as nothing substantial occurs to the family except the general's death and the bequest that will keep the wolf from the door for another day, their future is seen to be one of decline and ultimate extinction. Whether or not one agrees with such a view, it is evident that the focus of the work is not action, but character, revealed primarily as so often in Fontane through dialogue. The paucity of plot notwithstanding, the English critic S. S. Prawer has maintained that *The Poggenpuhl Family* in particular "could figure as exhibit A in any attempt to establish Fontane's claim to be regarded as the greatest master of the conversation piece of the European novel." Fontane, responding to the remarks of a reviewer, freely conceded the work's lack of action: "The book is not a novel and has no content, the 'how' has to do the work of the 'what'—nothing more pleasing can be said to me." Acknowledging the naturalists' tendency to dwell only on the lurid side of life, he replied to another review with the hope that others "would be found, who discover it to be well-crafted in its rambling style, as well as realistic, despite the absence of Jack the Ripper."

*The Poggenpuhl Family* enjoyed relative success upon its initial serialization in the illustrated magazine *Vom Fels zum Meer (From the Cliffs to the Sea)* in the fall of 1895 and the spring of the following year. In the summer of 1896 the book was published by the house owned by Fontane's son, who gradually acquired the rights to all of his father's novels. Nevertheless, to the author's dismay, *The Poggenpuhl Family* had been initially rejected by the conservative weekly *Daheim (At Home)* in which Fontane had published his first novel *Before the Storm* some sixteen years earlier. Despite the author's indignant complaint that the novel really represented "a glorification of the nobility," which, he had to concede, "will take it in a stupid and petty manner so as not to sense the flattery inherent in it," it is not difficult to understand why. The picture of the petty Prussian nobility rendered essentially powerless, sometimes comical and frequently cynical, no matter how close to the truth it might have been, was scarcely the sort of vision the aristocracy of the Second Empire cared to harbor of itself.

Theodor Fontane was amazingly clear-eyed in his recognition of the faults as well as the strengths of the Prussian aristocracy. Notwithstanding his own middle-class origins, he always had a soft spot for the Prussian Junker class. "Whoever would want to do away with the nobility, would eradicate the last bit of poetry from the world," he wrote in 1860. Nevertheless by the 1890s he recognized that the aristocracy had become a fossilized institution, which, by unremittingly pursuing its own self-interests, essentially represented a detriment to the ultimate democratization and consolidation of the recently established German nation. "Our nobility must be passed over," he wrote in 1894, several years after completing *The Poggenpuhl Family*, "we can visit them like the Egyptian Museum and bow down before Rhamses and Amenophis, but to govern the country for their sake, in the illusion that *this nobility is the country,* therein lies our misfortune, and as long as this condition persists it is not possible to give even the slightest thought to the continued development of German power or German esteem beyond our borders." In *The Poggenpuhl Family* Fontane created a small monument to the passing of a class; *Der Stechlin,* his last novel, was to be a larger one.

Despite his recognition that the aristocracy had outlived itself, Fontane's own Prussian faith in what had been the rightness of their world and the poetry he saw in it was too deeply ingrained for him to completely abandon it. Yet there is something touching in the old Fontane's expectation that the nobility would admire him for his work; they did not. At the author's seventy-fifth birthday celebration, congratulatory messages from the Prussian aristocracy were notably absent, so much so that he was moved to compose a highly ironical poetic comment. What Fontane perhaps never fully wished to recognize was that it was precisely the class he most disdained, the German bourgeoisie of the Second Empire, hungry for status, open to everything new and suggestive of "culture," which most appreciated his novels. In their pages, whether the author cared to admit it or not, in addition to presenting a style of life the nouveau riche and social climbers eagerly sought to emulate, he had indirectly pictured their ultimate triumph.

Fontane could not know either that the traits of character he admired so much in the Prussian nobility would nevertheless live on long after the aristocracy itself was no longer a determinant social force. Indeed, in the most positive sense, it was to no small degree Prussian gallantry against overwhelming odds, devotion to duty, honor, and loyalty to nation that inspired the events of July 20, 1944, when Colonel Klaus von Stauffenberg, representing a resistance movement with a strong core in the conservative officer class, placed a bomb in Hitler's bunker, which, although wounding him, failed to kill the Nazi dictator. By the same token, however, it was also the more dubious aspects of Junker character, unthinking loyalty, rigid authoritarianism, and unremitting militarism, which in the final analysis led to the extirpation of the old Germany, including the Prussia Theodor Fontane loved so well.

WILLIAM L. ZWIEBEL

# DELUSIONS,
# CONFUSIONS

# 1

In the middle of the 1870s, just at the crossing of the Kurfürsten-
damm and the Kurfürstenstraße, diagonally across from the
"Zoological," could still be found a large vegetable garden, stretching a distance away from the street. Despite compactness and seclusion, its small three-windowed dwelling, located some hundred
paces back, could nevertheless still be made out quite easily from the
passing street.[1] Anything else still belonging to the entire spread of
the truck garden, in fact what was really its main part, was hidden
by this very dwelling as if by a stage drop. Only a small wooden
turret, painted red and green, with its clock face half-broken away—
of the clock itself naught can be said—led one to suspect that behind
this stage drop something else might indeed be hidden, a suspicion
likely to find confirmation in the flock of pigeons which from time
to time circled the tower, and even more so, in the occasional
barking of a dog. Where this dog actually might be hiding defied
observation, even though the house door, located to the far left and
open from dawn to dusk, permitted a view of a small corner of the
courtyard. By and large nothing seemed purposefully intended to
hide anything, yet anyone who at the beginning of our tale were to
come by that way would have had to content himself with the sight
of the three-windowed cottage and a few fruit trees standing in the
garden before it.

It was the week after Pentecost, that time of long days whose
blinding light at times never seemed to want to come to an end. But
today the sun already stood behind the Wilmersdorf church tower

and in place of the rays which it had sent down throughout the day, evening shadows lay already in the garden. Its fairy-tale stillness was exceeded only by that of the little house itself, rented and occupied by Frau Nimptsch and her foster daughter, Lene. Frau Nimptsch herself sat as usual at the large, low hearth of her front room which took up the entire forepart of the house. Squatting and bent forward, she watched a rusty old teapot, whose top rattled continuously back and forth even though steam poured from its spout. At the same time the old woman held both hands towards the fire, so lost in thoughts and fantasies that she did not hear that the entry door was suddenly opened and a robust woman rather noisily entered. Not until the latter cleared her throat and called her friend and neighbor—none other than our aforementioned Frau Nimptsch—by name, did the former turn around and in a friendly manner, yet also with a touch of roguishness, reply, "Well now, that's real nice, Frau Dörr, that you've come by again. And from the 'castle' too. For a castle it is and a castle it'll always be. After all, it's even got a tower. Now you just sit down. . . . I just saw that dear husband of yours going off. And of course, that's as it should be. Tonight's his bowling night."

The person just greeted so amicably as Frau Dörr was not merely robust but above all an extremely imposing looking woman, who along with an air of kindness and dependability, at the same time gave off one of rather limited intelligence. Frau Nimptsch obviously did not seem to find any problem in that, however, and merely repeated, "Yes indeed, his bowling night. But what I really meant to say, *liebe* Frau Dörr, that old hat of Dörr's, it really can't go on like that anymore. Why it's worn just about as shiny as an old fox's hide, and it's really a disgrace. You just ought to take it away from him and slip another one in its place. Maybe he won't even notice it. . . . And now, you just pull up a chair, Frau Dörr, or better yet, just take that footstool over there. Lene, well, you know how it is, she's gone off 'n left me here all alone again."

"He was here, I s'pose."

"Course, he was here. And the two of them have gone off part way towards Wilmersdorf. Along the path. Nobody goes that way. But any minute now they can be back."

"Well then, I guess, I really better go."

"Oh no, oh no, Frau Dörr. He certainly won't be staying. And even if he does, you know, he's not like that."

"I know, I know. How do things really stand then?"

"How should they stand? It looks to me like she thinks there might be a chance, even if she doesn't want to admit it to herself, and she's getting ideas."

"Oh, goodness sakes," said Frau Dörr, drawing up a somewhat higher stool instead of the proffered footrest. "Goodness sakes, that's bad. Whenever they start getting ideas, that's when things start to get bad. That's just as sure as 'Amen' in church when the prayer's over. You know, *liebe* Frau Nimptsch, it was just like that with me too, only there wasn't no getting ideas. And that's just why it turned out completely different."

Frau Nimptsch apparently did not quite comprehend what Frau Dörr was getting at for which reason the latter went on, "And because I never got no fancy ideas in my head, everything worked out just fine and dandy, and now I got Dörr. Sure, ain't much, I know, but it's something, and respectable enough so that a body can hold up their head anywhere. And that's why I made sure we got married in church and not just at the Civil Court. There's still always talk, when it's just at the court."[2] Frau Nimptsch nodded.

Frau Dörr repeated herself, however, "Yes sir, in church. St. Matthias's, with Pastor Büchseln himself. But what I was really going to say, you see, Frau Nimptsch, I was probably a bit bigger and more attractive than Lene. And even if I wasn't prettier—and you really can't know about them things, tastes really do differ a lot, you know. Well, anyway, I was sort of more filled out, and that's just what lots of them like. Yes sir, that's for sure. But even if I was, so to speak, a bit more solid, and a bit heftier and had a certain somethin', and well I sure enough had somethin', even so, I was always nothin' fancy, just down-to-earth, you might say. And as far as he goes, that count of mine with his fifty years on him, well, he was always real down-to-earth too, just always a little tipsy, and wanting to fool around. If I told him once, I told him a hundred times, nope, nope, Count, that's out. I won't put up with that kind of stuff. . . . And it's always the old ones that are like that. And I can sure tell you, Frau Nimptsch, you just can't imagine somethin' like that. It was awful. And these days, when I see that baron of Lene's, why I'm downright ashamed even now, when I think how mine was. And when you look at Lene herself. Good Lord, an angel she ain't, that's for sure, but she's neat'n hard working and can do just about anything. And she's for orderliness'n respectability too. And you know, *liebe* Frau Nimptsch, that's just the sad part. The kind that fool around all over, one day here, next day there, well, they're the ones that never get hurt. Always land on all fours, just like a cat. But such a sweet thing like her, who takes it all real serious, and does it all for love, yes indeed, *that's* bad. . . . Or maybe it ain't so bad after all; you really did just take her in, and she ain't really your own flesh'n blood. Why maybe she's a princess or somethin'."

Frau Nimptsch shook her head at this assumption and seemed on the verge of making a reply. But Frau Dörr had already gotten up, and looking down the garden walkway, cried, "Oh Lord, here they come. And him, only in regular clothes, jacket and pants that match. But you can make out the difference anyway! And now he's whisperin' somethin' in her ear, and she's laughin' to herself. But she's started blushing all over. . . . And now he's goin'. And now, why really, I think he's comin' back again. Nope, nope, he's just waving one more time, and she's blowin' him a kiss. . . . Yes, sir, that's the thing for me . . . nope, mine was never like that."

Frau Dörr went on talking until Lene came in and greeted both of them.

# 2

Next morning the sun, already quite high, shone upon the courtyard of the Dörr garden, illuminating there a world of structures, among which was also the "castle" of which Frau Nimptsch had spoken with a touch of teasing and mockery. Ah, yes, this "castle"! In the twilight with its relatively large outline it might really have been possible to take it for something of the sort, but standing there in the harsh bright light of day one could see only too clearly that the whole thing, painted right up to the roof with Gothic windows, was nothing but a miserable wooden box, into the two gabled walls of which a framework of timbered beams with a filling of loam and straw had been set, so that these two relatively sturdy insertions more or less corresponded to a pair of gabled rooms. Everything else was nothing but a stone-floored space from which a tangle of ladders ascended, first to an attic and from there up to the tower which served as a pigeon loft.

Formerly, in a pre-Dörrean era, the whole enormous wooden box had served as a mere storage shed for bean poles and watering cans, perhaps even as a potato cellar. For an indeterminate number of years, however, since the entire complex had been purchased by its present owner, the real living quarters had been rented to Frau Nimptsch and the box with its Gothic ornamentation, following the addition of the previously mentioned attic rooms, had been arranged as living quarters for Dörr, who in those days was a widower.

It was a highly primitive arrangement which was in no wise altered by his remarriage shortly thereafter. In the summer the

7

nearly windowless storage shed with its stone flooring and cool atmosphere was not at all an unpleasant place to live. In the wintertime, however, Dörr and his wife, along with a somewhat weakminded twenty-year-old son from his first marriage, would simply have frozen to death were it not for the two large greenhouses located on the other side of the yard. It was in these that all three Dörrs spent the time from November to March exclusively.

But even during the warmer and better part of the year, provided they were not seeking asylum from the sun, the life of the family took place for the most part before and within the greenhouses because everything lay comfortably at hand. Here stood the shelves and racks on which the flowers taken from the greenhouses each morning might absorb the fresh air. Here too was the stable with its cow and goat and the hut for the cart dog. It was from here as well that the twin hotbeds, with a narrow walkway between them, extended nearly fifty paces to the large vegetable garden that lay further back.

Things did not look particularly orderly in the latter. For one thing because Dörr had no sense of orderliness, but especially because he had so great a passion for chickens, that he permitted his favorites to peck about wherever they chose, regardless of the damage they caused. Of course, said damage was never very great, since, with the exception of the asparagus beds, anything of a finer sort was completely absent from the truck garden. Dörr considered that which was the most commonplace to be at the same time the most advantageous. For this reason he cultivated marjoram and other sausage herbs, but especially, leeks. Regarding the latter, he was of the opinion that a real Berliner had need of only three things: a *Berliner Weiße*, a *Gilka*, and leeks.[1] "Nobody," he maintained regularly, "ever came up short with leeks."

He was, all in all, a genuine character, possessing views uniquely his own and exhibiting firm indifference to what anybody said about him. In keeping with this was his second marriage, a love match, in which the idea of a special beauty on the part of his wife was a contributing factor. Her former relationship to the count, instead of being harmful, had had exactly the opposite effect, tipping the scales, in fact, by providing overwhelming proof of her irresistibility. If in that case one might justifiably speak of overrating a person, it certainly could not be with regard to the personage of Dörr. Nature, as far as appearances go, had done exceedingly little for him. Emaciated, of middle stature, and with but five strands of grey hair on his head, he would have been a wholly commonplace figure, were it not for a brown mole between the corner of his eye and left temple, which gave him something out of the ordinary. For this reason too his wife was by no means wrong when in her typically uninhibited way she was in the habit of saying, "He's a bit wrinkled, for sure, but when you look at him from the left, there's something about him like a *Bosdorfer.*"[2]

That really hit the nail on the head. He would have been easily recognizable by this description, which was good enough for a wanted poster, if day in, day out he did not wear a linen cap with a large visor pulled down deeply over his face, hiding not only the common qualities of his physiognomy, but the special ones as well.

And so, cap and visor drawn over his face, he stood again today, the day after the conversation between Frau Dörr and Frau Nimptsch, in front of a flower rack which leaned against the foremost greenhouse, putting aside various wallflower and geranium pots which were to go to market tomorrow. The whole lot of them had not been grown in their pots but merely transplanted, and thus, laughing in advance about those "madams" who tomorrow would haggle the price down by the traditional five pfennige and still be the losers in the end, he looked them over with a special sense of satisfaction and joy. That counted as one of his greatest pleasures and was actually the chief intellectual activity in which he indulged. "That little bit of grumbling. . . . If only I could get to hear that some time."

Just as he was saying this to himself, he heard the yelping of a small mutt intermingled with the desperate crowing of a rooster. Sure enough, if he wasn't mistaken it was *his* rooster, his favorite, the one with silver plumage. Glancing over toward the garden, he indeed did see a group of chickens scurrying about. The rooster, however, had flown up the pear tree from which point he ceaselessly cried for help against the yapping dog below.

"Thunder and damnation," cried Dörr enraged, "that's Boll-mann's little . . . got through the fence again. Oh, if only the devil'd . . ." Quickly putting down the geranium he had just been inspecting, he rushed to the doghouse, grasped the snap and released the cart dog. The latter immediately bolted madly toward the garden. Before he could reach the pear tree, however, "Bollmann's little . . ." had showed his heels, disappearing under the fence and into the open—the yellow cart dog after him in huge bounds. But the hole in the fence, just large enough for a small terrier, blocked his way and forced him to give up the pursuit.

Things went no better for Dörr himself, who in the meantime had approached with a rake and exchanged glances with his dog. "Well, Sultan, nothing this time." Hearing that, Sultan trotted back to his quarters slowly and with embarrassment, as if he had perceived a mild reproach. Dörr, however, watched the terrier rushing down a furrow in the field across the way and after a few minutes remarked, "Devil take me, if I don't get me an air gun at Mehle's or someplace. Then I'll quietly blow that little beast right away. And nary a chicken or a rooster'll crow about it. Leastways not mine."

As for the tranquility Dörr had in mind for him, the rooster in question seemed for the time being not in the least concerned. Instead, he continued to employ his voice in a highly expansive fashion, while at the same time raising his silvered neck proudly, as if he wished to demonstrate to the hens that his flight into the pear tree had been nothing but a well-planned strategic measure or a mere whim.

Dörr, however, remarked, "Gad, what a rooster. An' he always thinks he's such a wonder. An' yet his courage ain't nothin' special at all." And with that he tramped back to his flower stand.

# 3

The entire affair had been observed by Frau Dörr, who was just then cutting asparagus. She looked on only casually, however, for a similar event took place every third day. She went on with her work and did not give up searching, until after inspecting the asparagus beds closely, no more "white tips" could be found. Only then did she hang the basket on her arm, place the harvesting knife in it, and shooing a few errant chicks before her as she went, slowly make her way on down the middle path of the garden and from there to the courtyard, in the direction of the flower racks, where Dörr had once more taken up his preparations for market.

"Well, Suselchen," he remarked to his better half, "there you are. Did you see that? Bollmann's mutt was here again. . . . Listen, he's going to get what's coming to him. I'll make a roast out of him. He must have a bit of fat on him. And Sultan can have the gristle. . . . And y'know, Susel, dog fat . . ." It looked as if he were about to expand on a method of treating gout for which of late he had shown a preference, but at that very instant, catching sight of the asparagus basket on his spouse's arm, he interrupted himself, and said, "Well now, let's see what you've got there. Anything worthwhile?"

"Wouldn't say that," said Frau Dörr, holding the scarcely half-filled basket towards him. Shaking his head, he let its contents slip through his fingers. It was mostly thin stalks with a good deal of broken pieces among them.

"Listen, Susel, the truth is, you just ain't got eyes for asparagus."

"Oh, I got them all right. But I just can't do no magic."

11

"Well, we won't argue about it, Susel. It won't make no more. But you could starve to death on that."

"Oh, nobody's about to do that. Cut out that constant complaining, Dörr. There's plenty there. And whether they get picked today or tomorrow don't make no difference. A good shower, like we had before Pentecost, and you'll see. And there'll be rain for sure. The water barrel smells like it again already, and the big garden spider's crawled into the corner. But you're lookin' for somethin' every day; you can't expect that."

Dörr laughed. "Well, tie it all up real good. And them little ones too. Then you can take a little off, if you have to."

"Oh, don't talk like that," interrupted Frau Dörr, constantly irked by his miserliness. Today again, however, she gave a tug at his earlobe—something he always took as an indication of affection— and went off towards the "castle," where she sought to make herself comfortable in the stone-tiled entry in order to tie up the asparagus bundles. No sooner had she pulled the stool, which always stood ready for use, over to the threshold, than across the way she heard a rear window of the three-windowed cottage occupied by Frau Nimptsch being opened with a vigorous push and immediately hooked in place. In the same instant she saw Lene who, clad in a jacket with a broad lavender pattern above her closely woven skirt and with a little bonnet covering her ash blond hair, greeted her amicably from across the way.

Frau Dörr returned her greeting with equal friendliness and then said, "Windows always open, that's the way, Lene. And it's getting hot already. There'll be some rain today, for sure."

"I know. And mother has a headache already from all this heat, and so I'd rather iron here in the back room. Anyway, its nicer here. Up front you don't see a soul."

"You're right there," responded Frau Dörr. "Well then, I'll just push over here a little closer to the window. Things always go better when you're talking like this."

"Oh, that's really nice of you, Frau Dörr. But there's a blazing sun right here at the window."

"Oh, that don't hurt nothin', Lene. I'll just go get my market umbrella. It's just an old thing, nothing but a bunch of patches, but it still does the job."

And before five minutes had passed, good old Frau Dörr had pulled her stool up to the window and sat under her umbrella as comfortably and confidently as if she had been on the Gendarmenmarkt.[1] And inside, Lene had set up her ironing board on two chairs placed right up to the window, and now stood so close that both could easily reach out and touch hands. All the while, the iron went busily back and forth. Frau Dörr too was busy at selecting and tying, and when now and then she looked up from her work into the window, she could see the small oven meant to provide new fillers for the iron glowing at the back of the room.

"You might get me a plate, Lene, a plate or maybe a platter." And when Lene immediately brought what Frau Dörr requested, the older woman poured into it the broken pieces of asparagus which she had kept in her apron while sorting. "There, Lene, that'll make a nice asparagus soup. And these are just as good as the others. That business that it's always supposed to be the tips is just a lot of nonsense. Same with cauliflower. Only the buds. Always the buds. Nothing but pure imagination. The stalk's really the best. That's where the strength lies. And the strength's always the main thing."

"Lord, you're always so kind, Frau Dörr. But what will your husband say?"

"Him? Good grief, Lene, what he says don't make no difference at all. It's always just talk, that's all. He always wants me to tie up the little'ns as if they was real stalks, but I don't go for cheatin' like that, even if the broken pieces and the little ones do taste just as good as the rest. People ought to get what they pay for. And it really gets me mad that somebody who's got so much of it right there for the pickin' is such 'n old miser. But that's the way they all are, them gardners, pinchn' 'n squeezn', and never getting enough."

"I know," laughed Lene, "he is stingy, and a little odd. But he really is a good husband though."

"Sure, Lene honey, so far, so good, and even that stinginess of his wouldn't be so bad. It's always better than him squandering everything. If only he weren't so lovey-dovey. You wouldn't believe it, but he's always right there hangin' around. But just you take a look at him. He really is a sorry lookin' sight, and all of fifty-six in the bargain, maybe even a year more. He tells lies too, y'know, whenever it suits him. And there's nothin' can be done about it, not a single thing. I keep telling him about this one gettin' a stroke and that one gettin' one, and I show him them that go limpin' around with a droopin' mouth, but he just laughs and don't believe it. But it'll happen anyways. Yes sir, Lene honey, I believe it for sure, it'll happen just like that. And maybe soon. Oh sure, he's made everything over to me, so I don't say no more about it. The way you make your bed, is the way you're gonna' lie in it. But what are we doing, talking about strokes and Dörr and how he ain't got nothin' but bowlegs. Good Lord, Lene honey, there's other folks who're just as straight as a fir tree. Right, Lene?"

Lene became even more flushed than she usually was and remarked, "The iron's gotten cold." Stepping back from the ironing board, she went over to the little oven and shook out the iron filler into the coals in order to insert a new one. It was all the work of but an instant. With an iron hook she skillfully proceeded to slide the glowing new filler into the flatiron, and only then noticed that Frau Dörr still waited for her reply. Just to make certain, however, the good woman asked the question anew, immediately adding, "Is he coming today?"

"Yes, at least he promised to."

"Well now tell me, Lene," continued Frau Dörr. "How did it really ever come about? Mother Nimptsch never says a thing, and when she does, it's always well, well, a little of this'n a little of that. And always just the half of it, and all mixed up in the bargain. Now you tell me. Is it really true that it happened in Stralau?"

"Yes, Frau Dörr, in Stralau it was. On Easter Monday, but it was already as warm as if it were Pentecost. And because Lina Gansauge felt like going rowing, we got a boat and Rudolph, who I'm sure you know, he's Lina's brother, decided to take the rudder."

"Good God, Rudolph. Why Rudolph's still just a boy."

"Exactly. But he said he knew all about it and just kept on saying, 'Girls, all ya gotta do is sit still, yer rockin' the boat too much'—he's got such a Berlin way of talking, you know. But we never had any intention of doing anything like that, because we saw right off that he wasn't much when it came to steering. Finally though, we forgot about it and just let ourselves drift along and teased anybody that came by and splashed water on us. And in one of the boats that was going in the same direction as us, there were some real fine gentlemen who kept on waving at us. And for fun we waved back. Lina even waved at them with her handkerchief and pretended she knew the gentlemen, which wasn't so at all. She just wanted to show off, because she's still so young. And while we were still laughing and joking like that and just sort of fooling with the rudder, all of a sudden we saw the steamer from Treptow coming toward us.

"You can imagine, Frau Dörr, we were scared to death and shouted at Rudolph to steer us away. But that boy was just plain scared stiff and only began steering, so that we just kept on going around in circles. And we started screaming and would have been run over for sure, if right at that instant the two gentlemen in that second boat hadn't felt sorry for us. They were next to us with a few pulls of their oars and while the one towed us over quickly with a boat hook and pulled us fast to their own boat, the other one rowed all of us out of the way. But even so one time it seemed as if the big waves from the steamer's wake were going to capsize us. The captain actually shook his finger at us—I saw him even though I was so frightened—but even that passed, and only a minute later we made it to Stralau and the two gentlemen, to whom we owed our being saved, jumped up on the bank and held out their hands to us and helped us climb out just like real cavaliers.

"And so there we stood then on the landing dock at Tübbecke's and were embarrassed something awful. Lina cried terribly to herself and only Rudolph, who ain't nothing but a stubborn and boastful kid and always has something against soldiers anyway, well, he just kept looking down real stubbornly as if he wanted to say, 'Nothing but a lot of foolishness. I could have rowed you out too.'"

"Oh sure, that's just the way he is, the loudmouthed brat. I know him all right. But them two fine gentlemen. That's really the main thing. . . ."

"Well, first they took care of us and then they stayed at the next table and kept on looking over at us. And around seven, when it was starting to get dark and we were getting ready to go home, one of them came over and asked if he and his comrade might not offer their services and accompany us. And I just laughed right out and said, they'd saved our lives and you certainly couldn't refuse somebody who'd saved your life. And I also told them that they ought to think it over again, because we lived just about at the other end of the world, and it really would be a trip. And he answered real obligingly, that was all the better. In the meantime the other one had come over too. . . . Oh, Frau Dörr, maybe it wasn't the right thing just to have spoken out so boldly and be so open like that, but I liked one of them. And I've never been one to be coy or prissy. I just can't do something like that. And so we walked the whole way, first along the Spree and then along the canal."

"And Rudolph?"

"He walked along behind as if he didn't belong with us at all. But he saw everything and kept his eye on us too. And that was the right thing too. After all, Lina's only just turned eighteen and she's still just a sweet, innocent thing."

"Think so?"

"Oh sure, Frau Dörr. You just have to look at her. You can see something like that right off."

"Yeah, mostly, I suppose. But now'n again, you can't neither. So then they brought you home?"

"Yes, Frau Dörr."

"And afterwards?"

"Yes, afterwards. Well, you know how it turned out afterwards. He came by next day and inquired. And since then he's come lots of times and it always makes me happy when he does. God, it does make a person happy when something like that happens to you. It's often so lonely way out here. And of course you know, Frau Dörr, Mother doesn't have anything against it. She always says, 'Child, it don't hurt anything. Before you know it, you're old.' "

"Yes indeed, yes indeed," responded Frau Dörr, "I've heard Mother Nimptsch say the likes of that before. And absolutely right she is too. I mean, whatever way you want to take it. The way it is in the catechism is always really better, really best of all, so to speak. You can sure believe me on that. But I know perfectly well, that it don't always work out like that. There's some that don't even want to have it that way. And if somebody don't want it that way, well then, they just don't, and it has to work out the other way. And most of the time it does too. Main thing is that a person's honest and respectable and keeps his word. And naturally, whatever comes afterwards, well, you just have to put up with it and can't wonder how come. And when somebody knows all that and really takes it to heart, well then, it ain't so bad. The only real bad thing's gettin' ideas."

"Oh, dear Frau Dörr," laughed Lene. "Whatever are you thinking? Ideas! I'm not getting any ideas at all. If I love somebody, I just love him. And that's enough for me. And I don't want nothing else from him, nothing, not a single thing. Just that my heart beats like it does and that I count the hours until he comes and can't wait until he comes again—that's what makes me happy. That's enough for me."

"Yes sir," smiled Frau Dörr to herself, "that's the right way, that's how it ought to be. But is it really true, Lene, that his name is Botho? Nobody can really have a name like that. Why that ain't no Christian name at all."

"Oh but it is, Frau Dörr," responded Lene, who was on the point of proving further to Frau Dörr that such names really do exist. Before she could go on, however, Sultan began barking, and at the same instant one could clearly hear from the entry of the house that someone had come in. Sure enough, the postman appeared and brought two orders for Dörr and a letter for Lene.

"Good Lord, Hahnke," cried Frau Dörr to the latter, who stood in the doorway covered in great pearls of sweat. "Just look at the way you're dripping there. Really that hot already? And only nine-thirty. Well, one thing sure is clear, being a postman certainly ain't no pleasure."

And the dear old soul wanted to go off and get a glass of fresh milk, but Hahnke gratefully refused. "Got no time, Frau Dörr. Another time." And off he went.

In the meantime Lene had opened her letter.

"Well, what does he say?"

"He's not coming today, but he'll be here tomorrow. Oh, it's such a long time until tomorrow. It's a good thing that I have my work. The more work I have to do, the better. And I'll come over to the garden this afternoon and help you with digging. But make sure Dörr isn't there."

"Oh, heaven forbid!"

After that they parted, and Lene went to the front room to bring her mother the plate of asparagus she had gotten from Frau Dörr.

# 4

And now it had come, the next evening, for which Baron Botho had announced himself. Lene walked back and forth in the front garden. Inside, in the large front room, Frau Nimptsch sat as usual at the hearth, around which again today the entire Dörr family had grouped itself. With large wooden needles Frau Dörr was knitting a blue wool jacket destined for her husband. As yet it had not acquired its right shape so that it lay in her lap like a large sheepskin. Next to her, his legs comfortably crossed, Dörr puffed on a clay pipe, while his son sat in the grandfather's chair close to the window, leaning his red head on its arm. Up at cock's crow every morning, he had dozed off from weariness once again this evening. Scarcely anyone spoke and nothing was to be heard but the clicking of the wooden needles and the gnawing of the squirrel, which now and then emerged from its little sentry box cage and peeped about curiously. Only the fire in the hearth and the reflection of the evening twilight provided any light.

Frau Dörr sat in such a way that she could see down the garden walk, and the twilight notwithstanding, recognize whoever might come along the hedge.

"Ah, here he comes," she said. "Now then Dörr, you just put out that pipe of yours. You're at it like a chimney again, smokin' and puffin' the whole day. And that awful gunpowder of yours ain't to everybody's taste."

Dörr paid little heed to such remarks and before his wife could say more or repeat one of her old saws, the baron himself entered.

He was visibly tipsy, having just come in fact from partaking of a wine punch which had been the object of a bet at his club. Extending his hand to Frau Nimptsch, he said, "Hello there, old girl, in good shape, I hope. Ah, Frau Dörr, and Herr Dörr too, my old friend and benefactor. Now tell me, Dörr, what have you got to say about this weather? Ordered up just for you, and for me as well. Those meadows of mine at home, the ones that are under water four out of every five years and never yield anything but buttercups, can certainly use weather like this. And Lene can use it too, so that she gets outside more. Or else she'll be getting too pale for me."

While he was speaking, Lene pulled over a wooden chair next to her mother, for she knew that this was Baron Botho's favorite place. Frau Dörr, however, firm in the conviction that a baron should have the place of honor, had in the meantime leapt up, and with her blue sheepskin dragging continuously behind her, set in on her stepson: "Ain't you gonna' get up? Naw, just like I say. Where there's nothin' inside, nothin's gonna' come out either." Half-asleep and with a silly look, the poor lad jumped out of the chair and was ready to give it up. The baron, however, refused to hear of it. "For Heaven's sake, dear Frau Dörr, let the poor boy be. I'd really rather sit on a stool, like my old friend Dörr here."

As he spoke, he pushed the wooden chair which Lene continued to hold ready, next to the old woman and, as he sat down, said, "Here, right next to Frau Nimptsch. That's the best place of all. I don't know of another hearth that I'd rather look on. Always a fire, always nice and warm. Yes indeed, old girl, this is the place for me."

"Oh my Lord," said the old woman. "The place for you. Next to n'old washerwoman."

"Certainly, why not? Every class has its honor. Washerwomen too. Why do you know, old girl, that there was once a famous poet, right here in Berlin, who wrote a poem about his old washerwoman?"[1]

"Can that be possible?"

"Sure it's possible. It's even certain. And do you know what he said at the end? Why he said he'd like to live and die just like that old washerwoman. Yes sir, that's exactly what he said."

"Can that be possible?" simpered the old woman to herself anew.

"And do you know, old girl, just so we don't forget to mention that either, he was absolutely right, and I say the exact same thing.

Oh sure, go ahead and laugh to yourself. But you just take a look around here. How do you live? Like the Good Lord in Paradise itself! For one thing you've got this house and this hearth and then you've got the garden and Frau Dörr. And to top it off you've got Lene. Am I right? But where the devil is she?"

He would have gone on, but in the same instant Lene reappeared with a coffee tray on which stood a carafe with water along with apple wine, for which, because he ascribed to it a miraculous healing power, the baron had an otherwise incomprehensible preference. "Oh Lene, how you spoil me. But you mustn't present it to me so ceremoniously. Why it's as if I were at the club. You've got to give it to me from your very own hand. It tastes best that way. Now give me your little paw, so that I can pet it. No, no, the left one, that one comes from the heart. Now just sit right down there between Herr and Frau Dörr, then I've got you right across from me and I can look at you all the time. I've been looking forward to this hour all day."

Lene laughed.

"You don't believe that I was? Oh, but I can prove it to you, Lene. I've brought something for you from that fancy high-society affair we had yesterday. And when you have something you've brought for somebody, that means you're looking forward to the persons who're getting it. Am I right, Dörr, old boy?"

Dörr smiled. Frau Dörr, however, remarked, "Good Lord, him. Him and presents. All he ever thinks about is grabbin' money'n pinchin' pennies. Them gardeners are all like that. But I really am dying to see what the Herr Baron has brought."

"Well then, I won't keep you waiting, or else our dear old Frau Dörr will start thinking that it's a golden slipper or something else like that from a fairy tale. It's nothing but this."

As he spoke, he handed Lene a paper bag from which, if looks were not deceiving, the fringed crepe paper of party snappers peeked out.

And in fact, that's exactly what they were, party snappers. The bag was passed around from one to the other.

"But now we've got to pull them, Lene. Hold tight and eyes closed."

Frau Dörr was delighted when there was a sharp bang and even more when Lene's index finger began to bleed. "That don't hurt none, Lene. I know all about things like that. Why that's like when the bride pricks her finger. I knew one once who got so carried away with it that she just kept on stickin' herself and suckin' at it 'n' suckin' at it like crazy."

Lene blushed. Frau Dörr, however, took no note of that and went on, "Now read the verse, Herr Baron."

And the latter read:

> Selflessness when consumed in love,
> Is joy to God and the angels above.

"Oh Lord," said Frau Dörr, folding her hands. "Why that's just like it came out of a hymn book. Them things always so pious?"

"Oh, heaven forbid," said Botho, "Not always. Come on now, Frau Dörr, my dear, let's try again and see what we get."

And he pulled another one and read:

> When Cupid's dart its deed's done well,
> It opens the portals of heaven and hell.

"Well now, Frau Dörr, what do you say to that? That sounds a bit different, doesn't it?"

"I'll say," replied Frau Dörr, "it sounds different. But somehow it don't quite please me. . . . When I pull on a party snapper. . . ."

"Well?"

"Then I don't want nothin' about hell. I don't even want to hear that there is somethin' like that."

"Neither do I," laughed Lene. "Frau Dörr is absolutely right. She's always right. But it is true, that when you read verses like that, you've got something to start with. I mean to start the conversation with. Starting is always the hardest part, just like with letters, and I really can't imagine how anybody can just start a conversation right off like that with so many strange ladies. After all, all of you people really don't know every other one of you."

"Oh, my darling Lene," said Botho, "that's not as hard as you think. As a matter of fact it's really very easy. Why, if you want, I'll act out a dinner conversation for you right now."

Frau Dörr and Frau Nimptsch expressed their pleasure at the idea. Lene too nodded approvingly.

"Well then," continued Botho, "just pretend that you were a little countess and I've just brought you in to dinner and we've sat down, and now we're up to the first spoon of soup."

"Good, good. But now?"

"And now I say, 'If I'm not wrong my dear Countess, I saw you yesterday at the flower show, you and her ladyship, your Frau Mama. And by no means surprising, at that. This weather is just too enticing every day. Why, a person could even consider it just the right thing for traveling. Do you have any plans, for the summer I mean, my dear Countess?' And now you answer, that unfortunately nothing is quite firm yet, because your papa, the Count, is absolutely set on the Bavarian Alps, but that your heart's desire is really Saxon Switzerland with the Königstein and the Bastei."[2]

"It really is too," laughed Lene.

"Well, you see, there's a lucky coincidence. And so then I go on: 'Yes, indeed, my dear Countess, our tastes certainly do agree there. I prefer Saxon Switzerland to any other part of the entire world too, including the real Switzerland. Why, you can't always revel in the grandeur of nature, or clamber around always out of breath. Ah, but Saxon Switzerland! Heavenly! Ideal! One's got Dresden; why you're there in just a quarter or half hour at the most, I can see paintings, theater, the *Großer Garten,* the *Zwinger,* the *Grünes Gewölbe.*[3] And don't forget to have them show you the pitcher with the foolish virgins and especially the cherry pit with the whole *Our Father* inscribed on it. The whole thing's visible only with a magnifying glass.' "

"And that's the way you talk?"

"Just like that, my sweet. And when I'm through with my neighbor on my left, Countess Lene, I just turn to my neighbor on my right, Frau Baroness Dörr. . . ."

Frau Dörr slapped her knee with such delight that there was a loud clap.

"And now for Frau Baroness Dörr. And what do I talk about? Well then, let's say mushrooms."

"Oh my Lord, mushrooms. About mushrooms. Oh, Herr Baron, you really can't do that."

"Oh, why not? Why can't we do that, dear old Frau Dörr? Why that's a very serious and instructive topic and for some it has a greater significance than you think. I visited a friend in Poland one time, an old regimental comrade of mine from the war. He lived in a big castle, red, with two big turrets, and so awfully old that they just don't come like that any more. And the very last room was his living room. He wasn't married, you know, because he hated women."

"Is that possible?"

"And all over the place were these rotten floorboards that had fallen through, and wherever a few floorboards were missing, there was a mushroom bed, and I had to pass all of those mushrooms till I finally got to his room."

"Is that possible," Frau Dörr said again, then adding, "Mushrooms. But you can't talk about mushrooms all the time."

"No, not all the time. But lots of times, or at least some of the time. And really, it doesn't make even the slightest difference, what you talk about. If it's not mushrooms, its champignons and if it's not the red Polish castle, why then it's Tegel Castle or Saatwinkel or Valentinswerder. Or Italy, or Paris, or the *Stadtbahn* or whether the Panke ought to be filled in. It's all the same, really. And you can say something about every one of those things for sure, whether it pleases you or not. And yes means just as much as no."

"But," said Lene, "if it's all nothing but empty talk, I don't understand why all of you put up with such affairs."

"Oh, you do get to see beautiful women and fancy clothes, and now and again, if you pay close attention, you get to see a look that tells you a whole story. And anyway, it doesn't take all that long, so that you always have time to make up for it at the club. And it really is splendid at the club. That's where the empty talk stops and the realities begin. Just yesterday I relieved Pitt of his Graditz black mare."

"Who is Pitt?"

"Oh, that's just one of those names we use among ourselves. We just call one another things like that when we're together. After all, the Crown Prince says Vicky when he means Victoria. It really is a joy to have nicknames of friendship and endearment like that. But listen. The concert's just beginning across the way. Can't we open the windows to hear it better? Why you're already swinging your foot back and forth. How would it be if we stepped right up and tried a Contre or a Francaise? We've got three couples; Father Dörr and my dear Frau Nimptsch and then Frau Dörr and me—may I have the honor?—and then there's Lene and Hans."

Frau Dörr agreed instantly. Dörr and Frau Nimptsch, however, begged off, the latter because she was too old and the former because he was not acquainted with anything so elegant.

"All right, Father Dörr. But then you'll have to provide the rhythm. Lene, give him the coffee tray and a spoon. And now, ladies, take your places, Frau Dörr, your arm. And now Hans, wake up—snappy, snappy."

And in fact both pairs took their places and Frau Dörr really even grew more stately as her partner proclaimed in solemn dancemaster's French, *"En avant deux, Pas de basque."* The freckled gardener's boy, unfortunately still half-asleep, found himself pushed back and forth in machinelike fashion as if he were nothing but a doll. The three others, however, danced like people who really knew what they were doing and delighted Dörr so much that he got up from his stool and in place of the spoon, began tapping on the tray with his knuckle. Frau Nimptsch too was infused with the joy of earlier days and, having nothing better to do, kept stirring around with the poker until the flame finally sprang up.

They continued in this fashion until the music across the way came to an end. Botho led Frau Dörr back to her seat and only Lene remained standing because the clumsy gardener's boy had no idea what he was to do with her. That suited Botho to perfection; as soon as the music started anew, he began to waltz with Lene, whispering to her how charming she was, more charming than ever before.

They had all become warm, most of all Frau Dörr, who was now standing at the open window. "Good Lord," she suddenly said, "I'm getting such a chill." On hearing that, Botho obligingly jumped up to close the window, but Frau Dörr would not hear of it, maintaining that real high-class people went in for fresh air, some so much that their bedcovers froze to their mouths in winter. After all, breath was the same as steam, and exactly like what comes from the spout of the teakettle. And so the windows would have to stay open, she refused to give in on that. But if Lene were to have something for one's insides, so to speak, something to warm heart and soul. . . .

"Certainly, dear Frau Dörr, anything, whatever you'd like. I can make some tea or punch, or even better, I've still got that *Kirschwasser* you gave me and Mother Nimptsch last Christmas to go along with that big almond cake."

And before Frau Dörr could decide between punch or tea, the

bottle of cherry brandy was brought out with glasses large and small. All took as much as they judged best, while Lene went from one to another, the sooty teapot from the hearth in her hand, pouring the bubbling and boiling water into each glass. "Not too much, Lene, honey, not too much. Always go for the real thing. Water takes away the strength." In an instant the room was filled with the ascending aroma of cherry kernels.

"Ah, that was well done," said Botho, nipping from the glass. "God knows I didn't have anything yesterday and certainly not a single thing today at the club that tasted so good. To Lene! But the real credit belongs to our good friend, Frau Dörr, because she took such a chill. Well then, I'll straightaway raise my glass once more. Frau Dörr, to your health and happiness."

"To your health and happiness," they all cried, and old Dörr rapped once more on the tray with his knuckles.

Everybody agreed that it was a splendid drink, much finer than that punch extract you got in the summer which always tasted like bitter lemon because it was mostly old bottles that had been standing in the blazing sun in shop windows since Shrovetide. *Kirschwasser,* on the other hand, was good for your health and never spoiled, and before anybody might poison himself with the bitter stuff, one really ought to enjoy at least one bottle of something first-rate.

This remark was made by Frau Dörr, and her husband, perhaps because he knew his wife's chief weakness only too well, and did not care to take a chance on it, urged that they break up: "After all, tomorrow is another day."

Botho and Lene attempted to persuade them to stay, but Frau Dörr, who well knew that one had to give in now and again if one wanted to keep good friends, merely said, "Oh let him go, Lene honey, I know him. He goes to bed with the chickens." "Well," said Botho, "if that's how it is, that's how it is. But then we'll accompany the Dörr family to their door."

And so they all broke up, leaving only Frau Nimptsch behind, who looked after those who were going with a kindly glance and nod of her head. She then got up, and seated herself again, this time in the grandfather's chair.

# 5

Before the "castle" with its green-and-red-painted turret, Botho and Lene halted, and with all due formality, requested Dörr's permission to enter his garden and stroll there for half an hour. The evening, they said, had been such a lovely one. Old Father Dörr muttered something to the effect that he could not leave his property in better hands, whereupon the young couple, cordially bowing, then took their leave and strolled toward the garden. Everything had long since become quiet except for Sultan, whom they had to pass. He stood up and kept on whining until Lene petted him; only then did he return to his shed.

Within the garden everything was fragrant and cool; all along the entire length of the main path, between currant and gooseberry bushes, stood stock and mignonette, their delicate odors intermingling with the stronger aroma of the thyme beds. Nothing moved in the trees and only glowworms circled through the air.

Lene had taken Botho's arm. Together they walked towards the rear of the garden where a bench was to be found between two silver poplars.

"Shall we sit down?"

"No," responded Lene, "not now." She turned onto a side path, where tall raspberry bushes grew almost higher than the garden fence. "I like to walk on your arm so much. Talk to me about something. But something really nice. Or ask me some questions, if you'd rather."

"All right. Does it bother you when I start up with the Dörrs?"

"I don't care."

"A strange couple. And yet, they're happy, I think. He has to do whatever she wants, even though he's far more clever."

"Yes," said Lene, "he is more clever, but he's miserly and hard-hearted too. Always having a bad conscience about it, that's what makes him so malleable. She keeps a close eye on him and won't put up with it when he tries to pull something over on someone. That's the thing he's afraid of and what makes him so accommodating."

"Nothing else?"

"Perhaps love too, as strange as it might sound. I mean, love on his part. The fact is, regardless of his being fifty-six or more, he's still crazy about his wife, just because she's so imposingly built. Both of them have made the strangest confessions to me about it. I'll admit right off, she certainly wouldn't be to my taste."

"Oh, you're wrong there, Lene. She cuts quite a figure."

"I suppose," laughed Lene, "she cuts quite a figure, but she really doesn't have one. Haven't you ever noticed that her hips are too high by a hand's breadth? But you men never see things like that. 'Cutting a figure' and 'well built,' that's always your every other word, without giving the slightest thought to where all that imposing stateliness comes from."

Chatting and teasing in this way, she suddenly stopped and bent down over a long and narrow strawberry bed which ran in front of the fence and hedge to look for an early strawberry. Finally she found what she was looking for, and taking the stem of a really magnificent specimen between her lips, she stood before him and looked at him.

He was not slow to react. Picking the berry from her lips, he embraced her and kissed her.

"My sweet Lene, that was well done, very well done. But just listen how Sultan is yelping. He wants to be with you. Shall I unhook him?"

"No, when he's here, I've only got you by half. And then when you talk about Frau Dörr and her shapeliness, it's almost as if I didn't have you at all."

"Fine," laughed Botho, "Sultan can stay where he is. It's all right with me. But I've really got to know more about Frau Dörr. Is she really so good-hearted?"

"Yes, that she is, despite the strange things she says. Things that sound like they have double meanings, and maybe they do. But she doesn't know anything about that and there's not the slightest thing in her conduct that could even suggest her past."

"Does she have one?"

"Yes indeed. At least for years she had an affair and 'went out with him,' as she usually says. And there's absolutely no doubt that there's been an awful lot of talk about this affair and naturally about our good Frau Dörr herself as well. And she really must have caused one stir after another. But in her naive way she's never given it a thought, and reproached herself about it even less. She talks about it like some sort of uncomfortable service which she provided, loyally and honestly, but just out of a sense of duty. You're laughing. It sounds strange too, I know, but there's no other way to express it. But now let's forget about Frau Dörr and sit down here instead and look at the moon."

It was true, across the way the moon stood above the elephant house, which in the silvery light that streamed down upon it looked even more fantastic than usual. Lene called his attention to it, and pulling the hood of her coat more tightly, lay her head on his breast.

A few minutes passed, silent and blissful, and only as she again raised her head, as if waking from a dream which she could somehow not hold on to, did she say, "What have you been thinking about? But you have to tell me the truth."

"What was I thinking about, Lene? Well, I'm almost ashamed to admit it. I was getting sentimental notions and thinking of our vegetable garden back home at Castle Zehden. It's just like Dörrs' here, the same lettuce beds with cherry trees in between, and I'll bet even the same number of nesting boxes for titmice. Even the asparagus beds are laid out the same. And I used to walk between them with my mother. Whenever she was in a good mood she would give me the knife and allow me to help her. But heaven help me if I was clumsy and cut an asparagus stalk too long or too short. My mother had a quick hand."

"I'll bet she did. And it always seems to me as if I ought to be afraid of her."

"Afraid? How so? Why, Lene?"

Lene laughed heartily and yet there was a trace of something forced in her laughter. "Don't go thinking right off that I'm planning to present myself to her ladyship. You mustn't take it any differently than if I'd said I'm afraid of the empress. Would something like that make you think I was planning to present myself at court? No, don't worry, I'm not going to make any accusations against you."

"No, you wouldn't do something like that. You're much too proud to do anything of that sort. You really are a little democrat and every kindly word of yours comes right from the heart. Am I right? But however that may be, let's take a chance and see if you can picture my mother. What does she look like?"

"Exactly the same as you; tall and slender, blue-eyed and blond."

Now it was his turn to laugh. "Poor Lene! This time you've missed completely. My mother is a little woman, with lively dark eyes and a big nose."

"Don't believe it. It can't be so."

"And yet it is so. You've got to remember, you know, that I have a father too. But you women never give that a thought. You always think that you're the main thing. But now, see if you can tell me something about my mother's character. But do a better job at guessing."

"I think that she is very concerned about her children's happiness."

"Right."

". . . and that all of her children will find rich matches, which is to say very rich matches. And I also know who she has in mind for you."

"Some unfortunate woman, whom you . . ."

"How little you know me. Believe me, just having you, having this hour, that's happiness enough for me. Whatever will come of it doesn't bother me at all. One of these days you'll have flown away . . ."

He shook his head.

"Don't shake your head. It's really so, just as I say it is. You love me and you're true to me. At least I'm naive and vain enough in my love for you to think that you are. But you'll fly away. I can see that clear and certain. You'll have to. They always say, 'Love is blind,' but it makes us see clearly and off into the future too."

"Ah, Lene. You don't know how much I love you."

"Oh, but I do. I do know. And I know too that you consider your

Lene something special and that every day you think, 'If only she were a baroness.' But it's too late for that now. There's no chance anymore that I'll be able to turn that trick. You love me and you're weak. There's no changing that. All handsome men are weak, and whatever is stronger than they are controls them. And the thing that's stronger. . . . Well, either it's your mother, or what people say, or circumstances in general. Or perhaps it's all three. . . . But just look there."

She pointed over toward the zoo. At that very moment a rocket hissed into the air from the leafy darkness of the trees and with a bang scattered into innumerable sparks. A second followed the first, continuing in this matter as if they were trying to pursue and overtake one another, until suddenly it was over and the bushes across the way began to glow in a green and reddish light. A few birds screeched intermittently in their cages and after a long pause the music began anew.

"You know, Botho, if I could take you like this and stroll up and down Slanderers' Boulevard[1] just as comfortably as here among these box tree hedges and if I could say to everyone, 'Go right ahead and be surprised, every one of you, he is who he is and I am who I am and he loves me and I love him,'—really, Botho, what do you really think I'd give for that? No, don't try to guess. You wouldn't guess it anyway. All your kind know about is yourselves and your club and your life. Oh, this poor little bit of life."

"Don't talk like that, Lene."

"Why not? A person's got to look everything straight in the face and not let yourself be made a fool of. And above all, not make a fool of one's self. But now it's getting cold and everything's over across the way too. That's the finale they're doing now. Come on, let's sit inside by the hearth, the fire won't be out yet and mother's long since in bed."

And so they walked slowly up the garden path, while she leaned lightly on his shoulder. No light burned in the "castle" any more and only Sultan, stretching his head out of his hut, looked after them. But deep in gloomy thoughts he remained still and did not stir.

# 6

I t was the following week and the chestnut blossoms had already faded everywhere, including Bellevuestraße. Here, between a front balcony and one overlooking the garden, Baron Botho von Rienäcker maintained a ground-floor apartment: study, dining room, bedroom. All were distinguished by tasteful furnishings which exceeded his means by no small measure. Two still lifes by Hertel graced the dining room. Between them hung a valuable copy of a *Bear Baiting* by Rubens, while in the study, surrounded by several smaller pictures of the same master, a *Storm at Sea* by Andreas Achenbach stood on parade. The seascape had fallen into his hands on the occasion of a raffle and through this costly and beautiful acquisition he had cultivated himself into becoming a connoisseur and specifically an Achenbach enthusiast. He liked to make jokes about it and was in the habit of asserting that his good fortune in the lottery had cost him dearly, since it constantly lured him into new purchases. He always added that perhaps it was like that with every bit of luck.

In front of the sofa, its plush covered by a persian rug, stood a coffee service on a small malachite table. On the sofa itself all sorts of political newspapers lay scattered about, among which were the sort whose presence in such a place might have raised eyebrows. This could be explained only by Baron Botho's favorite saying, "Witty chatter tops political matter." Stories which bore an inventive stamp, "pearls," he called them, amused him most. A canary, whose cage always remained open at breakfast, flew again today about the hand and shoulder of his far too indulgent master, who, instead of becoming impatient, put the paper aside each time to stroke his tiny favorite. Whenever he failed to do so, however, the little creature forced itself upon his master's neck and beard as he read, chirping long and stubbornly until it got its way. "Lovers are all alike," said Baron Rienäcker, "they all demand obedience and subjugation."

At this moment the corridor bell rang and the servant entered, carrying letters which had just been delivered. One, a grey squarish envelope, was unsealed and bore a three-pfennig stamp. "Hamburg Lottery tickets or new cigars," remarked Rienäcker, throwing the envelope aside without further attention to its contents. "But this one here . . . ah, from Lene. Well then, this one I'll save for last unless the third one here with a seal doesn't take precedence over it. The Osten coat of arms. That means Uncle Kurt Anton. Postmarked Berlin, which is to say he's here already. Whatever does he want? Ten to one I'm supposed to breakfast with him or to buy a new saddle, or else accompany him to Renz's, or maybe Kroll's as well. Most probably he'll want to do the one and not forget the other."

With a small knife that had been lying on the windowsill, he cut open the envelope on which he had recognized Uncle Osten's handwriting and took the letter from it. It read as follows:

*Hotel Brandenburg, Number 15*

*My dear Botho.*

    Arrived intact an hour ago at the East Station under that old Berlin motto of yours, 'Beware of Pickpockets' and have taken quarters at the Hotel Brandenburg, in other words at my old stamping grounds. A real conservative keeps his eye on the little things too. I'll be staying just two days. The atmosphere here is too oppressive for me. This place is a stifling dump. I'll tell you the rest when I see you. I'll be expecting you at Hiller's at one. Afterwards we'll buy a saddle. We can spend this evening at Renz's. Be on time.

Your old uncle,
*Kurt Anton*

Rienäcker laughed. "Thought so! And yet that's a new touch. It used to be Borchardt's, now it's Hiller's. Well, well, dear old uncle, a real conservative keeps his eye on the little things too. . . . And now for my darling Lene. . . . What would Uncle Kurt Anton say, I wonder, if he knew in what sort of company his letter and his orders had arrived."

While talking to himself he opened Lene's letter and read:

It's been five whole days since I've seen you. Is it going to be a whole week? I was so happy that evening, I thought you would be sure to come back the next day. And you were so sweet and dear. Mother keeps teasing me and says, 'he won't be back.' How that really cuts me right to the quick, because some day it really has to happen like that and because I feel that it can be any day at all.

I was reminded of it again yesterday. You see, when I just wrote that it's been five days since I've seen you, I wasn't telling the truth. I *did* see you, yesterday, in secret, from in hiding at the flower festival. Just think, I was there too, naturally way off in a side ayle, and I watched you riding back and forth there for a whole hour. I was really happy. You were the most imposing one of them all (almost as imposing as Frau Dörr, who sends her complements). I was so proud just seeing you that I wasn't the least bit jealous. Only once. Who was that pretty blond with the two white horses all wrapped in garlands? And those flowers were so thick, no leaves or stemms. I've never seen anything more beautiful than that in my whole life. When I was a little girl I would have thought she must be a princess. Now I know that princesses aren't always the most beautiful. But she was beautiful and you fanceed her, I could easily see that. And she fanceed you too. But her mother, who was sitting next to her, she fanceed you even more. That really bothered me.

If I have to, I can give you up to a real young one. But an older lady! And one who's a regular Frau Mama as well? No, no, she's had her due. Anyways, my one and only Botho, you see that you're going to have to cheer me up and make me calm again. I'll be waiting for you tomorrow or day after. And if you can't come in the evening, come during the day, even if it's only for a minute. I'm so worried about you. That means I'm really worried about myself. I know you understand.

*Your Lene*

"Your Lene," he said, repeating the signature again to himself. And a sense of disquietude overpowered him as violently conflicting emotions, love, concern, fear, passed through his heart. He read the letter a second time. At two or three places he could not refrain from making a little mark with a silver pencil, not so much out of pedantry as for the sheer joy of it. "How well she writes! Her handwriting is really fine and her spelling too, almost. . . . *Stemm* for *stem*. Well why not? There was a frightful old school official named Stemm, but I'm not that sort, thank God! And *complements*. Should I be angry with her because of an *e* or an *i*? Good Lord, who can write *compliments* correctly? Not always the young countesses and the old ones never. Anyway, what's the harm of it? In all reality this letter is just like Lene herself, kind, true, dependable, and its mistakes make it only all the more charming."

He leaned back in his chair, putting his hand over his eyes and brow. "Poor Lene, what's to become of it all? It would have been better for both of us if this time there had never been an Easter Monday. Why do there have to be two holidays anyway? What good has come of Treptow and Stralau and going rowing? And now my uncle! Either he's come as an emissary of my mother or he's got plans for me on his own. Well, we'll see soon enough. He's never been to any school of diplomatic dissimulation, and, even if he's sworn ten oaths not to say a word, it will come out anyway. I'll find out even though I'm no better than he is in the art of intrigue."

As he spoke he opened a compartment of his desk where other letters of Lene already lay bound with a red ribbon. He rang now for his servant, who was to assist him while dressing. "There, Johann, that's been taken care of. . . . And now, don't forget to lower the blinds. And if anyone comes looking for me, until twelve I'm at the barracks. After one at Hiller's and this evening, I'll be at Renz's. And don't forget to raise the blinds at the right time, so that I don't find an oven in here again. And leave the front lamp burning. But not in my bedroom, the bugs are like crazy this year. Understood?"

"As ordered, Herr Baron."

Carrying on this conversation, which took place half in the corridor, Rienäcker passed into the entryway of the building. Reaching the front garden, he gave a little tug at the pigtail of the thirteen-year-old daughter of the housemaster, who was at that moment bending over her little brother's wagon. In response he received a look of rage, which the instant he was recognized, transformed itself just as quickly into one of tender admiration.

Only then did he proceed through the wrought-iron gate into the street. Here, under the green foliage of chestnut trees, he looked alternately towards the Brandenburg Gate, then towards the Tiergarten where, as if on the screen of a camera obscura, people and vehicles silently moved back and forth.[1] "How beautiful. Really, I suppose it probably is one of the best of all possible worlds."

# 7

Duty at the barracks was over at twelve, and Botho von Rienäcker strolled down Unter den Linden towards the Brandenburg Gate, merely intending to fill the hour until his appointment at Hiller's as well as possible.[1] Two or three picture galleries along the way offered a welcome interlude as he walked. At Lepke's, a few Oswald Achenbachs stood in the show window, among them a scene of a dirty and yet sun-filled street in Palermo, almost stunning in the truthfulness of its vitality and colors. "There are things that you can really never quite figure out. The Achenbachs for example. Until just a short while ago I'd have sworn by Andreas, but when I see something like this, I really don't know whether Oswald is his equal or hasn't even surpassed him. In any case he's more colorful and varied. But I can only let myself think about things like that; to say so in front of anybody would mean to cut the value of my *Storm at Sea* in half for no reason at all."

Lost in such reflections, he stood a while in front of Lepke's window. Then, crossing Pariser Platz, he proceeded toward the Gate and the Tiergartenalle, which ran diagonally to the left, until he came to a stop in front of Wolff's *Lion Group*. Here he looked at his watch. "Twelve thirty. Still some time." Thus he again turned to make his way back towards Unter den Linden along the same route. In front of Redner's Palais he spotted Lieutenant von Wedell of the Dragoon Guards coming his way.

"Where to, Wedell?"

"The club. And you?"

"To Hiller's."

"A bit early."

"I know, but what can you do? I'm supposed to breakfast with an old uncle of mine, *Neumark* blood, comes from that corner of the world where Bentsch, Rentsch, and Stentsch are all located—nothing but names that rhyme with *Mensch*—of course without having the slightest consequence or obligation.[2] By the way, you know he—my uncle, I mean—used to be in your regiment. Of course, that was a long time ago. Early forties. Baron Osten."

"The one from Wietzendorf?"

"The very same."

"Oh, I know him, at least by name. Distantly related. My grandmother was an Osten. Isn't he the one who's on a war footing with Bismarck?"

"None other. Say, do you know what, Wedell? Why don't you come along? The club certainly won't run away on you and neither will Pitt or Serge. You'll find them there just as well at three as at one. The old boy still raves about dragoon's blue and gold, and he's *Neumarker* enough to be happy to meet any Wedell."

"Fine, Rienäcker. But on your responsibility."

"With pleasure."

As they continued to converse, they arrived at Hiller's, where the old baron was already standing at the glass door keeping lookout, since it was one minute past one. He refrained from any sort of comment, however, and was visibly pleased when Botho made his introduction, "Lieutenant von Wedell."

"Your Herr nephew . . ."

"No apologies, Herr von Wedell, anybody named Wedell is always welcome, and when he's wearing this uniform in the bargain, two or three times over. Come along, gentlemen, we'll just withdraw from this parade of tables and chairs and concentrate our forces in the rear. Not usually the Prussian thing to do, but advisable here."

As he said that, he charged off ahead of them looking for good seats, and after glancing into various small rooms, finally picked a moderately large one with leather-colored wall coverings. Despite a wide triple window, the room was dimly lit because it opened on a dark and narrow court. The extra place setting was instantly removed from the table, which had been set for four, and while the two officers placed sword and saber in the corner near the window, the old baron turned to the head waiter, who had followed them at a distance, and ordered a lobster and a white Burgundy. "But which one, Botho?"

"Let's say, Chablis."

"Fine. Chablis. And fresh water too. But not right out of the tap. Preferably so that the carafe is fogged up. And now, gentlemen, please take your places. My dear Wedell here, and Botho, you sit there. If only we didn't have this heat, this premature dog day weather. Fresh air, gentlemen, fresh air! This beautiful Berlin of yours—which is getting more beautiful every day, at least that's what we're assured by everyone who doesn't know any better—this beautiful Berlin of yours has everything, except fresh air." With that he tore open the large windows and seated himself so that he had the wide middle opening directly in front of him.

The lobster had not yet arrived but the Chablis stood before them. Brimming with restlessness, old Osten took one of the rolls from the basket and, merely to have something to do, cut it into diagonal pieces with an equal measure of virtuosity and haste. Then, letting the knife fall, he extended his hand to Wedell. "Really obliged to you, Herr von Wedell. Brilliant inspiration of Botho's to have torn you away from your club for a few hours. I take it as a good omen to be able to greet a Wedell right on my first sally in Berlin."

No longer able to control his restlessness, he now began to pour the wine, following which he ordered a Cliquot put on the ice. He then continued, "Actually, dear Wedell, we're related. There isn't a single Wedell with whom we're not related, even if only through a peck of peas. Neumark blood in the whole lot. And when I see that old dragoon's blue of mine, well, my heart goes right into my throat. Yes, indeed, Herr von Wedell, old love never dies. But here comes the lobster. . . . Please, the large claw here. The claws are always the best. . . . But as I was just saying, old love never dies, nor that certain soldierly flair either. Thank God, I always say. In the old days we still had old Dobeneck.[3]

"Goddamn! *There* was a man! Sweet as a baby. But if something ever went wrong and didn't come off, if he looked at you then, well I'd just like to have seen the fellow who could endure that look. A real old East Prussian still left over from the days of 1813 and 1814.

Scared stiff of him we were, but we loved him too. Like a father to us he was. And do you know, Herr von Wedell, who my *Rittmeister*[4] was . . . ?"

At this instant the champagne arrived.

"My *Rittmeister* was Manteuffel, the very same to whom we all owe everything. The man who created our army, and with our army our victory."[5]

Herr von Wedell bowed while Botho offhandedly remarked, "Of course, one can say that."

But as immediately became evident, that was neither witty nor wise on Botho's part. The old baron, who in any case suffered from high blood pressure, went red all over his bald pate and the little bit of curly hair at his temples seemed to curl even more tightly. "I don't understand you, Botho. What's that supposed to mean, 'one can say that?' Why it's the same as saying, 'one *can't* say that.' And I know exactly what you're driving at. You're suggesting that a certain reserve officer of the cuirassiers, who otherwise never held anything *in* reserve, least of all when it came to revolutionary measures, you're suggesting, I say, that a certain Halberstadt Cuirassier in that sulphur yellow collar of his, stormed St. Privat and completed the encirclement at Sedan all by himself in his very own high and mighty personage.[6] Don't give me that, Botho. He was nothing but a clerk who worked in the provincial government in Potsdam, under old Meding as a matter of fact, who never had a good word to say about him. I know that for a fact. And he really never learned a thing except how to write dispatches. That much I'll grant him. *That* he understands. Or to put it another way, he's a pen pusher.[7] But it's not pen pushers who've made Prussia great. Was there a pen pusher at Fehrbellin? Was that a pen pusher at Leuthen? Was Blücher a pen pusher or Yorck?[8] *Right here's* where you'll find the Prussian pen. I can't endure this cult."

"But my dear uncle . . ."

"But, but . . . no buts about it! Believe me, Botho, questions like that take years. I understand things of that sort much better. After all, how do things stand? He's kicking over the ladder he's climbed up on, even banning the *Kreuzzeitung*.[9] Plain and simple, he's ruining us. He's got a small opinion of us and insults us. And when he feels like it, he accuses us of theft or embezzlement and puts us in confinement in some fortress. Ach, what am I saying, in a fortress. Fortresses are for respectable people. No indeed, he's packing us off to the poorhouse, so that we can all spin wool. . . . But, fresh air, *meine Herren,* fresh air. You've got no fresh air here. Damnable little dump!"

Leaping up, he opened the two side windows in addition to the middle one, so that the curtains and tablecloth began to blow in the ensuing draft. Sitting down once more, he took a piece of ice from the champagne bucket and pressed it to his brow.

"Ah," he went on, "this piece of ice here, best part of the whole breakfast. . . . And now, tell me, Herr von Wedell, am I right or not? Botho, come on, be honest now, am I right? Isn't it true that as a member of the nobility from the *Mark,* a body's ready to talk himself right into being tried for high treason, just out of pure aristocratic indignation? To take a man like that . . . from one of our best families . . . better than the Bismarcks, and so many of them have already given their lives for throne and the Hohenzollerns, that you could form a whole company of royal guards out of them, regular royal guards, fancy brass helmets and all, and Boitzenburg himself in command. Yes, indeed, *meine Herren.* Such an affront to a family like that! And why? Embezzlement, indiscretion, violation of official secrets. I ask you! The only thing missing is infanticide and moral turpitude, and by heavens, it's amazing enough that that hasn't been added to the list to boot.[10] But you're silent, gentlemen. I beg you, speak up. Believe me, I can listen to other opinions and put up with them. I'm not like he is. Speak up, Herr von Wedell, speak up."

Wedell, in ever-growing embarrassment, groped for some phrase that would interject a note of agreement and pacification. "Of course, Herr Baron, it's just as you say. But, *pardon,* at that time, when the matter was being resolved, I heard it said many times, and the phrase has remained quite fixed in my memory, that the weaker party ought to yield rather than seek to cross the path of the stronger. That's forbidden in politics as well as in life. That's simply how it is—might before right."

"And there's nothing to contradict that, no appeal?"

"Oh, of course, Herr Baron. Under certain circumstances there's an appeal to be sure. And to be perfectly candid about it, I know of such cases of justified opposition. What the weak are not permitted, is granted to the pure of heart, those who are pure in conviction, or pure in motivation. Such purity has the right to resistance, even the obligation to do so. But who *possesses* such purity? Did he who . . . ? But I can say no more, because I wouldn't wish to insult either you, Herr Baron, or the family, of whom we're speaking. But you know, even without my saying so, that *that* particular individual who dared such a thing, did *not* possess this purity of motivation. Someone who is merely weaker has no right to anything. Only the pure of heart may venture all."

"Only the pure of heart may venture all," repeated the old baron with such a sly look, that it was doubtful whether he was filled with the truth of this thesis or its contestability. "The pure of heart may venture all. Capital phrase. Must take it back home with me. My pastor will really get a kick out of it. Last fall he got after me and demanded a piece of one of my fields back. Not for his own sake, of course. Oh, dear me, heaven forbid! Simply for the principle of the thing, and for the sake of his successor. Wouldn't want to give anything away that might turn out to be his. Sly old fox. But the pure of heart may venture all."

"But you'll certainly give in on this business with the pastor's field," remarked Botho. "I know Schönemann from the old days at Sellenthins."

"Yes indeed. He was still the tutor in those days and didn't know any better than to cut down on school hours and prolong the play time. Why, he could play a game of hoops just like a young marquis. Really! It was a joy just to watch him! But now he's been vicar for seven years, and you'd never recognize the Schönemann who paid court to her ladyship. One thing I've got to admit though, he certainly educated both of those missies, best of all your Käthe . . ."

Botho looked embarrassedly at his uncle, almost as if he were pleading for discretion. The old baron, however, overjoyed at having got hold of such a delicate topic so artfully, went right on, brimming over with growing good humor. "Oh, come on, stop that, Botho. Discretion. Nonsense! Wedell is a fellow countryman and probably knows as much about the whole affair as everybody else. Why keep quiet about such things? You're as good as bound already. And the Good Lord knows, my boy, when I just imagine those missies passing in revue, why 'a better'n ne'er you'll find.' Teeth like pearls, and always laughs so that you can see the whole string of 'em. A flaxen blond, good enough to kiss. And I'll tell you, if I were thirty years younger . . ."

Wedell, noticing Botho's embarrassment, sought to come to his assistance. "The Sellenthin ladies are all quite the beauties, mother and daughters. I was with them last summer at Norderney. Charming. But I'd give preference to the second . . ."

"All the better, Wedell. Then you won't get in each other's way, and we can have a double wedding right off. And Schönemann can perform the ceremony, provided Kluckhuhn, who's a bit touchy like all old-timers, permits it. What's more, I'll not only provide the team and wagon, but I'll deed that bit of the pastor's acre over to him without further ado, if I get to see such a wedding within the year. You're rich, my dear Wedell. And when you get right down to it, you're not in any hurry either. But just take a look at our friend Botho here. The fact that he looks so well fed certainly isn't due to that sandbox of his. Except for a few meadows, it really isn't much more than a nursery for pine trees. Even less that 'Eel Lake' of his. 'Eel Lake,' that sounds wonderful, almost poetic you might even say. But that's all there is to it. Nobody can live on eels.

"I know, you don't like to hear about things like this, but since we're discussing it, it's got to come out. What's the situation? Your grandfather had the moor cleared and your late father—a capital fellow, but I never saw anybody play such a terrible game of *l'hombre,* and for such high stakes in the bargain—your late father, as I was saying, divided up the five hundred acres of marshland and sold it to the Jeseritz peasants. And what's left of good ground isn't much and those thirty thousand Taler are long gone as well. If you were on your own, it might work out, but you've got to share with your brother. And for the time being your Frau Mama, my dearly beloved sister, still has the whole thing under control. Splendid woman, intelligent and clever, but she's not one who ever landed on the thrifty side either.

"Botho, why are you serving with the Imperial Cuirassiers, and why have you got a rich cousin, who's only waiting for you to come, with a plain, old-fashioned proposal so that you can sign, seal, and deliver what your parents already agreed to when you were still children? Why go on just thinking about it? Listen, if on the way home tomorrow I could just stop by at your Mamma's and bring her the good news, 'Josephine, my dear, Botho's willing, everything's arranged.' I tell you, my boy, that would really be something to give a real lift to an old uncle who means well by you. Say something, Wedell. It's time that he parts company with this bachelor's existence of his, or else he'll throw away the little fortune that he's got, or maybe even get himself involved with some sweet little thing from the bourgeoisie. Am I right? Of course. Agreed. And we'll have to raise our glasses on it. But not with what we've got left here . . ." He pressed the button for the waiter.

"Bottle of Heidsieck. Best you've got."

# 8

At this very moment two young cavaliers were passing time at the club. One, a member of the Gardes du Corps, was slim, tall, and beardless. The other, posted from the Pasewalk Regiment, of somewhat smaller stature, wore a full beard. Only his chin—as specified by regulations—was clean-shaven. The white damask tablecloth on which they had breakfasted was thrown back, and on the cleared half of the table the two of them sat at a game of piquet.

"Six with a four."

"Fine."

"And you?"

"Fourteen aces, three kings, three queens . . . and you won't take a trick." And he laid his hand out on the table, in the next instant pushing the cards together while the other shuffled.

"Did you know Ella's getting married?"

"Too bad."

"Why too bad?"

"She won't be able to jump through rings anymore."

"Nonsense. The more they marry, the slimmer they get."

"True, but with exceptions. Lots of famous families from the circus aristocracy are already flourishing in their third or fourth generation, which to a certain extent sort of points to conditions of change like slim and not so slim, or, if you will, new moon and first quarter, et cetera."

"Wrong. Error *in calculo*. You're forgetting adoption. All of those circus people are secretly Gichtelians.[1] The whole lot of them bequeath their fortune, their reputation, and their name according to a prearranged plan. It looks like they're the same, but yet they're different. Always fresh blood. Cut the cards. . . . By the way, I've got some more news. Afzelius is being transferred to the general staff."

"Which one?"

"The one from the Uhlans."

"Impossible."

"Moltke puts great store in him. He's supposed to have written a superb study."[2]

"Doesn't impress me. Nothing but library sniffing and copy work. Anybody who's the least bit resourceful can scribble books like Humboldt or Ranke."[3]

"Four. Fourteen aces."

"Five on the king."

And as the tricks were made, one could hear the clicking of the balls and the sound of their falling into the pockets in the neighboring billiard room.

All in all, only six or eight gentlemen had assembled in the two rear rooms of the club, which on their narrow end opened onto a sunny but rather uninteresting garden. All were silent, more or less engrossed in their whist or domino, not the least of them the two engaged in piquet, who had just been chatting about Ella and Afzelius. The stakes had become rather high for which reason neither looked up from his game until they noticed a new arrival approaching through the open archway of the adjoining room. It was Wedell.

"Well now, Wedell, if you don't bring a whole world of news with you, we'll excommunicate you in grand style."

"*Pardon,* Serge, we hadn't definitely agreed to meet."

"But nearly so. In any case, you find me personally in the most conciliatory mood. How you'll be able to square it with Pitt, who's just lost one hundred and fifty points, is your affair."

As they talked, the two pushed their cards aside. The officer who had been addressed as Serge by the newly arrived Wedell, drew his pocket watch. "Three fifteen. Well then, coffee time. Some philosopher or other, and it must have been one of the greatest, once said that the best thing about coffee was the fact that it fits every situation and hour of the day. Really true. Words of wisdom. But where should we have it? I think we ought to sit outside on the terrace, right out in the sun. The more one defies the weather, the better one can deal with it.

"Right then, Pehlecke, three cups. I can't put up with listening to those balls falling anymore, it's making me nervous. Of course we've got noise outside too, but it's different. Instead of that irksome clicking, we can listen to the rumble and thunder of our subterranean bowling alley and in the process imagine we're sitting on Vesuvius or Aetna. And why not, I ask you? In the final analysis all pleasure is nothing but imagination, and whoever's got the best imagination has the greatest pleasure. Only the unreal has any true value and is really the only reality."

"Serge," replied his partner, who in the piquet game had been addressed as Pitt, "if you keep on like this with these famous great statements of yours, you'll punish Wedell even worse than he deserves. And besides, you ought to have a bit of consideration towards me for losing. Well then, here we'll stay, the lawn at our rear, this ivy on the flank and a bare wall *en vue*. A splendid spot for his majesty's guards! I wonder what old Prince Pückler would have said about this club's garden?[4]

"Pehlecke . . . right, bring the table over here, that's fine. And for the final touch, one of those Cuban beauties from your choicest stock. And now Wedell, if you're to be forgiven, you'd better just shake your sleeve until a new war falls out or come up with some other juicy news. You're supposed to be related through the Puttkamers to our Lord God Almighty Himself! I needn't add which one. What's he cooking up now?"

"Pitt," responded Wedell, "I implore you. Just no Bismarck questions, please. First of all, you know that I don't know a thing, because seventeenth-degree cousins don't quite belong to the prince's confidants and intimate acquaintances. And secondly, because instead of straight from the prince, I've just come from a little target shooting during which there were a few bull's-eyes and a large number of misses—all of which were directed at none other than His Highness himself."

"And who was our bold marksman?"

"Old Baron Osten. Rienäcker's uncle. Charming old fellow and *bon-garçon*, but foxy as well, to be sure."

"Like all of those from the Mark."

"I'm one too."

"*Tant mieux.* Then you know it all the better. But out with it. What does the old boy say?"

"Quite a bit. His political views are scarcely worth talking about. But there's another thing that's all the more important. Rienäcker's in a tight corner."

"What kind of a corner?"

"He's supposed to get married."

"You call that a tight corner? Come on, Wedell, Rienäcker's in a much tighter one than that. He gets nine thousand a year and spends twelve. That's the tightest corner of all, at least tighter than the marrying corner. Marriage isn't a danger for Rienäcker, it's his rescue. Anyway, I've seen it coming. Who is it, by the way?"

"One of his cousins."

"Of course. Rescuers and cousins are nearly identical these days. I'll bet that her name is Paula too. Cousins are all called Paula lately."

"Not this one."

"What then?"

"Käthe."

"Käthe? Aha, got it. Käthe Sellenthin. Hm, not bad. Splendid catch. Old Sellenthin—isn't he the one with the patch on his eye?—he's got six estates and if you count the outlying properties it's even thirteen. They'll be divided between both parties and number thirteen goes to Käthe as a little bit extra. My congratulations . . ."

"You know her?"

"Of course. Wonderful flaxen blond hair with forget-me-not eyes. But not the sentimental type nevertheless, more for the sun than the moon. She was here at Madame Zülow's girls' school and the fellows were all courting her at fourteen."

"At the girls' school?"

"Not directly, and not every day, but on Sundays for sure, whenever she went to dinner at old Uncle Osten's—the very same from whom you've just come. Käthe, Käthe Sellenthin . . . in those days she was like a little wagtail. That's what we called her. She was the most charming little cutie you ever could imagine. I can still see her hair knot. The distaff we called it. So Rienäcker's going to do his spinning with that? Well, why not? Things won't be so difficult for him at all."

"In the end maybe more difficult than some seem to think," answered Wedell. "As surely as he needs improvement in his finances, I'm still not so certain that he would just go out and pick this especially selected blond compatriot without a second thought. For some time now Rienäcker's been specializing in another color, more in the line of ash blond, and if what Balafré recently told me is true, he's given serious thought to the idea whether or not he ought to raise the lady who does his whites to his Lady in White. Whether it's Castle Avenel or Castle Zehden makes no difference to him. A castle's a castle. And you know that Rienäcker, who goes his own way in lots of things, was always partial to the natural."[5]

"Yes," laughed Pitt, "That he was. But Balafré's exaggerating and making up interesting tales for himself. You're the sober sort, Wedell, and certainly don't believe that kind of invented nonsense."

"No, not if it's invented," responded Wedell. "But I believe in what I know to be true. That six-foot stature of his notwithstanding, or maybe just because of it, Rienäcker is weak and can be easily controlled. He has an extraordinary sort of softness and good-heartedness in his nature."

"That he does. But circumstances will force his hand. He'll break off and get free of this, if worst comes to worst, like a fox gets out of the trap. It's painful, and some of the life stays caught. But the main thing is getting out, breaking free. *Vivat* Käthe. And Rienäcker. How does the saying go? 'God helps those, who help themselves.' "

# 9

On the same evening Botho wrote Lene that he would visit her on the following day, perhaps earlier than usual. He kept his word, arriving an hour before sunset. Naturally he encountered Frau Dörr as well. It was a splendid evening, not at all too warm, and after they had chatted for a while, Botho said, "Perhaps we could take a walk in the garden."

"Yes, the garden. Or somewhere else?"

"What do you mean?"

Lene laughed. "Don't start worrying again, Botho. No one is waiting in ambush, and the lady with the white horses and the flower garlands won't jump out on you."

"Well, where would you like to go, Lene?"

"Just out into the fields. Somewhere where it's green and where you won't have anything except daisies and me. And Frau Dörr too, if she'll have the goodness to accompany us."

"If she'll have the goodness," said Frau Dörr. "Of course, she will. Honored, I'm sure. But I'll have to get dolled up a bit first. I'll be right back."

"Not necessary, Frau Dörr. We'll pick you up."

And thus it was that when the young couple made their way towards the garden a quarter of an hour later, Frau Dörr stood ready at the door, a shawl on her arm and a magnificent hat on her head, a present from Dörr, who like all misers now and again bought something ridiculously expensive.

Botho made a flattering remark to their splendidly decked-out companion after which all three made their way down the walk. Passing through a small hidden gate, they proceeded onto a path which, before turning into the open meadows, here at least still ran along the garden fence, nearly hidden by nettles on its outer side.

"We'll stay here," said Lene. "This is the prettiest path and it's the most isolated too. Nobody comes this way."

In fact, it was the most isolated path, by far quieter and more empty than three or four others, which ran parallel to it across the field towards Wilmersdorf, each of which exhibited to some extent a peculiar sort of suburban activity. On one of these paths all sorts of sheds could be seen, between which stood scaffolds, seemingly intended for gymnasts. Botho's curiosity was awakened. Before he could ask what it really was, however, the activity in the distance answered his question. Across the scaffoldings, rugs and carpets were spread, and in that instant such a knocking and beating with large cane paddles started up that the path soon lay hidden in a cloud of dust.

Botho pointed it out and was about to engross himself in conversation with Frau Dörr about the value or worthlessness of the carpets, which seen in broad daylight seemed to be nothing but dust catchers. "If a fellow didn't have a strong chest," he commented, "he'd come down with consumption before he knew what happened." In the middle of his remark he broke off, however, for just at this moment the path they had taken passed by a spot where rubble from a sculptor's studio must have been dumped. All sorts of stone ornaments, especially angels' heads, lay about in great numbers.

"That's an angel's head," said Botho. "Look, Frau Dörr, here's one that's even got wings."

"So I see," said Frau Dörr. "And fat little dimples too. But is it really an angel? It seems to me if it's so little and it's got wings, that it's really Cupid."

"Angel or Cupid," said Botho, "it all amounts to the same thing. Just ask Lene. She'll tell you. Right, Lene?"

Lene reacted as if her feelings had been hurt. He took her hand, however, and everything was quickly smoothed over again.

Directly behind the rubble pile the path turned down towards the left, immediately intersecting with a somewhat larger one. Its black poplars had just come into full bloom and strewn their flakelike catkins about the meadows, on which they now lay like tufts of pulled cotton.

"Look at that, Lene," said Frau Dörr. "Do you know that they stuff beds with that nowadays, just like feathers. They call it wood wool."

"Yes, I know, Frau Dörr. And it always makes me happy whenever I see people figure out something like that and put it to good use. But that wouldn't be anything for you."

"No sir, Lene, that wouldn't be nothin' for me. You're right there. I go more for something good and firm, like horse hair and springs, and when it really gets bouncing . . ."

"Oh, of course," said Lene, for whom this description was beginning to get a bit embarrassing. "I'm just afraid maybe we're in for some rain. Just listen to the frogs, Frau Dörr."

"Oh sure, the bullfrogs," agreed the latter. "Sometimes at night there's so much croaking, you can't even sleep. And what's the cause of it all? Because there ain't nothing but swamp around here, and just looks like it's meadows. Just look at that pond over there, where that stork's standing and looking at us. Well, he sure ain't looking at me. He'd have to look a long time for that. And that's just fine with me too."

"We really do have to turn around," said Lene, embarrassed, although really merely to have something to say.

"Heaven forbid," laughed Frau Dörr. "And not just now for sure. You can't really be afraid and certainly not of somethin' like old Adebar the stork? Adebar, my joy, bring me a . . . Or should I sing, Adebar, you pearl . . . ?"

And so it went on for quite a while, because Frau Dörr needed a bit of time to give up on such a favorite theme. Finally, however, there came a pause, during which they walked on at a slow pace until at last they reached a ridge which spread like a plateau from the Spree towards the Havel. At this very point the open meadows came to an end and fields of corn and rapeseed began, extending to the foremost rows of houses from Wilmersdorf.

"Let's just go up there," said Frau Dörr, "and then we'll sit down and pick some buttercups'n weave us a wreath. Good Lord, it's always real fun to fit one stem to another 'till ya' got a whole wreath or a chain put together."

"Indeed it is, indeed it is," remarked Lene, who today seemed destined not to escape a single minor embarrassment. "Indeed it is. But come along now, Frau Dörr, the path goes this way."

Conversing in this manner, they ascended the low rise and arriving at the top, sat down on a pile of quick grass and nettles which had been dumped there in the previous autumn. This weed pile was a splendid place to rest, and at the same time offered a lookout point. Here, beyond a ditch edged by mounds and meadows, one could not only view the northernmost row of houses in Wilmersdorf, but also with perfect clarity make out the falling of the pins and especially the sound of the balls rolling back along two rickety lattice boards from a nearby open-air bowling establishment. Tremendously pleased by the sight, Lene took Botho's hand, remarking, "Look there, Botho, I know ever so much about those places! When I was a little girl we lived right next to one. All I have to hear is the ball land and I can tell right away, how many they'll get."

"Well," said Botho, "then we can bet on it."

"For what?"

"We'll find something."

"All right. But I only have to get it right three times. If I don't say anything, it doesn't count."

"Fine with me."

Now all three listened intently and Frau Dörr, becoming more excited by the moment, swore by all that was high and holy that her heart was absolutely pounding, and that she felt exactly as if she were sitting before the curtain in a theater. "Lene, Lene, you've taken on too much. Child, that ain't even possible."

She might have continued in that vein had they not at that very instant heard a ball strike the floor and, after a single dull impact against the gutter edge, once again become still. "A miss," cried Lene. And so it was.

"That was easy," said Botho. "Too easy. I could have guessed that too. Let's see what comes now."

Sure enough, two more throws followed without Lene as much as saying a word or even making a move. Only Frau Dörr's eyes seemed to be popping more and more out of her head. At this moment, however, came a firm rolling sound, and with a peculiar combination of elasticity and hardness, the ball could be heard humming and dancing over the boards. "All nine," cried Lene. And in an instant they heard the sound of falling pins from across the way and the pin boy confirmed what scarcely needed any confirmation.

"It looks like you've won, Lene. We'll eat a *Vielliebchen* before the day's over and then things will all work out. Right, Frau Dörr?"[1]

"Sure," said the latter with a wink of her eye, "things will all work out." And as she spoke she untied her hat and made circles with it as if it were the hat she wore on market day.

In the meantime the sun sank behind the Wilmersdorf church tower. Lene suggested they begin to head home; she was getting cold. On the way, however, she suggested that they play tag. She was certain Botho would never catch her.

"Oho, we'll just see about that."

And now began a game of chasing and grabbing after one another in which Lene really did manage to escape time after time until, totally exhausted from laughing and excitement, she took refuge behind the stately form of Frau Dörr.

"Now I've got my tree," she laughed. "Now you really won't get me." Holding tightly to Frau Dörr's protruding coattail, she pushed the good old soul skillfully to the right and left, so that for a while she was able to keep herself covered. Suddenly, however, Botho stood next to her, grasped her firmly, and gave her a kiss.

"That's against the rules; we didn't agree to anything like that."

Despite such a rejection, however, she held tightly to his arm, and while imitating the gravelly voice of the guards, gave the order, "Pass in revue! . . . Forward march!" all the while taking delight in the seemingly endless expressions of wonder and amazement with which dear old Frau Dörr accompanied the game.

"Can you believe that?" said the latter. "Nope, it ain't to be believed. And he's always like that, never a bit different. When I just think of mine. Ain't to be believed, I tell you. And yet he was one of them too. And always that way."

"What's she talking about?" asked Botho quietly.

"Oh, she's thinking back again. . . . But, you know . . . I told you all about it."

"Oh, *that's* it. *Him.* Well, he probably wasn't so bad."

"Who knows? When you get right down to it, one's just the same as the other."

"Think so?"

"No." As she spoke she shook her head and in her eyes lay a mixture of tenderness and emotion. But she resisted such a mood taking hold of her and said quickly, "Let's sing, Frau Dörr. Let's sing something. But what?"

"Morning's glow . . ."

"No, not that. . . . 'Tomorrow in the cool, cool grave.'[2] That's too sad for me. No, let's sing 'In a year, in a year,' or better yet, 'If you remember.' "[3]

"Yes, *that's* the thing, *that's* beautiful, that's my most favorite song."

And with well-practiced voices all three sang Frau Dörr's most favorite song. They had already reached the vicinity of the truck garden as "I'll remember . . . I'll be grateful all my life," still rang over the field, while from the other side of the road, where the barns and sheds were located, the echo could be heard resounding.

Frau Dörr was overjoyed. Lene and Botho, however, had become serious.

# 10

I t was already getting dark when they once again stood before Frau Nimptsch's living quarters and Botho, who had quickly regained his cheerfulness and good humor, intended merely to look in for a moment and then be on his way. When Lene reminded him of all sorts of promises, however, and Frau Dörr by means of emphatic looks and gestures recalled the *Vielliebchen* which was still to be disposed of, he gave in and decided to remain for the evening.

"That's fine," said Frau Dörr. "And I'll stay now too. That is, if I'm allowed to stay and don't interfere with the *Vielliebchen*. Because, you can never tell, you know. I'll just take my hat home and my shawl. An' then I'll be back."

"Of course, you've got to come back," said Botho, extending his hand to her. "We won't be this young when we meet again."

"No, no," laughed Frau Dörr, "we won't be this young when we meet again. An' it's really impossible too, even if we got together tomorrow already. A day's a day and already makes a difference. So it really is true that we won't be this young when we meet again. And we all gotta' put up with it."

The conversation continued in this tone for a bit, and the fact of daily aging, disputed by no one, so fascinated Frau Dörr that she returned to it several times over. Only then did she depart. Lene accompanied her to the hallway, while Botho sat down next to Frau Nimptsch and, while adjusting the shawl which had fallen from her shoulder, asked her if she was still angry that he had once again abducted Lene for a few hours. But it had been so nice up there on the weed pile, where they had stretched out and chatted, that they had completely lost track of time.

"Yes, people lose track of time when they're happy," replied the old woman. "And young folk are happy'n that's fine'n as it should be. But when you get old, *lieber* Herr Baron, then the hours start to drag'n you wish the day was over and your life along with it."

"Oh, you're just saying that, old girl. Everybody enjoys living, old or young. Right, Lene, we all enjoy living?"

Lene had just entered the room from the hallway and, as if struck by his words, ran to him and embraced and kissed him as if completely possessed by a passion otherwise utterly alien to her.

"Lene, what's gotten into you?"

But she had once more collected herself and with a quick gesture of her hand, warded off his concern, as if wanting to say, "Don't ask." Then, while Botho continued speaking with Frau Nimptsch, she went to the kitchen cupboard, rummaged about for a bit, and her face now cheerful, came back holding a small notebook covered in blue paper which looked exactly like those in which housewives kept their daily accounts. In fact the book served this very purpose while at the same time being used for questions with which Lene also occupied herself now and then, whether out of curiosity or as a result of a deeper interest. She opened it and pointed to the last page and Botho's glance immediately encountered the heavily underlined title: *Things That Need to Be Known.*

"Good grief, Lene, that sounds like some kind of religious tract or the title of some comedy."

"It is, sort of. Just keep on reading."

"Who were the two ladies at the flower show? Is it the older one or the younger? Who is Pitt? Who is Serge? Who is Gaston?"

Botho laughed. "If I'm supposed to answer all of that for you, Lene, I'll be here until morning."

It was a stroke of good fortune that Frau Dörr was not present to hear this answer or else there would have been a new embarrassment. But their otherwise alert friend, alert at least when it came to the baron, had not yet returned. Thus Lene replied, "Fine, I'm open to bargaining. As far as I go, we can talk about the two ladies some other time. But what do these foreign names mean? I asked just the other day when you brought the bag. But your answer wasn't really an answer, just sort of half of one. Is it a mystery?"

"No."

"Well then, tell me."

"Glad to, Lene. Those are nothing but nicknames."

"I know. You told me that already."

". . . well then, names we've given ourselves for convenience's sake, whether they have some relevance or not, just as they happen to occur to us."

"And what does Pitt mean?"

"Pitt was an English statesman."

"Is your friend one too?"

"For heaven's sake."

"And Serge?"

"That's a Russian first name. A saint's name, a lot of Russian princes have it too."

"Who don't have to be saints though, do they? And Gaston?"

"That's a French name."

"Yes, I remember that. Once, when I was just a little thing, even before I was confirmed, I saw a play: *The Man in the Iron Mask*. And the one with the mask was named Gaston. And I cried something awful."

"And now, you'll laugh, when I tell you: *I'm* Gaston."

"No, I'm not laughing. You've got a mask too."

Jokingly and seriously Botho sought to assure her of the opposite, but Frau Dörr, who entered just at that moment, cut off the conversation by excusing herself for having made them wait so long. An order had come, however, and she had quickly had to prepare a funeral wreath.

"A big one or a little one?" asked Frau Nimptsch who enjoyed talking about funerals and had a real passion to hear about everything and anything pertaining to them.

"Well," said Frau Dörr, "it was middle-sized. Lower-class folk. Ivy with azaleas."

"My Lord," continued Frau Nimptsch, "everybody wants ivy with azaleas. Except for me. Ivy is fine when it grows on the grave and gets all twisted up green'n thick, so that the grave is all peaceful and whoever's lying beneath it there too. But ivy in a wreath just ain't right. In my day we used to take everlastings, yellow ones, or orange, and when it was supposed to be something really fancy, then we took red or white ones and made wreaths out of them, or maybe we just took one and hung that on the cross, and it used to hang there the whole winter. And when spring came it was still hanging there. Some of them hung there even longer. But that business with ivy and azaleas ain't no good. And why not? Why, because they don't last long. Why, I always think to myself, the longer the wreath hangs up above there, the longer people think of their dead beneath it. Sometimes even a widow does too, if she ain't too young. So that's why I'm for everlastings, yellow or red or white ones too. And anybody can add some other wreath whenever he wants to. That's sort of just for appearances. But the one made of everlastings, that's the real one."

"Mother," said Lene, "you're always talking so much about wreaths and graves."

"Well, child, everybody talks about what's on their mind. When somebody thinks about weddings, they talk about weddings and when somebody thinks about funerals, then they talk about the grave. Anyway, it wasn't me that started talking about graves and wreaths. Frau Dörr started talking about that, and she was right too. I just talk about it a lot, because I always get worried'n think, that's all well and good, but who'll bring you one?"

"Oh Mother . . ."

"Sure Lene, you're kind, you're a good girl. But man proposes'n God disposes, 'n' here today 'n' gone tomorrow. And you can die just as well as me, every day that God gives us, even if I don't believe you will. And Frau Dörr can die too or maybe she'll be living somewhere else when I die, or maybe I'll live somewhere else and just have moved in. Oh, my dearest Lene, nobody's sure of anything, not one single thing, not even a wreath on their grave."

"Oh no, no indeed, Mother Nimptsch," interjected Botho. "You'll have one for sure."

"My oh my, Herr Baron, if that was only true."

"And if I'm in Petersburg or in Paris, and I hear that my old Frau Nimptsch has died, I'll send a wreath. And if I'm in Berlin or somewhere nearby, I'll bring it myself."

The old woman's face became simply radiant with joy. "Well now, I'll take your word on it, Herr Baron. That means I'll get a wreath on my grave and it sure does make me glad that I will. Y'know, I can't stand them bare graves that look like an orphan's cemetery or for prisoners or even worse. But now make some tea, Lene, the water's boiling and bubbling away, and there's strawberries and milk too, and sour cream. Good Heavens, our poor Herr Baron must be downright famished. Just looking at somebody all the time makes you hungry, why even I still know that. Yes indeed, Frau Dörr, we was young once too, even if that was a long time ago. But people were just the same then as they are today."

Frau Nimptsch, who was having one of her philosophical days, went on in this vein for a while, during which Lene brought in the evening meal and Botho continued teasing good old Frau Dörr. It was a good thing, he maintained, that her "official hat of state" had been put to bed in good time. That was really something for Kroll's fancy restaurant or the theater, but not for the likes of a weed pile in Wilmersdorf. Where had she ever gotten that hat? Not even princesses had hats like that. He had never seen something as flattering in his entire life. He certainly didn't mean to talk of himself, but even a prince could have been carried away just looking at it.

No doubt the good woman could hear perfectly well that he was joking. Nevertheless she responded, "Yep, when Dörr gets started, he gets so fast and fancy that I ain't at all sure where he gets it from. On regular days there ain't much about him, but all of a sudden he gets like a changed man, and he just ain't the same person. So I always say, there really is something about him, but he just can't show it so easy."

Thus they continued to chat over tea until ten had rolled around. Botho then got up to go and Lene and Frau Dörr accompanied him as far as the front garden gate. As they stood there, Frau Dörr again reminded them that the *Vielliebchen* was still forgotten. Botho, however, apparently did not care to notice her remark, and merely emphasized anew how fine the afternoon had been. "We ought go for walks like that more often, Lene, and when I come back, we'll give some thought about where. Oh, I'm sure I'll find something, someplace that's pretty and quiet, and nice and far away too, not just across the fields."

"And then we'll take Frau Dörr along again too," said Lene, "or we'll ask her. Won't we, Botho?"

"Certainly, Lene. Frau Dörr's always got to be there. Couldn't do something like that without Frau Dörr."

"Oh, Herr Baron, I just can't accept that. I can't ask for the likes of that at all."

"Oh, but you can, dear Frau Dörr," laughed Botho. "You can ask for anything. A woman like you."

And with that they separated.

# 11

The outing which had been agreed upon or at least planned after the walk to Wilmersdorf now became the favorite topic of conversation for several weeks, and whenever Botho came, the question of where they should go was pondered greatly. Every sort of possible place was considered: Erkner and Kranichberge, Schwilow and Baumgartenbrück, but all were still too crowded. Thus it came about that Botho finally suggested Hankel's Depot,[1] about whose beauty and isolation he had heard nothing but truly miraculous things. Lene was in agreement; the only thing that mattered to her was to get out in the open for a change, as far as possible from the bustle of the city in God's free and open spaces, and to be together with the man she loved. Where was unimportant to her.

It was settled then. The next Friday was set for the outing, and with the afternoon train to Görlitz they rode out to Hankel's Depot, where they intended to stay overnight and enjoy the next day in complete tranquility.

The train had only a few cars and these too were but sparsely occupied. Thus Botho and Lene found themselves alone. In the adjoining compartment a lively discussion was taking place, at the same time loud enough to make out clearly that it was a group of travelers who were going further and not stopping at Hankel's Depot.

Lene was happy. She extended her hand to Botho and looked out silently at the landscape of forests and heath. Finally she said, "I wonder what Frau Dörr will say, that we've left her at home?"

"She mustn't ever find out."

"Mother will let it slip out."

"True. That would be bad. And yet we couldn't do otherwise. Look, just the other day, on the meadow, that was fine, we were completely alone. But even if we find just as much isolation at Hankel's Depot, we'll still come across an innkeeper and his wife or maybe even a Berlin waiter. And a waiter like that, the sort that's always laughing to himself, or at least laughing on the inside, I can't stand, they ruin my pleasure. When she's sitting next to your mother or lecturing old Dörr, Frau Dörr is priceless, but not when other people are around. With others, she's just comical, an embarrassment."

Towards five the train stopped at the edge of the forest. No one really did get off except for Botho and Lene, and with frequent pauses, the two of them ambled comfortably along towards an inn, which some ten minutes distant from the little station building, had its place right on the Spree. This "establishment" as it was characterized on the tilted signpost, had originally been nothing but a fisherman's house, which more through years of additions rather than renovations, had been gradually transformed into an inn. The view over the river, however, made up for anything else which might be lacking, so that the glowing reputation which the place enjoyed among its devotees, seemed not to be exaggerated in the slightest. Lene too felt immediately at home and seated herself in a verandalike wooden porch attached to the front, half of which was hidden by the branches of an old elm standing between the house and the riverbank.

"Here's where we'll stay," she said. "Just look at the boats, two, three of them . . . and further up there's a whole fleet coming. Oh yes, it was a good idea to come here. Look over there, how they're running back and forth on that boat and leaning against the oars. And at the same time, everything's so quiet. Oh, my one and only Botho, how beautiful it is and how much I love you."

It pleased Botho to see Lene so happy. A resolute quality, something almost severe, that otherwise lay in her character, seemed to have been taken from her and had given way to an otherwise foreign tenderness, a change which seemed to do her infinitely good.

The innkeeper, whose title to the "establishment" went as far back as his father and grandfather, put in his appearance after a while to ask about the wishes of his guests, especially if they would be "staying the night." On receiving an affirmative response he then requested that they be so kind as to decide which room they might care to have. Several were at their disposal, he informed them, among which the mansard room was undoubtedly the best. It was perhaps a bit low, he added, but otherwise quite large and roomy and it had a view over the Spree as far as the Müggelgebirge.

His suggestion accepted, the innkeeper went off to make the necessary preparations, and Botho and Lene were not only once again alone with one another, but reveled completely in their solitude. A finch, nesting in the neighboring bushes, gently rocked on one of the low-hanging branches of the elm. Swallows darted back and forth, and last of all a black duck with a long train of ducklings sauntered solemnly past the veranda towards a dock built far out into the river. Halfway out on the walkway, however, she remained standing, while her ducklings plunged into the river and swam away.

Lene eagerly took everything in. "Just look, Botho, how the current is running there between those piles." But in fact, it was neither the walkway nor the swiftly running current which held her attention, but rather the two boats which lay tied up before them. She looked lovingly at them, indulging in all sorts of little questions and hints, and not until Botho continued to remain deaf and seemed utterly uncomprehending, did she finally come out with it and say straightaway that she would like to go for a row.

"You women are incorrigible. Absolutely incorrigible in your frivolity. Just think of the day after Easter. Just a hairbreadth . . ."

"And I'd have drowned. Of course. But that was just the one thing. Besides that came the acquaintance I made with a certain good-looking gentleman, whom you might just recall. His name was Botho. You wouldn't, I imagine, care to look upon the day after Easter as an unlucky day, would you? I'm more polite than that and a bit more tactful too."

"Now, now. . . . But tell me, can you really row, Lene?"

"Of course, I can. And I can even steer and set a sail. Just because I nearly drowned, you don't think much of me and my talents. But it was that boy's fault, and anyway, when you finally get down to it, anybody can drown."

As they spoke they left the veranda and made their way along the walkway towards the two boats whose sails were furled, while atop their mastheads pennants fluttered with names embroidered on them.

"Which one should we take," asked Botho, "the *Trout* or the *Hope?*"

"The *Trout,* of course. What business do we have with the *Hope?*"

Botho clearly perceived that Lene's remark was intended to needle, for her delicate sensibility notwithstanding, she never denied her nature as a genuine child of Berlin, who found pleasure in barbed little remarks. He forgave this little dig, however, said nothing, and assisted her into the boat. He then jumped in after her. Just as he was releasing the boat, the innkeeper appeared with a jacket and plaid blanket, explaining that it would get colder as the sun set. Both offered their thanks, and in a few moments found themselves in the middle of the river, which here constricted by islands and spits of land jutting into it, could scarcely have been three hundred paces across. Lene pulled at the oars only now and then, but even these few strokes were soon enough to bring them to a meadow, standing in tall grass, which also served as a boatyard, on which, some distance from them, a Spree River barge was under construction and old and leaky boats were being tarred and caulked.

"Let's go over there," cried Lene joyfully, pulling Botho along. But even before they reached the boatyard the hammering of the shipbuilder's ax ceased and the sound of bells beginning to toll announced that the working day had ended. Thus, still a hundred paces from the boatyard, they turned off onto a path which cut diagonally across the meadow and led to a forest of pines. Their reddish trunks glowed splendidly in the reflection of the already-low sun, while a bluish mist lay on their crowns.

"I'd like to pick a really beautiful bouquet for you," said Botho, as he took Lene by the hand. "But just look, a real meadow, nothing but grass. Not a single flower. Not a one."

"Not at all. There are lots of them. You just don't see any because you're too choosy."

"Even if I were, it's because it's for you."

"Oh, no excuses. You'll see. I'll find some."

And bending down she looked right and left, saying, "Just look, here . . . and over there . . . and here again. There are more here than in Dörr's garden, you just have to have an eye for them." Thus she went swiftly and busily to work, pulling up all kinds of weeds and blades of grass, until after a short time she had gathered a bundle of usable and unusable things in her hands.

In the meantime they had reached a fisherman's hut which must have stood empty for years. The forest began directly behind it and in front, on a strip of sand strewn with pinecones, a boat lay upside down.

"That's just what we need," said Botho. "We'll sit here. You certainly must be tired. Now let's see what you've picked. I think you don't know yourself, and I'm going to have to take over the role of the botanist here. Give them here. Those are buttercups, and that's mouse-ear, some call that false forget-me-not. Did you hear that? False. And this one here with the jagged leaves, that's tarax-acum, our good old dandelion, which the French use to make salad. Well, to each his own. But there is a difference between a salad and a bouquet."

"Just you give me that," laughed Lene. "You don't have any eye at all for these things, because you don't really love them, and having an eye for something and loving it always go together. First off, you decided that the meadow didn't have any flowers and now that we've got them, you don't want to admit that they're real flowers. But they are real flowers and very good ones at that. What will you bet that I can make something pretty out of them for you?"

"Well, I am just a bit curious to see which ones you'll choose."

"Just those that you agree to yourself. Now let's get started. Here's some forget-me-nots, not mouse-ear-forget-me-nots, in other words, no false ones, but the real thing. Agreed?"

"All right."

"And this one is veronica, a fine little flower. I imagine, you'll accept that too, won't you? I won't even ask you about it. And this big reddish brown one is devil's-bit. They grew it just for you. Oh yes, go right ahead and laugh. And this one here," and she bent towards a few yellowish flowers growing right in front of her on the sand, "these are everlastings."

"Everlastings," said Botho. "Of course, they're good old Frau Nimptsch's passion. Of course, we'll take those for sure, *they* definitely can't be left out. Now just tie it all up in a little bouquet."

"Fine. But with what? We'll let it go until we find some rushes."

"Oh no, I won't wait that long. And a piece of rush isn't good enough for me, too thick and coarse. I want something really fine. You know, Lene, you have such beautiful, long hair. Pull one out and braid that around the bouquet."

"No," she said firmly.

"No? Why not? Why no?"

"Because the saying goes, 'hair binds.' And if I bind it around the bouquet, that means you're bound along with it."

"Oh, that's just superstition. That's what Frau Dörr says."

"No, Mother says so. And whatever she's told me since I was a girl, even if it looked like superstition, it was always right."

"Well, I don't care. I won't argue about it. But I don't want any other ribbon around the bouquet except a hair of yours. And you certainly won't be so stubborn as to refuse."

She looked at him, pulled a hair from her head, and wound it around the bouquet. Then she said, "It's what you wanted. Here, take it. Now you're bound."

He tried to laugh, but the seriousness with which she had pursued the conversation and spoken the last words nevertheless did not fail to make an impression on him.

"It's getting cool," he remarked after a while. "The innkeeper was right in giving us this jacket and blanket. Come on, let's go back."

And so they walked back to the place where their boat lay and hurried to get across the river.

Only now, while rowing back, as they came closer to it with each stroke of the oar, did they really see how picturesquely the inn was situated. Like a tall and grotesque cap its thatched roof sat upon the low timbered beam structure, whose four front windows were just beginning to show light. At the same moment several lanterns were carried onto the veranda and through the branches of the old elm, which in the darkness resembled a fantastic grillwork, all sorts of luminous beams glittered over the river.

Neither spoke. But each one was lost in thoughts of happiness and the question of how long that happiness would last.

# 12

I t was already growing dark as they landed.

"Let's take this table," said Botho, as they again entered the veranda. "The wind won't bother us here and I'll order a grog or some mulled wine for you, all right? I can plainly see the cold's gotten to you."

He suggested all sorts of other things to her as well, but Lene asked to be allowed to go up to their room. When he came up, she told him, she would be fine again. She was just a little worn-out and really didn't need anything. Once she'd gotten a bit of rest, it would pass.

Thus she left him and ascended the stairs to the mansard room, which in the meantime had been prepared for them, accompanied by the innkeeper's wife, who, laboring under completely false impressions, immediately began asking inquisitively what was really the matter. Without needing a reply, she went on to the effect that, yes indeed, as she well knew from her own case, it was often that way with young women, and before her oldest had been born—right now she had four, but it had really been five because the middle one had been early and died right off—it had been just the same for her too. It came over you just like that and you felt like you were going to die. But a cup of mint tea, especially Cloister mint, and it would pass in no time and just like that you'd feel as happy as a fish in water, all set to go and real affectionate too. "Yes indeed, mam, but when you got four of 'em hanging around you, not even counting the little angel up there . . ."

Only with effort was Lene able to repress her embarrassment. Merely to have something to say, she asked for some mint tea, Cloister mint, about which she'd also heard a lot.

While this conversation was taking place in the mansard room above, Botho had seated himself. He did not sit, however, on the veranda, which was shielded from the wind, but in front of it instead, at an ancient table hewn from local timbers, nailed to four heavy posts, with an unimpeded view. Here he decided to take supper. He ordered a fish dinner, and as the "carp with dill" arrived for which years ago the inn had gained a reputation, the innkeeper appeared as well to ask which wine the "Herr Baron"—purely trusting to luck he had addressed him with this title—might care to have.

"Well," replied Botho, "I think that a Braunsberger, or let's say a Rüdesheimer, ought to go with this exquisite carp. And as a sign that it's good, you've got to sit down here and be my guest for your own wine."

The innkeeper bowed with a smile and soon returned with a slightly dusty bottle while the maid, a pretty girl of Wendish extraction, in a full skirt and black headcloth, brought the glasses on a tray.

"Well, let's just see," said Botho. "This bottle seems to promise all sorts of good things. Too much dust and cobwebs always look suspicious, but this one . . . ah, superb! Vintage 70, right? Well then, now we've got to drink a toast. Right. But to what? To Hankel's Depot!"

The innkeeper was obviously delighted and Botho, who plainly saw what a good impression he was making, continued in his typically affable and easygoing manner. "I really find it delightful here. There's only one thing you can say against Hankel's Depot: its name."

"Yes," replied the innkeeper by way of confirmation, "its name. It does leave a lot to be desired and it really is a problem for us. And yet, it's actually perfectly right, you know. Hankel's Depot really was a depot and that's why it's got a name like that."

"Fine. But that doesn't get us very far. Why did they call it a depot? What is a depot anyway?"

"Well, we could just as easily say loading and receiving post. This whole bit of land around here"—he pointed backwards as he spoke—"was always a large crown domain and under Old Fritz and even before that, under the Soldier King, it was called the Wusterhausen Estate.[1] There were probably about thirty villages that belonged to it, forests and fields included. Well, you see, those thirty villages, they naturally produced quite a bit, and they needed quite a bit too, or to put it differently, they had their exports and imports. And from the very beginning they needed a port or marketplace for both and it was only a question of what spot they would pick for it. Well, this place right here is the one they picked. This inlet became a port, marketplace, a 'depot' for everything that came or went. And since the fisherman who lived here in those days was named Hankel, my ancestor by the way, they arrived at 'Hankel's Depot.' "

"Too bad," said Botho, "that it can't be explained to everybody so nice and neatly." The innkeeper, presumably considering himself encouraged to do so, was about to go on. Before he could continue, however, the cry of a bird could be heard from high above, and as Botho peered inquisitively upward, he could make out two large birds, scarcely perceptible in the darkening twilight, gliding over the surface of the water.

"Were those wild geese?"

"No, herons. The whole forest around here is full of them. It's a real hunting preserve in general. Boar and deer by the hundreds, and here in the reeds, ducks, snipe, and marsh snipe."

"Splendid," cried Botho, whose hunting instincts began to make themselves felt. "Do you know that I envy you? What difference does the name make, anyway? Ducks, snipe, and marsh snipe. Why it makes you want to have it so good yourself. But it must be lonely here, really lonely."

The innkeeper chuckled and Botho, who instantly noticed it, became inquisitive. "You're smiling. But isn't it true? For the last half hour I haven't heard anything but the water gurgling under the dock and just this minute the call of those herons up there. I'd call that lonely, as pretty as it may be. Now and then a few Spree barges pass by, but they're all the same or at least they look the same. Anyway, each one of them is like a phantom ship. It's really as silent as the grave."

"Of course," replied the innkeeper. "But it's all like this only for as long as it lasts."

"What do you mean?"

"Yes," the other repeated, "just as long as it lasts. You talk of loneliness, Herr Baron, and for days on end it really is lonely here. And it can go on for weeks. But no sooner than the ice breaks and spring comes than the visitors arrive, and the Berliners are back."

"When do they come?"

"Unbelievably early. Four weeks before Easter and they're here. You see, Herr Baron, when I, weather-beaten as I am, still keep to my parlor because the east wind is kicking up and the March sun is burning, your Berliner pulls up a chair in the open, puts his summer topcoat over it and orders himself a *Weiße*. After all, as soon as the sun starts shining, the Berliners start talking about beautiful weather. And that pneumonia or diphtheria might be lurking in every draft doesn't mean a thing to them. They like to play hoops most of all, a few of them go in for boccie, and when they leave, all blistered up from the burning sun, sometimes I feel downright sorry for them. There's not a single one of them whose skin won't at least be peeling by the next day."

Botho laughed. "Ah yes, the Berliners. And it also occurs to me, your Spree around here must of course be the area where the oarsmen and sailors get together and hold their regattas."

"Certainly," said the innkeeper. "But that doesn't really mean much. When there's a crowd, there's at most fifty, or maybe now and then a hundred. And then it all gets quiet again and the whole water sports business is over for weeks and months. No, the rowing clubs are comparatively easy, you can put up with them. But when the steamers come in June, that's when it gets bad. And it stays that way the whole summer long, or at least for a long, long time."

"I can believe you," said Botho.

"Then every evening there comes a telegram: 'Tomorrow morning, arriving nine o'clock, Spree steamship Alsen. Excursion party. 240 persons.' And then come the names of whoever has arranged it all. That's all right once. But it just keeps on and on.

"When you get right down to it, what goes on at one of these outings? Until dark they're outside in field and forest, then comes supper and then they dance until eleven. Well then, you'll say:

'That's not such a big thing,' and it wouldn't be if we had the next day off. But the next day is just the same as the first, and the third is like the second. Every night at eleven off goes a steamer with 240 people on board, and every morning at nine there comes another with just as many. In between we've got to clean up and get everything ready again. And so the whole night is spent airing things out, cleaning and polishing, and just when the last doorknob is nice and shiny, there comes the next ship pulling up.

"Naturally, everything's got its good side. At midnight, when you're counting up your returns for the day, you know why you've put yourself through it all. 'Nothing ventured, nothing gained,' as they say, and that's true too. If I had to fill up all the bowls of May punch that have been drunk around here, I'd have to get myself a Heidelberg Keg.[2] It pays, for sure, that's all well and good. But to get ahead, you have to go backwards as well. You pay with the most important thing you've got, your life and your health. After all, what good is life without a bit of sleep?"

"True, I can certainly see that well enough," replied Botho. "Nothing's perfect. But then comes winter and you can sleep like a log."

"That's so, providing it isn't New Year's Eve or Epiphany or Shrove Tuesday. And they come around more often than the calendar says. You ought to see what goes on when everybody from ten villages around here comes on sleighs or skates and they all get together in the big ballroom I've added on. Then you don't see a single face from the big city and the Berliners leave us in peace. It's the hired men and the servant girls who get to have their day then. That's when you see otter fur caps and manchester jackets with silver buckles, and all kinds of soldiers, who are on leave just at that time, they show up too, Schwedt Dragoons, Fürstenwald Uhlans, and probably even Potsdam Hussars.[3] And they're all jealous of one another and just spoiling for a fight, so that you don't know what they'd rather do, dance or brawl. Just the smallest thing and whole villages are at one another, carrying on regular battles. And they rage and roar like that the whole night long, and whole mountains of pancakes disappear, until finally come the dawn, and off they go home again across the ice on the river or through the snow."

"I can certainly see that you really can't talk much about loneliness and the silence of the grave," said Botho. "Lucky that I didn't know anything at all about it, otherwise I'd never have had the courage and would have stayed away. And I really would have been sorry not to have ever seen such a pretty corner of the world. . . . But you were just saying, a minute ago, 'what good is life without a bit of sleep.' I think you're right. I'm a bit tired, even though it's still early. Comes from the air and water, I think. And then I've got to go and see . . . your dear wife took such pains. . . . Good night, innkeeper. Been talking too much."

With that he arose and strode off towards the now-silent house.

Her feet diagonally across the chair she had pulled up, Lene had sat down on the bed and drunk a cup of the tea brought to her by the innkeeper's wife. The rest and warmth had done her good, her spell had passed, and in a short while she could have gone down to the veranda to take part in the conversation between Botho and the innkeeper. But she did not really feel like talking, and thus she merely got up to look around the room which until now she had hardly noticed.

It turned out to be worth the trouble. The ceiling beams and clay-stuccoed walls had been preserved from the old days. The white-washed ceiling hung so low that she could touch it with her fingers, but wherever improvement had been needed, it had been carefully carried out. In place of the small panes which could still be seen on the ground level, a large window had been set in, reaching almost to the floor. Just as the innkeeper had described, it offered a splendid view of the entire water and woodland landscape. But this huge mirror-sized window was not the only thing which modernity and comfort had added to the room. A few good pictures, presumably acquired at auction, also graced the old, bulged and blistered clay walls. Near the back of where the protruding window gable met the slope of the roof, in other words, towards the room itself, two elegant toilette tables stood facing one another. Everything revealed that the fisherman's and boatman's hostelry had been con-scientiously preserved, while at the same time it had been trans-formed into a comfortable guest house for the rich sportsmen from the sailing and rowing clubs.

Lene felt comfortably reminded of home by everything she saw. At first she began to study the two wide-framed pictures hanging right and left over the night tables. They were engravings whose subjects aroused a lively interest in her. She would gladly have known what the titles beneath them meant. *Washington Crossing the Delaware* stood before one, *The Last Hour at Trafalgar* under the other.[4] But she was unable to get beyond merely deciphering syllables, which, as trivial as it was, pained her deeply, for it made her aware of the abyss which separated her from Botho. Of course, he poked fun at knowledge and "culture," but she was sensible enough to understand how to interpret such mockery.

Close to the door which led into the room, above a rococo table on which red glasses and a water carafe were standing, hung a colorful lithograph with an inscription in three languages: "*Si jeunesse savait.*" It was a picture she recollected having seen in the Dörr household as well. Dörr loved things of that sort. Seeing it here made her feel put out. Her delicate sensuality felt violated by the lewdness in the picture, as if it represented a distortion of her own feelings. To free herself of such an impression, she went to the gable window and opened both sides to let in the night air. Ah, how that refreshed her! At the same time she sat down on the windowsill, but two hand's breadth from the floor, wrapped her left arm around the window post, and listened towards the nearby veranda. She could hear nothing. Deep silence prevailed. Only in the old elm tree could a rustling and whispering be heard. Everything left from the unpleasantness which had just touched her soul now disappeared, as she looked more closely and with growing delight at the scene spread out before her. The water flowed quietly on, forest and field lay in an evening twilight and the moon, which was just again showing its first sicklelike form, cast a ray of light over the river so that one could make out the gentle undulations of its waves.

"How beautiful," said Lene, with a deep sigh. "And I really *am* happy."

She did not want to tear herself away from the view but at last she arose, pushed a chair before the mirror and began to undo her beautiful hair. Then she began to braid it. While she was still occupied with the task, Botho entered.

"Lene, still up! I thought I'd have to awaken you with a kiss."

"You've come too early for that, as late as you are."

And she stood up and walked toward him. "My one and only Botho. How long you've taken . . ."

"Your fever? Your spell?"

"Gone, and now I'm fine again. For half an hour already. I've been waiting for you all that time." And she drew him to the still-open window. "Just look. Wouldn't any poor human heart feel longing at such a sight?"

She nestled close to him and closing her eyes, turned up towards him with an expression of exalted happiness.

# 13

B oth were up early. The sun was still dueling with the morning mist as they descended the stairs to breakfast below. A gentle wind was blowing, a morning breeze of the sort which boatmen do not care to let pass unused. Thus an entire flotilla of Spree barges glided by, just as our young couple stepped out into the open.

Lene was still in her morning clothes. She took Botho's arm and strolled with him along the bank to a spot standing high with reeds and rushes. He gazed at her affectionately. "Lene, you really look like I've never seen you look before. Really, how can I describe it? There's no other word for it. Lene, you look so happy."

And so it was. She was happy, completely happy and saw the world in a rose-colored light. She had the most wonderful, the most beloved of men on her arm and reveled in a precious moment. Was that not enough? And if this moment were the last, well then, it was the last. Had she not been favored already just being able to have such a day? Even if only for once, one single time.

Thus all the thoughts of sorrow and concern, which despite herself, usually weighed heavily on her soul, had disappeared. She felt only pride, joy, gratitude. But she said nothing; she was superstitious and had no desire to risk her happiness by talking about it. Only a slight trembling of her arm revealed to Botho how deeply his remark, "I think, you're happy, Lene," had penetrated to her innermost heart.

The innkeeper appeared and inquired courteously, although with a touch of embarrassment, about their night's rest.

"Excellent," replied Botho. "That mint tea prescribed by your dear wife worked miracles, and the new moon shining right into our window and the nightingales singing so softly that you could just about hear them, well, who couldn't sleep with all that as if in paradise. I hope no Spree steamer's been arranged with 240 guests for this afternoon though. That would really be an expulsion from paradise. You're smiling and thinking, 'Who knows?' and maybe I really am asking for trouble by even suggesting it. But it isn't here yet. I don't see any funnel, and I can't make out any smoke yet. The Spree is still clear and even if the whole of Berlin were bearing down on us already, at least we can still have our breakfast in peace. Am I right? But where?"

"My guests have but to command."

"Well then, I think under that elm. The porch, as nice as it is, is really only good when the sun starts to get hot. And it isn't hot yet, it looks like it's still involved with the mist over there in the forest."

The innkeeper went off to see to the breakfast. The young couple, however, continued their stroll towards a point jutting out on their side of the river from which they could make out the red rooftops of a neighboring village and to the right, the tapered church tower of Königswusterhausen. On the edge of the point lay a willow trunk which had been washed ashore. Here they seated themselves, and proceeded to watch two fishermen, a man and a woman, as they cut the surrounding reeds and threw the large bundles into their boat. They took pleasure in the idyllic scene. When they returned after a while, breakfast was spread out before them. It was more of an English breakfast than a German one: coffee and tea along with eggs and meat, and on a silver rack, even slices of toasted white bread.

"Ah, just look at that, Lene. We'll have to breakfast here more often. What do you think? Heavenly! And take a look over there at the boatyard. They're caulking again and they've really got a regular rhythm going. I say, a working rhythm like that is really the most beautiful music there is."

Lene nodded, but she was only half-listening. Her gaze was again directed at the dock, but not at the boats moored there, which had aroused her interest on the previous day, but instead at a pretty serving girl, kneeling on the middle of the boarded platform next to her copper pots and pans from the kitchen. With spirited enthusiasm for her work which found expression in every movement of her arms, she scoured the jugs, kettles, and saucepans. Whenever she finished, she let the water splashingly rinse out the piece, which had been scrubbed until it gleamed. Then she lifted it, holding it up to flash for an instant in the sun, and placed it in a basket next to her.

Lene seemed fascinated by the scene. "Just look," she said, as she pointed towards the pretty young girl, who, to all appearances could not get enough of her work.

"You know, Botho, it's not just chance that she's kneeling there. She's kneeling there for me. I feel clearly that it's a sign for me, an act of fate."

"Lene, what's wrong with you? Why, you look changed. You've suddenly turned pale all over."

"Oh nothing."

"Nothing? And yet your eyes are trembling as if you're close to tears. You've certainly seen kitchenware before and a scullery maid polishing it. It looks almost as if you envy that girl that she's kneeling there and working as hard as she is."

The appearance of the innkeeper interrupted the conversation. Lene once more recovered her composure and was soon her cheerful self again. Then she went upstairs to change.

When she returned she found that an itinerary suggested by the innkeeper had been unconditionally accepted by Botho: a sailboat was to take the young couple to the next village, the town of Nieder-Löhme, charmingly situated on the Wendish Spree, from there they would make their way on foot to Königswusterhausen, where they would visit the park and castle, returning by the same route. It was a half-day's outing. As for the afternoon, that could be decided later.

Lene was satisfied with the idea, and a few blankets had already been brought to the quickly readied boat, when voices and hearty laughter could be heard from the garden, seeming to suggest visitors and that a disturbance of their isolation was in prospect.

"Ah, people from the sailing and oarsman club," said Botho. "Thank God that we can get away from them. Let's hurry, Lene."

As quickly as possible the two of them hastened to get to the boat. Before they could even reach the dock, however, they found themselves surrounded and captured. It was some of Botho's comrades, in fact, his most intimate friends: Pitt, Serge , Balafré. All three of them with their ladies.

"*Ah, les beaux esprits se rencontrent,*" said Balafré, full of high spirits, which quickly yielded to a more composed bearing as he realized that he was being observed from the threshold of the inn, where stood the innkeeper and his wife. "What a lucky encounter at a spot like this. Permit me, Gaston, to introduce our ladies to you. Queen Isabeau, Mistress Joan, and Mistress Margot."[1]

Botho immediately recognized what code word was in use today. Quickly adjusting to it, with a light gesture towards Lene, he now made his introduction, "Mademoiselle Agnes Sorel."[2]

All three gentlemen bowed courteously, in fact, to all appearances downright respectfully. The two daughters of Thibaut d'Arc, however, made an exceedingly abrupt little curtsy, leaving it to Queen Isabeau, who was at least fifteen years older, to extend a warmer greeting to Agnes Sorel, who, since they did not know her, made them visibly uncomfortable.

The whole thing was an intrusion, perhaps even one that had been planned. Nevertheless, the more this seemed to be the case, the more necessary it was to put up a good front. And Botho succeeded at it completely. He asked one question after another, learning in the process that earlier in the day they had come as far as Schmöckwitz on one of the smaller Spree steamers and from there had taken a sailboat to Zeuthen. From Zeuthen they had made their way on foot, scarcely a twenty-minute walk; it had been really charming, old trees, meadows, and red rooftops.

The entire party of new arrivals informed them of this, especially Queen Isabeau, a lady extremely well upholstered in the posterior, who distinguished herself almost as much through her loquaciousness as her rotundity. They casually strolled as they talked and having reached the veranda, seated themselves at one of the long tables.

"Delightful," said Serge. "Far away, free and open, yet nicely secluded. And those meadows over there are just made for a moonlight stroll."

"You're right," added Balafré, "a moonlight stroll. Charming, really charming. But it's just ten in the morning—that leaves an even twelve hours that we've got to dispose of until it's time for a moonlight stroll. I propose a boating party."

"No," replied Isabeau, "No boating parties. We've had the likes of that over and over already today. First the steamer, then a sailboat, and now another boat, that's too much. I'm against it. Anyway, I fail to understand what all this constant paddling about is supposed to achieve. The only thing left is that we all go fishing or start pulling those creatures out with our bare hands and get all excited about the little beasties. No indeed, there'll be no more paddling today. I've really got to put my foot down there."

The gentlemen, at whom she directed these words, were obviously much amused at the queen mother's decisiveness and came up with several other suggestions. Their fate was, however, the same. Isabeau rejected everything, and when finally half jokingly and half in earnest some began to disapprove of her behavior, she simply demanded silence. "Gentlemen," she said, "patience. I ask that you permit me to speak at least for a moment." Ironic applause was the reply, for it was she alone who had spoken up to that moment. Unconcerned, however, she went on, "Gentlemen, I beg you, teach me to comprehend your gentlemanly ways. What is an outing anyway? An outing is supposed to be breakfast and a game of cards. Am I right?"

"Isabeau is always right," laughed Balafré giving her a pat on the shoulder. "We'll have a game. This spot right here is splendid; why, I almost think that everyone will come up a winner here. And the ladies can go for a promenade while we're playing or perhaps take a little morning snooze. They say that's the healthiest thing and an hour and a half will certainly be enough. Reunion at twelve. Menu according to the choice of our queen. Yes, my queen, life is beautiful indeed. True, that's from *Don Carlos,* but then does everything have to be from the *Maid?*"

That made a hit, and the two younger ladies giggled, although they had really only understood the code word. Isabeau, on the other hand, who had grown up hearing suggestive and allusive remarks of the sort, maintained her dignity to the fullest and, while turning to the three other ladies, remarked, "If you will follow me, ladies. We have just been dismissed and have two hours for ourselves. By no means the worst of things."

With that they arose and went off toward the house, where the queen entered the kitchen and with a friendly yet superior tone asked for the innkeeper. The latter was not present, for which reason the young servant girl promised to have him called from the garden. Isabeau, however, would not hear of it. She would go herself. And go she did, constantly followed by her cortege of three ladies—Balafré described it as the hen with her chicks—making her way to the garden where she discovered the innkeeper laying out new asparagus beds. Directly next to them stood an old-fashioned greenhouse, very low in front with large slanting windows. On its somewhat-crumbling masonry, Lene seated herself along with both daughters of Thibaut d'Arc, while Isabeau directed the negotiations.

"We've come to discuss the midday meal with you, innkeeper. What can we have?"

"Anything the ladies and gentlemen care to order."

"Anything? That's a lot, almost too much. Well then, I'm for eel. But not like this, but like this instead." As she spoke, she pointed first at the ring on her finger and then to her broad, tightly fitting bracelet.

"Sorry, ladies," replied the innkeeper. "Nothing doing with eel. Fish in general. Can't help you there. Only have it now and then. Yesterday we had carp in dill sauce, but that was from Berlin. If I want to have a fish, I've got to get it from the fish market in Kölln."

"Too bad. We could have brought one along. Well, what then?"

"Saddle of venison."

"Hm, that sounds like something. And some vegetables first. Too late for asparagus, or just about. But you've got some young beans, as I see. And in your hotbed, I'm sure you'll find something, a few cucumbers or some lettuce. Then something sweet. Something with whipped cream. Personally, I'm not interested in anything like that, but the gentlemen, who always act as if it didn't mean a thing to them, they're always big on sweets. Well then, three, four courses, I think. And then bread and butter."

"And at what time do the ladies and gentlemen care to have it?"

"Well, soon, I think, or at least as soon as possible. Right? We're hungry and if the venison's on the fire for half an hour, that should do it. Well then, let's say, at twelve. And, if I may, a punch. One bottle of Rhine wine, three of Moselle and three bottles of champagne. But good brands. Don't think it will go to waste on the likes of us. I know my champagne and can taste right away whether it's a Moet or Mumm. But you'll do it up right, if I dare say so. You really inspire me with confidence. By the way, can't we get right out of your garden and into the woods? I hate any unnecessary steps. And maybe we'll find some champignons. That would be heavenly. They could go with the venison. Champignons never spoil anything."

The innkeeper not only responded positively to the question regarding the more commodious path, but even accompanied the ladies personally as far as the garden gate, from which point it was but a few steps to the edge of the woods. Nothing but a tree-lined road intervened. Once across the latter, they were in the shade of the forest and Isabeau, who suffered a good deal from the constantly increasing heat, considered herself fortunate to have avoided the relatively long detour across a treeless meadow. Shutting her elegant parasol, which was embellished however, with a rather large grease spot, and hanging it on her belt, she took Lene's arm, while the two other ladies followed. Obviously in the best of moods, turning to Margot and Joan, she remarked, "We've simply got to have a goal. Just woods and more woods is really awful. What do you think, Joan?"

Joan was the taller of the two d'Arcs, quite pretty, a bit pale, and simply but stylishly dressed. Serge expected as much. Her gloves fitted perfectly and one would have really thought she was a lady if she had not used her teeth to fasten one of the glove buttons that had come undone while Isabeau was conversing with the innkeeper.

"What do you think, Joan?" repeated the queen.

"Well, then I suggest that we go back towards the village from which we've come. Its name was Zeuthen, I think, and it looked so romantic and melancholy. It was such a pretty path to here too, and the way back must be just as pretty or maybe even prettier. And on the right, that is, on the left side going back, there was a cemetery with nothin' but crosses in it. There was a real big one made of marble too."

"Sure, Joan honey, that's all fine and dandy, but what are we supposed to do then? We've already seen the path. And the cemetery? Do you want to . . . ?"

"Sure I do. I've sort of got my feelings, especially on a day like this. And it's always a good thing to keep in mind that you've got to die. And when the lilac is in bloom like this . . ."

"But Joan, the lilac isn't in bloom anymore, at best it's the laburnum and that's already putting out seed pods. Goodness sakes, if you're so keen on cemeteries, why you can go see the one on Oranienstraße every day. But I can see, there's no use talking to you. Zeuthen and cemeteries, that's nothing but nonsense! We'd rather stay here and not see a thing. Come on, little girl, give me your arm again."

The little girl, who was by no means little, was Lene. She obeyed. Once again taking the lead, the queen now continued in a confidential tone, "Ach, that Joan, you really can't go around in public with her. She hasn't got a good reputation and she's nothing but a goose. Glory, kid, you'll never believe the kind that's running around in these circles nowadays. Oh sure, she's got a pretty figure and takes care of her gloves. But she really ought to take care of something else. And y'know, her kind are always talking about dying and cemeteries. But then you ought to see them other times! As long as things are going along like this, everything's just fine. But when the punchbowl goes around a couple of times, then she starts squealin' and hollerin'. No manners at all. But where should the likes of her get them from anyway? She was always with them lower-class people out there on the road to Tegel where nobody that's anybody ever comes, and the artillery just passes by once in a while. And artillery . . . well, you know . . . you'd never believe how different that all is. And now Serge has taken her out of there and wants to make something out of her. Goodness sakes! That just won't happen right off, at least not that snappy. Good things take time.

"But there's still some strawberries there. Well now, that's nice! Come on, little girl, we'll pick a few—if only it weren't for this damned bending—and when we find a real big one, we'll take it along. I'll pop it in his mouth later. He'll like that. After all, y'know, he's just like a little kid and really is the best."

Lene, who was well aware that she was speaking of Balafré, asked a few questions including once again why the gentlemen really had such strange names. She had asked before, she said, but never heard anything worth talking about.

"Good God," said the queen, "you got things goin' on like this, and nobody's even supposed to notice it, and all that's nothin' but a lot a' put-on anyway. First off, nobody makes anything of it, and if somebody does make something of it, it still goes on anyway. And why shouldn't it? Who's it gonna' hurt? They all don't have nothing to reproach themselves for and each one of them is just the same as the other."

Lene stared straight ahead and remained silent.

"And really, kid, and you'll come to see it too, really, it's all just nothing but a bore. For a while it's all right and I don't mean to say anything against it, and I'm not about to swear off it, either. But it gets to you after a while. When you've been at it since you was fifteen, even before gettin' confirmed. Really though, the sooner you're out of it, the better. I'm gonna' buy myself a little bar—I'm gettin' the money—I even know where from already. Then I'm gonna' marry a widower. I even know who already. And he's agreed too. Because, I've got to tell you, I'm for order and respectability and bringin' up the kids in the right way. Whether they're his or mine, don't make no difference. . . . And what's the real story with you?"

Lene did not say a word.

"Oh Lord, kid, why you're getting all red. I'll bet you've got it *here*"—she pointed to her heart—"and you're doing it all for love. Yeah, kid, *then* it's really bad, then you're really in for a smash."

Joan followed with Margot. They remained purposely behind, breaking off birch twigs, as if they intended to weave a wreath from them. "How do you like her?" said Margot. "The one with Gaston, I mean."

"Like her? Not in the least. That's all we need, that the likes of her start playing this game and come into style. Just look at how her gloves fit. And that hat sure ain't much either. He really shouldn't let her go around like that. And she must be dumb too, she never says a word."

"No," said Margot. "She's not dumb, she just hasn't caught on yet. And the fact that she's cosied right up to good old fatso, that's sure smart enough."

"Oh, good old fatso. Don't give me her! She thinks she's really it. But she's nothing at all. I su e don't want to say anything bad about her but she's false, as false as they come."

"No, Joan. If there's one thing she's not it's false. She got you out of a tight spot more than once. You know what I mean."

"Good God, and why? Because she was in it herself too and because she's always putting on airs and acting so important. Anybody as fat as that is never any good."

"Lord, Joan, the things you say. You got it backwards, the fat ones are always good."

"Well, whatever you say. But one thing you can't deny: she looks ridiculous. Just look at the way she waddles along there, like an overfed duck. And always buttoned right up to the top too, just because otherwise she couldn't let herself be seen in front of respectable people. And one thing I won't give in on, Margot, a bit of a trim figure really is the most important thing. We ain't no Turks, y'know. And why didn't she want to go along to the cemetery? Because she's scared? Heaven forbid, she wouldn't even think of it, just because she's got herself all stuffed in and can't hold out from the heat. And really, it ain't so terribly hot at all today."

And so the conversations went, until the two pairs finally came together again and sat down on a moss-covered mound at the side of a ditch.

Isabeau looked at her watch again and again. The hands did not seem to want to move.

When at last it was half past eleven, she said, "Well, ladies, the time has come. I think we've just about had enough nature for one day and can with complete justification pass on to something else. Not a bite since seven this morning. I really can't count that ham sandwich at Grünau. But—thank God—renunciation, as Balafré says, is its own reward and nothing makes you more hungry than an empty stomach. Come on, ladies, that saddle of venison is starting to become more important than anything else. Right, Joan?"

The latter deigned merely to shrug her shoulders and vigorously sought to refute the suggestion that things such as venison or punch could ever carry any weight with her.

Isabeau laughed, however. "Well, we'll just see, Joan. Oh sure, the Zeuthen cemetery would have been better. But you have to take what you've got."

And with that they started on their way, returning from the forest into the garden and from the latter, in which a few butterflies were just chasing one another, to the front of the inn, where they were to eat.

As they passed the restaurant, Isabeau caught sight of the inn-keeper busy pouring out a bottle of Moselle wine. "Too bad," she said. "That I would have to see just that. Fate could have granted me a better sight than that. Why did it have to be Moselle?"

# 14

Despite all of Isabeau's strenuous efforts, a real sense of cheer no longer seemed to return following this stroll. What was worse, at least for Botho and Lene, was that this same feeling of cheer also remained absent when both of them took their leave from his comrades and their ladies and had begun their return journey all alone in a compartment in which they were the sole occupants. An hour later, rather depressed, they arrived at the gloomily illuminated Görlitz station. Here, as she left the train, Lene at once urgently pleaded to be allowed to make her way through the city alone. They were tired and worn-out, she maintained, and that did not do them any good. Botho, however, was not to be dissuaded from what he viewed as due consideration and gentlemanly obligation. Thus, together they undertook the long, long trip along the canal in a rickety old hackney carriage, constantly endeavoring to start a conversation about the outing and "how nice it had been." It was a dreadful and forced conversation, during which Botho felt only too well how right Lene's feelings had been, as she in an almost pleading tone had urged that he not accompany her.

Yes, the excursion to Hankels' Depot, which had held such promise and really begun so beautifully and happily, had in the end turned into nothing but a mixture of ill-humor, weariness, and fatigue. Only at the last moment, when with gentle lovingness and a certain sense of guilt Botho bid her good night, did Lene once again rush to him. Grasping his hand, she kissed him with almost passionate impetuousness. "Oh, Botho," she cried, "it didn't turn out the way it ought to have today. And yet, it was nobody's fault . . . not even the others."

"Don't, Lene."

"No, no. No one was to blame. It's simply the way it is and there's no changing it. But its being like that is just what makes it so terrible. If somebody were to blame, then one could ask for forgiveness and it would be all right again. But that won't do us any good. There's nothing to forgive either."

"Lene . . ."

"You've got to listen for a minute more. Oh, my one and only Botho, you want to hide it from me, but it's coming to an end. And quickly, I know it."

"You don't know what you're saying."

"Of course, I only dreamed it," continued Lene. "But why did I dream it? Because it was in my heart all day. My dream was only what my heart told me was so. And there's one thing more I wanted to tell you, Botho, why I've run back to you like this: I meant what I said to you last night. Being able to live this summer was my happiness, and it will go on being my happiness, even if I'm never happy again from this day on."

"Lene, Lene, don't talk like that. . . ."

"You feel yourself that I'm right. In the goodness of your heart you don't want to admit it, you don't want to recognize that it's so. But I know it. Yesterday, when we were walking through that meadow and talked, and I picked that bouquet for you, that was our last bit of happiness, our last beautiful hour together."

With this conversation the day had come to an end. Now the next morning had arrived and the summer sun shone brightly in Botho's room. Both windows stood open, and in the chestnuts outside sparrows were chirping. Botho, smoking a meerschaum pipe, lay leaning back in a rocking chair, now and again swinging a handkerchief that lay next to him at a large horsefly, which, no sooner than it had gone out one window, immediately reappeared at the other, buzzing stubbornly and relentlessly around him.

"If only I could get rid of this pest! Torment it, torture it, that's what I'd like to do. These flies are always harbingers of bad news and they irk you so maliciously as if they took pleasure themselves in the tribulation they're announcing. In this instant he struck out at it once more. "Got away again. Nothing helps. Well then, resignation. Accepting your lot is always the best thing. The Turks are the smartest folk of all."

Hearing the little wrought-iron gate outside bang closed during this monologue made him look toward the front garden and as he did, he caught sight of the postman, who had just entered. With a quick, military salute and a "Good morning, Herr Baron," the latter passed first a newspaper and then a letter to him through the rather low ground-floor window. Botho threw the newspaper aside, while at the same time looking closely at the letter on which without difficulty he had recognized the tiny, closely spaced but nevertheless extremely legible handwriting of his mother. "Thought so. . . . I know already, even before I've read it. Poor Lene."

And now he opened the letter and read:

*Castle Zehden. June 29, 1875.*

*My dear Botho!*

What I informed you of in my last letter as something I feared might happen, has now taken place: Rothmüller in Arnswalde has given notice of foreclosing and merely added that "for the sake of old friendship" he would be willing to wait until New Year's, if it were to cause me any embarrassment. "He knows well," he says, "what he owes to the memory of the old Baron." Gratuitous comments of this sort, however well-meant they may be, are doubly irritating for me; there is so much pretentious solicitude associated with them which never has a very pleasant effect, least of all when it comes from such a quarter.

You may perhaps understand the unpleasant feelings and concern which these lines caused me. Uncle Kurt Anton would gladly help out, as he has already done on former occasions. He loves me and you above all. But to take advantage of his affection again and again has something particularly disconcerting about it, all the more since he ascribes the blame for our continual embarrassment to our entire family, but especially to you and me. Despite my honest efforts regarding the management of the estate, I am neither economical nor modest enough in my needs for him, in which he may be right, while you are not practical or worldly-wise enough, in which he is also probably on the mark.

Yes, Botho, that is the situation. My brother is a man with a highly developed sense of what is right and proper, and in financial matters possessing a really outstanding generosity. That is something one can say of only a very few of our noblemen. As you know, our dear old Mark Brandenburg is a province where thrift is called for and in situations of great need, penury as well; nevertheless as generous as your uncle is, he has his moods and eccentricities, and seeing himself persistently crossed in this matter has for some time now seriously displeased him. He told me, when I recently took the opportunity to remind him of the foreclosure which once again threatens us, "I'm happy to be of assistance, sister, as you well know, but I openly admit, always being expected to help out in a situation where one could assist one's self at any time if one were just a bit more sensible and a bit less obstinate, is something that makes strong demands on that side of my character which never was the most prominent: my tolerance."

You know what these words refer to, Botho, and I impart them to you today in the same way as they were imparted to me by Uncle Kurt Anton at that time. From your letters and remarks it would seem that there is nothing which you abhor more than sentimental indiscretions, yet I fear that you are yourself involved in one, more deeply in fact than you would care to admit or perhaps even know. I say no more.

Rienäcker put the letter down and paced back and forth in the room, while at the same time half mechanically exchanging the meerschaum for a cigarette. Then he picked up the letter again and continued to read:

Yes, Botho, the future of all of us is in your hands and it is up to you to determine whether this feeling of constant dependence is to go on or come to an end. It is in your hands, I say, but indeed I must add, only for a short while more, in any case not much longer. Uncle Kurt Anton also discussed this with me, especially in regard to the Sellenthin girls' Mama, who at his last visit in Rothenmoor made herself clear not only quite firmly but also with a touch of irritation in this affair, in which she is vitally concerned. Does the House of Rienäcker, she told him, perhaps believe that a fortune, which is constantly decreasing like the Sibylline Books (where she got that simile, I'll never know), is getting more and more valuable?[1] Käthe is going to be twenty-two, has become quite the sophisticated young lady, and with the help of an inheritance coming from her Aunt Kielmannsegge, has at her disposal a fortune whose interest is probably not considerably less than that of the entire principal of the Rienäcker heaths, their Eel Lake included.

Such a young lady is not to be kept waiting, least of all with such persistent indifference. If it were to suit Herr von Rienäcker to drop what had been previously planned and agreed to by his family and to view such earlier arrangements as nothing but child's play, she has nothing against it. Herr von Rienäcker is free the instant he wants to be free. If, on the other hand, he does not intend to make use of this unconditional freedom to withdraw, then it is about time he make that clear as well. It is not her desire that her daughter should become an object of gossip.

From the tone of this you will easily take it, that it is absolutely necessary to come to a decision and to act accordingly. You know what I wish. My wishes, however, are not to be considered obligatory for you. Do what your good sense tells you to do. Decide one way or the other, but for heaven's sake, do something! To withdraw would be more honorable than continued postponement. If you hesitate much longer, we will not only lose the bride, but the good will of the entire Sellenthin family, and what is worse, indeed what is worst of all, we also stand to lose the kindly and always helpful attitude of your uncle. My thoughts are with you, may they also be able to guide you. I repeat, this would be the path to your good fortune and to that of us all. Therewith, I remain, Your loving mother,

*Josephine von R*

Having read to the end, Botho became highly agitated. It was just as the letter said: a postponement was no longer possible. Things were not well with the Rienäcker fortune and there were debts, which to settle through his own wit or energy, he by no means felt in himself the necessary strength. "Who am I? An average person from the so-called upper sphere of society. And what am I capable of doing? I can break in a horse, carve a capon, and know how to gamble at cards. That's all. And so I've got a choice between a circus rider, a headwaiter, or a croupier. At best you can add on a trooper, if I feel like joining some sort of Foreign Legion. Then Lene can come along as Daughter of the Regiment. I can just see her now in a short jacket, military boots, and a little canteen strapped to her back."[2]

He continued in this tone, finding satisfaction in bitter remarks directed against himself. Finally, however, he rang and ordered his horse. He wanted to ride. In a few minutes his splendid chestnut mare stood outside, a present from his uncle and the envy of his comrades as well. He pulled himself into the saddle, gave the boy some instructions and rode off toward the Moabit Bridge. After crossing it, he turned off onto a broad path which led over fen and field to the Jungfernheide. Here he let his horse slow from a trot to a walk and with every passing moment, having up to now yielded to all sorts of unclear thoughts, he began to cross-examine himself increasingly firmly and sharply. "What is it that's keeping me from taking the step that the whole world expects? Do I want to marry Lene? No. Does she expect it? No. Have I promised her, I would? No. Or will our parting get any easier, if I put it off? No. Over and over, it's no. And yet I delay and defer doing the *one* thing which absolutely must be done. And why do I go on putting it off? What's the reason for all this hesitation and delay? Stupid question. Because I love her."

Cannon shots resounding from the Tegel artillery range interrupted his monologue at this point and not until he had once again calmed his horse, which had momentarily become restless, did he once more take up his train of thought and repeat: "Because I love her! Exactly, why should I be ashamed of such a feeling? Our feelings are sovereign and the mere fact that one is in love gives one the right to be in love, regardless of how the world may shake its head or talk of riddles. Anyway, it's not a riddle and even if it were, it's one that I can solve. Every single human being is drawn by nature to certain, sometimes very, very little things, which, regardless of how little they are, give life meaning or else count as the best things in life for him. And for me the best things are simplicity, truthfulness, naturalness. And Lene's got all of them. That's what she's charmed me with. That's the spell from which it's now so hard for me to free myself."

In this instant his horse pricked up its ears and he caught sight of a hare which, startled from a strip of meadowland, raced directly in front of him toward the Jungfernheide. Inquisitively he gazed after it, not returning to his thoughts until it had disappeared between the trees of the heath. "And anyway, was it really something so foolish and impossible that I wanted? No. It's not my way to take on the world and openly declare war on it and its prejudices. I'm completely against any tilting at windmills of that sort. The only thing that I wanted was a bit of discreet happiness, a bit of happiness, for which, sooner or later I expected society's tacit approbation, because of the affront it had been spared. That was my dream and the goal of my hopes and thoughts. And now I'm supposed to turn my back on this happiness and exchange it for something which, as far as I go, isn't happiness at all. I'm utterly indifferent to the atmosphere of the salon, and I abhor anything that's put-on, affected, sophisticated, chic, stylish, savoir faire—all hateful and foreign words to me."

Here his horse, which for the last quarter hour had scarcely been under rein, turned down a side path as if by itself. The path led across a field and immediately beyond it toward a grassy place, hedged in by undergrowth and a few oaks. Here, in the shadow of one of the older trees, stood a short, low-set stone cross, and as he rode closer to see what this cross actually stood for, he read: *Ludwig v. Hinckeldey, Died, 10 March 1856.* How that struck him! He knew that the cross stood somewhere around here, but he had never come as far as this place. Now he saw it as a sign that his horse, left to its own will, had brought him exactly to this spot.[3]

Hinckeldey! It was almost twenty years since that once-almighty personage met his end, and everything that had been said about the affair in his parents' house when the news reached them now stood clearly before him once more. One story above all came again to his mind. One of the middle-class officials who was particularly close to his chief had warned him, advising against it, calling dueling in general insanity and a crime, especially one of this sort and under such circumstances. But his superior, suddenly feeling in *this* affair compelled to play the aristocratic man of honor, had curtly and arrogantly replied, "Nörner, you just don't understand anything about things of this sort." An hour later he had gone to his death. And why? For the sake of an aristocratic idea, a class whim, that had been more powerful even than reason, even more powerful than the law whose guardian and defender it had in fact been his duty to be.

"Instructive. And what am I especially to learn from it? What does this monument say to me? One thing, in any case: our background determines our actions. Whoever obeys that may fall, but he will fall in a better way than whoever contradicts it."

As he continued his reflections, he turned his horse quickly around and rode diagonally across a field towards a large factory area, a steel rolling mill or a machine shop, where from innumerable chimneys dense smoke and columns of fire rose skyward. It was midday and some of the workers sat outside in the shadows to partake of their meal. The women, who had brought the food, stood by chatting. Some of them had infants on their arms and laughed amongst themselves when a roguish or suggestive remark was made. Rienäcker, who only too rightly had ascribed to himself a sense for the unsophisticated, was enchanted at the sight, which opened before him. With a touch of envy he looked at the group of happy people. "Work, daily bread, and order. When our Brandenburg folk marry, it's not passions and love they talk about. They just say, 'I've just got to have my order.' And that is a beautiful trait in the life of our people and not at all a prosaic one. Order means a great deal, sometimes it's everything. And now I ask myself: Has *my* life been in order? No. Order is marriage." He continued in this manner for a while and then he saw Lene again, standing before him. But in her eyes lay nothing of reproach and accusation, but rather just the opposite; she seemed to be agreeing in a kindly way.

"Yes, my dear Lene, you're for work and orderliness too, and you realize what has to be, and aren't making it hard for me. . . . But it's hard nevertheless . . . for you and for me."

He set his horse into a trot once again. For a while he stayed close to the Spree. Then, passing Unter den Zelten, lying still in the midday sun, he turned down a bridle path that brought him to the Wrangel Fountain and immediately thereafter led right to his door.

# 15

Botho wanted to go to Lene immediately, but feeling that he lacked the strength to do so, he at least wanted to write. But that too was impossible. "I can't do it, not today." Thus he let the day pass and waited until the next morning. Then he wrote a brief note:

*Dear Lene!*
Just what you told me day before yesterday has now really happened: parting. Parting forever. I've received letters from home that force me to it. It has to be, and because it has to be, let it be quickly. Oh, how I wish these days were behind us already. I won't say any more, not even how I really feel deep in my heart. It was a short, beautiful time and I'll never forget any of it. I'll be there around nine. I won't come earlier because it mustn't take long. *Auf Wiedersehen*. Just one more time, *auf Wiedersehen*.

*your B. v. R.*

And so he came. Lene stood at the wrought-iron fence and received him as usual. Not the slightest suggestion of reproach nor even of painful resignation lay in her countenance. She took his arm and thus they walked up the front garden path.

"It's good that you've come. I'm happy that you're here. And you've got to be happy too."

As they talked in this way, they reached the house and Botho was about to pass from the entryway into the large front room. Lene drew him past the door, however, saying, "No, Frau Dörr is in there."

"And still angry with us?"

"Not that. I've calmed her down. But what do we want with her today? Come on, it's such a beautiful evening, and we want to be alone together."

He agreed. They walked down the hall, across the courtyard and towards the garden. Sultan did not stir, merely squinting after them as they proceeded up the wide middle path and then made their way towards the bench situated between the raspberry bushes.

When they reached it, they sat down. It was quiet. From the fields one could hear the sound of chirping. Above them stood the moon.

She leaned on him, saying warmly and calmly, "And so this is the last time that I'll hold your hand in mine?"

"Yes, Lene. Can you forgive me?"

"The questions you ask. What should I forgive you for?"

"That I'm hurting you like this."

"Yes, it hurts, that's true."

She became silent again and looked up at the stars, rising palely in the sky above them.

"What are you thinking about, Lene?"

"How beautiful it would be to be up there."

"Don't talk like that. You mustn't wish your life away. From wishes like that, it's only a step to . . ."

She smiled. "No, not that. I'm not like that girl that ran to the well and threw herself in because her boyfriend danced with somebody else. Do you remember how you told me about that?"

"But what do you mean then? You're also not the sort who makes remarks like that, just for the sake of saying them."

"No, I meant it seriously too. Really,"—she pointed upwards— "I'd like to be up there. Then I'd have peace. But I can wait. . . . And now, come on, let's go out into the field. I haven't brought a shawl with me and it's cold sitting here like this."

And so they went up the same path that once before had led them to the foremost row of houses in Wilmersdorf. Under the starlit night the tower was clearly visible; only over the meadows was a thin veil of mist passing.

"Do you still remember how we walked here with Frau Dörr?" asked Botho.

She nodded. "That's why I suggested it. I really wasn't cold, or almost not at all. Oh, it was such a beautiful day that time. I've never been so cheerful and happy, never before and never since. Even at this moment it still makes me happy when I think back on it, the way we walked along and sang 'If You Remember.' Yes, memories mean a lot, they're really everything. And I have them now and they'll stay with me and can never be taken away from me. And my heart has such a wonderful feeling when I think of it."

He embraced her. "You're so good."

Lene went on in her calm way. "And because my heart feels this way, I don't want to let it just pass. I want to tell you everything. In reality it's the same thing I've always told you, even day before yesterday, when we were on that outing that went awry and then afterwards, when we parted. I've seen it coming like this from the very beginning. What's happening now is only what has always had to happen. When you've had a beautiful dream, you've got to thank God for it, and can't complain that it's over and reality's beginning again. It's hard right now, but everything can be forgotten, or things will look better again. One day you'll be happy again and perhaps I will too."

"Do you think so? And if not, what then?"

"Then you live without being happy."

"Oh Lene, you say that so easily, as if happiness were nothing at all. But it is something, and that's what torments me and makes me feel that I've done you a great wrong."

"I acquit you of anything like that. You haven't done me any wrong. You've not led me astray and you've never made me any promises. It was all of my own free choice. I loved you from the bottom of my heart and that was my destiny. And if there was any guilt involved, it was *my* guilt. Besides, I've got to tell you again and again, it was a guilt that makes me glad to the depths of my soul, because it's meant my happiness. If I've got to pay for it now, I'll pay gladly. You've done no harm, injured nothing, insulted nothing, or at most just what people call respectability and morality. Should I feel remorse for something like that? No. Everything will straighten itself out again, even that. . . . Come on now, let's turn back. Just look how the fog is rising. I think Frau Dörr has gone by now and we'll find the good old woman alone. She knows about everything and she's been saying the same thing over and over the whole day through."

"What?"

"That it's for the best this way."

Frau Nimptsch really was alone as Botho and Lene entered. Everything was quiet and dimly lit, only the fire from the hearth cast a glow over the broad shadows which slanted through the entire room. The goldfinch had long since gone to sleep in his cage and nothing was to be heard except for the occasional hissing of water as it boiled over.

"Good evening, old girl!" said Botho.

The old woman returned his greeting and was on the point of rising from her footstool to pull over the large easy chair. Botho, however, would not hear of it, and said, "No, old girl, I'll just sit down at my old place."

As he spoke he pushed his stool towards the fire.

A brief pause ensued. Soon, however, he began anew. "I've come to say good-bye and to thank you for all the dear and good things that I've had here for so long. Yes, old girl, right from the bottom of my heart. I really enjoyed being here and was truly happy. And now it's time to go. The only thing left to say is just that it probably really is best this way."

The old woman remained silent, nodding in agreement. "But I'm not leaving the world," said Botho, "and I won't forget you, old girl. Now, give me your hand. There. And now, good night."

With that he stood up quickly and strode to the door, Lene clinging closely to him. In this manner they went as far as the garden gate, without another word having been spoken. Then, however, she whispered, "Be quick, Botho! I can't hold out much longer. It's really been too much, these two days. Good-bye, my only one. Be happy, as you well deserve, and as happy as you've made me. Then you'll be truly happy. As for the rest, we won't say anything more about it. It's not worth talking about. There . . . there."

She kissed him once and then again and then she shut the gate.

Catching sight of Lene again as he reached the other side of the street, he seemed to want to turn back and exchange words and kisses with her once more. But she held him back with a sharp wave of her hand. Thus he walked further down the street, while she, her head on her arm and her arm resting on the gatepost, looked after him with wide eyes.

She stood in this way for a long while, until his footsteps ceased to echo in the stillness of the night.

# 16

The marriage had taken place at the Sellenthin estate Rothenmoor in the middle of September. Uncle Osten, otherwise no public speaker, raised his glass to the bridal couple in what was without doubt the longest toast of his life. Next day the *Kreuzzeitung* carried the following among its family announcements: "Botho, Baron von Rienäcker, First Lieutenant, Imperial Regiment of Cuirassiers, and Käthe, Baroness von Rienäcker, herewith respectfully announce their marriage which took place yesterday."

The *Kreuzzeitung,* as well can be imagined, was not the sort of journal which usually found its way to the Dörr's garden quarters and its adjoining structures. Nevertheless on the very next morning there arrived a letter addressed to Fräulein Magdalene Nimptsch, in which nothing was to be found except the newspaper clipping with the marriage announcement. Lene gave a start, but collected herself more quickly than the sender—in all probability an envious seamstress colleague—might have expected. That the missive originated from such a source could be easily deduced from the form of address which had been inscribed on the envelope: "To that most Highborn Lady." It was this very malice, however, intended to double the pain, which in fact stood Lene in good stead, helping to reduce the bitter feeling in her that this news might otherwise have caused.

Botho and Käthe von Rienäcker embarked for Dresden on their wedding day itself, after both had safely withstood the enticement of visiting cousins in the *Neumark*. They had, in fact, no cause to regret their choice, least of all Botho, who congratulated himself every day not only on their sojourn in Dresden, but even more on the possession of such a young wife, who seemed totally unacquainted with either caprice or bad humor.

It was really so, she laughed all day long. Her disposition was every bit as radiant and bright blond as her appearance. She took delight in everything and discovered the cheerful side of whatever she encountered. In the hotel where they were staying, for instance, there was a waiter with a toupee, which resembled the crest of a wave about to tumble over. This waiter, along with his coiffure, was her daily joy to such an extent that, despite being usually lacking in wit, she really outdid herself in images and comparisons.

Botho was enjoying himself too, and laughed along heartily, until all at once a note of uneasiness began to mingle with his laughter. He began to notice, in fact, that regardless of what might happen or come to her attention, she focused solely on the trivial or comical aspect of it. And so, when after a stay of fourteen days, the two embarked on their homeward journey to Berlin, it happened that a brief conversation, just as they were getting under way, imparted complete certainty to him regarding this side of his wife's character. They had a compartment to themselves, and as they were crossing the bridge over the Elbe and looking back once again to bid farewell to the Dresden Altstadt and the dome of the *Frauenkirche*, Botho took her hand and asked, "Now tell me, Käthe, what was actually the nicest thing here in Dresden?"

"Guess!"

"Well, that's difficult. You have your own sort of taste, so to speak, and church choirs and Holbein Madonnas really aren't your cup of tea."

"No. You're certainly right there. I won't keep my lord and master waiting and in torment about it either. There were three things that I found simply delightful: first off, that café at the corner of the Altmarkt and the Scheffelgasse with all those wonderful pastries and that liqueur. Just sitting there like that . . ."

"But Käthe, you couldn't sit there at all, you could scarcely even stand. Why, it was really as if one had to fight for every bite."

"That's it exactly. That's just it, dear boy. Everything that one has to fight for . . ."

She turned away and teasingly pretended to be pouting until he heartily gave her a kiss.

"I see," she laughed, "when all's said and done you really do agree with me, and as a reward you now get to hear the second and third things. My second was the open-air summer theater where we saw *Monsieur Herkules* and Knaack drummed the *Tannhäuser* March on a rickety old whist table. I've never seen anything as funny in my whole life and you probably haven't either. It was really just too funny. . . . And the third, well the third was *Bacchus on the Ile Goat* in the *Green Chamber* and *The Dog Scratching Himself* by Peter Vischer."[1]

"I thought as much, and if Uncle Osten hears of it, he'll say you're right and be more fond of you than he is already, and he'll say even more often than he does now, 'I tell you Botho, that Käthe . . .' "

"And shouldn't he?"

"Oh, of course, he should."

With that their conversation broke off for several minutes. But as tenderly and lovingly as he looked across at his young wife, its contents nevertheless echoed somewhat distressingly in Botho's soul. His young wife, however, did not have the slightest suspicion of what was going on in her husband's mind, and merely remarked, "I'm tired, Botho. All those pictures. It really does catch up with you. But"—at that moment the train came to a halt—"whatever is all that noise and commotion out there?"

"It's a Dresden amusement park, Kötzschenbroda, I think."

"Kötzschenbroda? What a name. Just too funny."

While the train steamed on, she stretched herself out, seeming to close her eyes. But she did not sleep. Instead, she looked over at her beloved husband through half-closed eyelids.

On Landgrafenstraβe, which in those days still had only one row of houses, Käthe's Mama had in the meantime readied their apartment. At the beginning of October, when the young couple once again returned to Berlin, they were delighted with the comfortable lodgings which they found. In both front rooms, each of which had a fireplace, a fire was burning. The doors and windows stood open nevertheless, for the fires had been started merely for the sake of appearances and ventilation. The most attractive thing, however, was the large balcony with its wide, low-hanging awning, from under which one could look straight out into the country, first over the little forest of birch trees and the Zoological Gardens, and beyond them, all the way to the northernmost corner of the Grunewald.

Käthe clapped her hands with joy at this splendidly unimpeded view, after which she embraced her Mama, and gave Botho a kiss. Suddenly she pointed towards the left. There, between occasional poplars and a few willows, a shingled tower could be seen. "Look, Botho, how funny. Why, it looks like it's bent in three places. And that village next to it. What's the name of it?"

"Wilmersdorf, I think," stuttered Botho.

"Well then, fine. Wilmersdorf. But what's this 'I think?' You certainly must know the names of the villages around here. Just look at him, Mama. Doesn't he look as if he'd just revealed some state secret to us? Really, nothing funnier than these men."

With that they once again left the balcony to take their first midday meal *en famille* in the adjoining room: only Mama, the young couple and Serge, who was the sole invited guest.

Rienäcker's apartment was scarcely a thousand paces from Frau Nimptsch's house. Lene knew nothing of the fact, however, and often made her way down Landgrafenstraße, something she would certainly have avoided, had she had even the slightest idea of their being neighbors.

But it couldn't remain a mystery to her for long.

It was already the third week of October, and the sun was shining with such warmth, that one hardly felt the sharper bite in the air. "I've got to go into town, mother," said Lene, "Goldstein has written me. He wants to discuss a pattern that's supposed to be embroidered on the things for the Princess of Waldeck. And when I'm in town, I want to visit Frau Demuth on Alte Jakobstraße. Otherwise you just lose touch with everybody. But I'll be back by noon. I'll say something to Frau Dörr, so that she looks in on you."

"That's all right, Lene. That's all right. I'd rather be left alone. Old lady Dörr talks so much, you know, an' always about that husband of hers. I got my fire here. And when the goldfinch chirps now and then, that's plenty for me. But, if you was to bring me back a little bag of something—I got such a raw feelin' in my throat these days, and them malt drops are always so soothin'. . . ."

"Fine, mother."

With that Lene left the quiet little dwelling, making her way first down Kurfürstenstraße and then down the long Potsdamerstraße towards the Spittelmarkt, where Goldstein Brothers had their business. Everything went as desired, and it was nearly noon as she made her way back, this time taking Lützowstraße rather than Kurfürstenstraße. The sun did her good and the bustle on the Magdeburger Platz, where it had been market day and everyone was now getting ready to shut up shop, so pleased her that she remained standing for a while, looking on at the colorful commotion. It was as if she were mesmerized by it all, and not until the fire brigade clattered past with a tremendous uproar did she arouse herself.

Lene listened until the clanging and banging had receded in the distance. Then she looked down towards the left at the clock of the Church of the Twelve Apostles. "Just twelve," she said. "It's time to get a move on. She always gets upset, whenever I get there later than she thinks I should." Thus she made her way down Lützowstraße towards the square of the same name. Suddenly, however, she stopped, not knowing where to turn. Not far from her she recognized Botho, walking directly towards her with a young and beautiful woman on his arm. The young woman was speaking in a lively manner and from the looks of it solely about comical things, for Botho was laughing continuously as he looked down at her. It was to this that she owed her not being long since noticed.

Quickly making the decision to avoid meeting him at any price, she turned away from the sidewalk to the right and headed towards the first large shop window which happened to be at hand. Before it lay a square corrugated iron plate, presumably a cover for a cellar opening. The shop window itself was that of an ordinary grocery store, with the usual display of paraffin candles and "mixed-pickle" jars—nothing special. Lene, however, stared at it as if she had never seen its like before. And, in fact, it was just in time; at that very instant the young couple passed so closely by her that not a word of the conversation between them escaped her.

"Not so loud, Käthe," Botho was saying, "people are looking at us already."

"Let them . . ."

"In the end they'll think we're having a quarrel."

"While we're laughing? Quarreling and laughing?"

She laughed once more.

Lene felt the trembling of the thin iron plate on which she was standing. A brass rail extended horizontally in front of the glass shop window for its protection; for an instant it seemed to her as if she would have to reach out to it for support and assistance. She continued to hold herself erect, however, and not until she could be certain that both were far enough away, did she again turn to go on. Gingerly she made her way along the houses, and for a short stretch was able to keep moving. Soon, however, she felt as if she were going to faint. Thus, no sooner had she reached the next cross street which led to the canal, than she turned into it and entered a front garden whose wrought-iron gate stood open. Only with effort was she still able to drag herself up the few steps of a small flight of stairs which led to a veranda and raised ground floor. Here, close to losing consciousness, she sat down.

As she again came to herself, she could see that a half-grown girl was standing next to her, looking at her with sympathy. In her hand was a spade with which she had been digging in the small garden beds. From the veranda railing an old nanny watched with scarcely less curiosity. Apparently no one else was at home except for the child and the servant. Thanking both, Lene stood up and made her way towards the gate once more. The half-grown girl gazed after her with a look of mournful astonishment, however, and it seemed almost as if for the first time an awareness of the sorrows of life had been awakened in the child's heart.

In the meantime, having crossed the street, Lene had now reached the canal. She walked along its embankment where she could be certain not to meet anyone. Now and then a Pomeranian yapped from the barges, and since it was noon, thin columns of smoke rose from the small cabin stovepipes. She, however, saw or heard nothing, or at least she was not aware of what was going on around her. Not until she reached the spot beyond the zoo, where the houses along the canal stopped, and the large sluice gate with water foaming over it came into sight, did she remain standing, gasping for air. "Oh, if only one could just cry," she said, as she pressed her hand to her breast and heart.

At home she found her mother in the usual place and seated herself across from her without a word being exchanged between them. Suddenly, however, the old woman, who until then had been staring constantly in the same direction, looked up from the fire, and gave a start as she perceived the change in Lene's countenance.

"Lene, child, what's wrong? Lene, you look so strange." And as difficult as it usually was for her to get around, in a flash she was up from her footstool, looking for the pitcher with which to sprinkle water on the girl, who remained sitting before her as if she were half-dead. But the pitcher was empty and thus she hobbled towards the hall and from there to the courtyard and into the garden to call for good old Frau Dörr, who was cutting wallflowers and honeysuckle to make bouquets for market. Her husband was standing next to her, saying, "Don't use too much string."

As she heard the old woman's pathetic cries coming from the distance, Frau Dörr turned pale. In a loud voice she responded, "Here I come, Mother Nimptsch, here I come." Throwing away all the flowers as well as the cord she held in her hand, she immediately set out for the little house in the front, because, as she told herself, "Something really must be wrong there."

"Right, . . . just as I thought, Leneken." As she spoke, she shook and shoved the girl, who remained sitting as before, lifeless. In the meantime the old woman came in slowly after her, shuffling through the hall.

"We got to get her into bed," cried Frau Dörr. Old Mother Nimptsch herself was getting ready to take hold, but that was hardly what the sturdy Frau Dörr had in mind when she said "we." "I'll handle this by myself, Mother Nimptsch," she said, and taking Lene in her arms, carried her into the next room and covered her up.

"There, Mother Nimptsch. Now a hot dish cover. I know about these things. It comes from the blood. First you gotta get a dish cover then a warm brick on the sole of the foot, right under the instep, that's where the life is. But what do you think is the cause of it? Must be excitement for sure."

"Don't know. She hasn't said a word to me. But I think, maybe, she's seen him."

"Sure enough. That's it. I know about things like that. . . . But now let's get them windows down and them blinds too. Some folks go in for camphor and Hoffmann's smelling salts but camphor makes you real weak and it really ain't good for nothin' but moths.

No sir, dear old Frau Nimptsch, anybody that's got a good constitution, and is still young in the bargain ought to be able to help themself. That's why I'm always for a good sweat. But it's got to be the right way. And what's the cause of it all? Men, that's what. And still you can't do without 'em. . . . There, she's gettin' some color back."

"Shouldn't we better send for the doctor?"

"Oh, God forbid. They're all out ridin' around right now makin' house calls. By the time one of them gets here, she could be dead'n resurrected again three times over."

# 17

Two and a half years had passed since that meeting, during which much had changed in our circle of friends and acquaintances, except on Landgrafenstraße.

Here the same good humor continued to prevail, the cheerfulness of what perhaps might have depressed other young wives—the fact that the couple continued to be merely a couple—was not for an instant an occasion of suffering for Käthe. She enjoyed life so much and found such complete satisfaction in chic and chatter, riding and driving, that she sooner shrank from an alteration in their domestic scene than wished for one. A sense of family, not to mention a longing for one, had not yet dawned in her and when her Mama made a remark about these matters in one of her letters, Käthe rather heretically replied: "Don't worry, Mama, Botho's brother has just gotten engaged too, and the wedding is to be in six months. I'll gladly leave it to my future sister-in-law to concern herself with the continuation of the House of Rienäcker."

Botho saw the thing somewhat differently, yet his happiness too was not especially dimmed by the missing element, and when nevertheless now and again a sense of dissatisfaction came over him, it was primarily because, while it was perhaps possible to exchange a passably reasonable word with Käthe, it was by no means possible to exchange a serious one. She was entertaining and at times let herself even be carried away to the point of making clever observations, but even the best things she said were superficial and facetious, as if she lacked the ability to distinguish between significant and insignificant matters. Worst of all, she viewed it all as an advantage, and was perfectly satisfied with herself about it without having the slightest intention of changing. "But Käthe, Käthe," Botho would then cry, allowing some of his disapproval to surface as well. Time and again, however, her cheerful nature was able to disarm him, in fact to such an extent that he almost felt himself to be pedantic because of the criticisms that he raised.

Lene, with her simplicity, truthfulness, and straightforwardness, often stood before his soul, disappearing, however, just as quickly. It was only when chance occurrences once again evoked a specific event in all its reality, that along with this greater sense of reality, stronger feelings arose as well, and sometimes even an embarrassing situation.

Such a chance occurrence took place right in the very first summer, as the young couple, having just come from a dinner with Count Alten, were taking tea on their balcony. Käthe lay back in her chair, having him read her an article from the newspaper about parsonage and surplice fees, which was crammed with statistics. Actually, she understood very little of the whole thing, all the less inasmuch as the large number of figures bothered her. Nevertheless, she listened rather attentively because all the young "missies" from the *Mark* spend half their girlhood "at the vicar's" and thus preserve an interest in parsonage affairs. So it was today as well. Evening came at last, and in the same instant as darkness began to fall, the concert over in the zoo commenced and a delightful Strauss waltz resounded from the distance.

"Just listen, Botho," said Käthe, sitting up, then adding highspiritedly, "Come on, let's dance." Without waiting for his acquiescence, she pulled him out of his chair, and waltzed him into the large room off the balcony and then several times around it. Then she gave him a kiss and said, as she nestled close to him, "You know, Botho, I've never danced as wonderfully before. Not even at my first ball, the one I was at when I was still at Zülow's, in fact, I might as well admit, before I was even confirmed. Uncle Osten took me on his responsibility and Mama doesn't know about it till this day. But even that wasn't as beautiful as this evening. But forbidden fruit always tastes the sweetest, doesn't it? But you're not saying a word. Why you're even embarrassed, Botho. See, I've caught you again."

Botho wanted to say something, but she never let him begin. "I really think, Botho, that my sister Ine has put a spell on you. And don't think you can try and console me by telling me that she's still just a schoolgirl, or not much beyond. They're always the most dangerous types. Isn't that so? Well, I'll pretend I haven't noticed a thing, and let you two have your little fling. But it's the old stories, the old, old stories, that I'm jealous about, much, much more than the new ones."

"That's odd," said Botho, attempting to laugh.

"And yet, in the end, not half as odd as it looks," continued Käthe. "You see, you've got the new stories more or less right in front of your eyes and it really would be awful and the other person would really have to be a master at deception, if you didn't notice anything, and just let yourself be fooled completely. But the old stories, you've got no control over them, there can have been a thousand and three of those and you'd scarcely know . . ."

"And what you don't know . . ."

"Can *still* hurt you anyway. But let's drop the subject. Read me some more from your newspaper. I had to keep thinking of the Kluckhuhns. That dear old woman doesn't understand a thing like that. And her oldest is supposed to be getting ready to go off to the university."

Such occurrences happened more and more frequently, and along with past events, also conjured up Lene's picture in Botho's soul. But her he never saw, which struck him as odd, since he knew, of course, that they were practically neighbors.

It struck him as odd and yet it would have been easy for him to understand, had he only learned betimes that Frau Nimptsch and Lene were no longer to be found at the old location. For so it was. From the day on which Lene encountered the young couple on Lützowstraße, she declared to the old woman that she could no longer stay in Dörr's house. When old Mother Nimptsch, who usually never protested, whimpered and shook her head and went on and on referring to the hearth, Lene replied, "Mother, you certainly must know me by now. I won't take your hearth and your fire away from you. You'll get them all back. I've saved up money for that, and if I didn't have enough already, I'd work until I got it all together. But we've got to leave here. I have to go by there every day, I can't endure that, Mother. I don't begrudge him his happiness. No, more than that, I'm happy that he has it. God knows that's true! He was always a good and dear person and did everything to please me, and there never was any arrogance or fancy airs about him. And to say it straight out, even though I usually can't stand fine gentlemen, he was a real nobleman, somebody who really had his heart in the right place. Yes, my one and only Botho, I want you to be happy, as happy as you well deserve. But I can't look on, Mother, I've got to get away from here, because every time I just take ten steps, I think he's standing there in front of me. And as a result, I'm constantly shaking all over. No, no, it can't go on like this. But you'll get your fireplace. That's a promise from me, your Lene."

After this conversation all resistance on the part of the old woman was abandoned. Frau Dörr too said, "Sure, you got to move out. And that old skinflint Dörr, it just serves him right. He was always grumblin' to me that you were sittin' here too cheap and that he wasn't even making enough to cover repairs and taxes. Well, now he can be happy, when the whole place stands empty on him. And that's just what'll happen. Who's gonna' move into a doll's house like this, where every cat that goes by can look in the window, and there ain't no gas or no water line either. Why sure, you got quarterly notice rights and can get out at Easter and none of his tantrums'll do him a bit of good. And it makes me downright glad, Lene, that's how awful I am. But I got to pay right off for my pleasure about it, 'cause when you're gone, honey, 'n good old Frau Nimptsch with her fire and her teapot and her water that's always boiling, well, Lene, who'll I have then? Nothin' but *him* 'n' Sultan 'n' that dumb kid who's just gettin' dumber. Outside of that, nobody at all. And when it gets cold and the snow starts fallin' sometimes it's enough to make you turn Cath'lic out'a sheer boredom 'n' loneliness."

Those were more or less the first discussions as the plan of moving became fixed in Lene's mind, and when Easter arrived, a furniture wagon actually did pull up to load their few possessions. Old Dörr behaved surprisingly well right to the last moment and after a solemn parting, Frau Nimptsch was packed into a cab along with her squirrel and her goldfinch and driven to the Luisenufer, where, three flights up, Lene had rented a small but attractive apartment. Not only had she purchased a few new pieces of furniture, but in keeping with her promise, she had also seen to it that a hearth was built onto the large stove in the front room. At first there had been all sorts of difficulties on the part of the landlord, because, as he argued, structures like that built on in front ruin the oven. Giving her reasons, however, Lene held her ground, which was something that made a great effect on the old and kindly cabinetmaker, who admired things of that sort, and so was convinced to give in.

Both now lived more or less in the same manner as they had lived before in Dörr's garden house, but with the difference that they now sat three floors up and instead of the fantastic towers of the elephant house, they now looked out at the pretty dome of St. Michael's Church. In fact, the view which they now enjoyed was really delightful. It was so beautiful and open that it even gained an influence over the habits of old Mother Nimptsch, inducing her not just to sit on her footstool in front of the fire anymore, but instead, when the sun shone, also to take a place in front of the open window, where Lene had arranged a raised step. All of that really did wonders for old Frau Nimptsch and improved her health to such an extent that since changing living quarters, she no longer suffered as much from rheumatic aches as before in Dörr's garden house, which, as poetically as it may have been situated, had really not been much better than a cellar.

Of course, not a single week passed in which, despite the endlessly long way, Frau Dörr did not appear, having come from the "Zoological" to the Luisenufer, just "to see how things stand." Like all Berlin married women, she then spoke exclusively about her husband, regularly striking a tone as if her marriage to him had been one of the worst mésalliances of all time and something that to her actually bordered on the inexplicable. In reality though, things were such that she not only felt herself extremely contented and satisfied, but actually pleased that Dörr was exactly as he was. She had nothing but advantage from the situation: on one hand that of becoming continuously richer, while on the other and just as important to her, being constantly able to exalt herself over the old skinflint and to reproach him for his meanness, without the slightest danger of any alteration or diminution of her capital.

Yes indeed, Dörr was the main topic of these conversations and Lene, whenever she was not at Goldsteins or somewhere else in town, laughed heartily too, all the more heartily since she, like Frau Nimptsch, had visibly recovered since their move. From the beginning, putting things in order, making new purchases and fixing what had to be fixed had, as can be imagined, drawn her away from her introspection. And what was still more important and really of primary advantage for her health and recovery, was that she no longer needed to fear an encounter with Botho. Who came to the Luisenufer? Certainly not Botho. All of that combined to keep her looking comparatively refreshed and cheerful once more. Only one thing remained which outwardly recalled the struggle which lay behind her: right in the middle of where she parted her hair now grew a streak of gray. Mother Nimptsch seemed not to notice it, or else made little of it. Frau Dörr, however, who in her way was in touch with the latest styles and uncommonly proud of her genuine braid, saw the white streak right off and said to Lene, "My God, Lene, right there on the left. But naturally, sure, that's where it is . . . it's gotta' be on the left."

It was shortly after the move that this conversation took place. Otherwise neither Botho nor the old days were generally mentioned. The reason was simply that whenever the conversation took a turn towards specifically *this* topic, Lene would break it off quickly or else more than likely leave the room. Frau Dörr noticed this after it occurred several times and thus remained silent about things of which it was plainly obvious that no one wished either to speak or hear.

Thus an entire year passed and by the time that year was up another reason had presented itself which no longer made it seem advisable to dig up old stories. Next door, in fact, adjoining Frau Nimptsch's, a new tenant had moved in, a man who by keeping with good neighborliness, promised from the outset to become more than just a good neighbor. Every evening he came to chat, so that now and then it reminded one of the times when Dörr sat on his stool, smoking his pipe, except that the new neighbor was different in many respects. An orderly and educated man, he possessed if not refined then at least very respectable manners and was a good conversationalist in the bargain. Whenever Lene was present, he would talk about all sorts of municipal affairs: schools, gas works, sewage systems, and now and then about his travels. If it happened that he found himself alone with the old woman, it did not bother him in the least; he played "Life and Death," or checkers or sometimes even helped her lay out a game of solitaire, although he actually despised cards altogether. He was a religious nonconformist, and after having first been active among the Mennonites and then later among the Irvingites, he had recently established his own independent sect.

As can well be imagined, all of this excited Frau Dörr's curiosity to the utmost, and as a result she did not weary in asking questions or making hints, although always when Lene was doing something about the house, or taking care of all sorts of purchases in the city. "Tell me, *liebe* Frau Nimptsch, what is he really? I looked it up, but he ain't in the city directory yet. Dörr's only got the one from last year. Franke's his name?"

"Yes, Franke."

"Franke. There was one of them in the Ohmgasse, a master cooper. Only had one eye. I mean, the other one was still there, but there wasn't nothin' left but just the white. Looked just like a fish bladder. And do y'know what was the cause of it? A ring jumped off, while he was puttin' it on and the point went right into his eye. That's what did it. Think he comes from that family?"

"No, Frau Dörr, he ain't from around here at all. He comes from Bremen."

"Oh, I see. Well then, then it's perfectly natural."

Frau Nimptsch nodded in agreement, without being further enlightened regarding the assurance that it was natural and went on, "From Bremen to America don't take no more than fourteen days. That's where he went. And he was something like a plumber or a locksmith or a machinist, but when he seen that it wasn't working out, he became a doctor and went around with nothin' but little bottles, and he's supposed to have done some preaching too. And because he preached so good, he was taken on by . . . well, now I forgot again. But they're supposed to be all nothing but real pious people and real respectable too."

"Good Lord in heaven above," said Frau Dörr. "He ain't one of them. . . . Good God, what do you call them, that got so many wives, always six or seven right off and some even more. . . . I don't know what they ever do with so many."

There was a topic that seemed to have been created just for Frau Dörr. But Mother Nimptsch calmed her friend and said, "No, dear Frau Dörr, it's something else again. I thought it might be something like that too at first, but then he just laughed an' said, 'Heaven forbid, Frau Nimptsch. I'm a bachelor. And when I get married, I expect that one'll be just about enough for me.' "

"Well, there goes a stone from my heart," said Frau Dörr. "And what happened then? I mean, over there in America?"

"Well, afterwards things turned out real fine, and in no time he was out of trouble. You know how them pious folk are, they always help one another out. And so he got back his old customers and his old trade too. And he's still got it and he's in a big factory here on Köpenicker Straße, where they make little pipes and burners and gas jets and everything that they need for gas. And he's a boss there, something like a carpenters' or a bricklayers' foreman, and he's probably got a hundred people under him. And he's a very respectable man with a top hat'n black gloves. And he's got a good salary too."

"And Lene?"

"Well, Lene, she'd take him all right. And why shouldn't she either? But, you know, she can't keep her mouth shut, and when he comes and says something to her, then she'll tell him everything, all the old stories; first the one with Kühlwein—and that's so long ago, as if it really never even happened—and then the one with the baron. And Franke, you know, is a fine and upright man, really actually a gentlemen."

"We've got to talk her out of it. He don't have to know everything. What for anyway? Even we don't know everything."

"True, true, but you know Lene . . ."

# 18

Now June 1878 had come. Frau von Rienäcker and Frau von Sellenthin had been visiting the young couple throughout May, and mother and mother-in-law convinced themselves more and more every day that they found their Käthe paler, more anemic, and weaker than ever. As one can well imagine, they did not cease urging that a specialist be consulted. With the latter's assistance, after what were incidentally, very expensive gynecological examinations, a four-week cure in Schlangenbad was determined to be absolutely indispensable. Schwalbach could then follow.[1] Käthe merely laughed and wanted to have none of it, least of all Schlangenbad. There was, she maintained, something in the name that gave her the creeps, so that she could already feel the viper at her breast.[2] But in the end she gave in, finding a satisfaction in the ensuing preparations for the journey which went beyond what she anticipated from the cure.

She went into town daily in order to make the necessary purchases, and did not weary in informing everyone, how she was only now at last learning to comprehend that "shopping" of the English ladies, which currently occupied such a high place in favor and esteem. Wandering about from shop to shop like that, always finding pretty things and polite people was, she declared, a real pleasure and highly instructive in the bargain; you got to see so much that you weren't yet familiar with, or hadn't even heard about. As a rule, Botho also took part in these expeditions and before the first week in June had arrived, half of the entire Rienäcker apartment had been transformed into a small exhibition of traveling things. A gigantic trunk with brass trimming, which Botho not unjustly entitled "the coffin of my riches," began the roundelay, then came two somewhat smaller ones of Russian leather, along with handbags, traveling blankets, and cushions. Spread out across the sofa lay the traveling wardrobe, a duster on top, along with a pair of marvelous, thick-soled, heavily laced boots, as if some sort of Alpine expedition were in the offing.

The trip was to get under way on St. John's Day, the 24th of June. But the day before, Käthe wanted to have the *cercle intime* gathered around her once again, and thus Wedell, one of the young Ostens, and of course Pitt and Serge had been invited for a relatively early hour. In addition, there was Käthe's special favorite, Balafré, who at Mars-la-tour and as a Halberstädter besides, had taken part in the famous charge and acquired his nickname as the result of a really magnificent slash right across his brow and cheek.

Käthe sat between Wedell and Balafré and did not look as if she was in particular need of Schlangenbad or any other water cure in the entire world; her color was excellent, she was laughing and asking a hundred questions, and whenever someone of whom she had asked a question started to respond, a minimum of words were all she needed by way of an answer. It was really she who led the conversation and no one took offense, for she practiced the art of pleasantly vacuous chatter with consummate mastery. Balafré asked how she pictured her life during the cure. Schlangenbad, he remarked, was not only famous for its miraculous therapy, but far, far more for its boredom, and four weeks of boredom at the baths would be a bit much, even under the best of therapeutic circumstances.

"Oh, my dear Balafré," said Käthe, "you really shouldn't frighten me like that and you wouldn't either, if you knew how much Botho's done for me. Why, he's even put eight volumes of novellas in my trunk—as the bottom layer, of course—and just so my imagination doesn't get too overheated in a way that would be harmful to the cure, he's thrown in a book on artificial fish breeding as well."

Balafré burst out laughing.

"Oh yes, go right ahead and laugh, dear friend, and yet you only know the half of it. The main thing is his motivation. Botho never does anything without a good reason, you know. What I just said

about my imagination being protected from harm by that fish brochure was, of course, just a joke; the serious thing about it is that
I've really *got* to read that kind of thing, the brochure, I mean,
for patriotic reasons in fact. The Neumark, you know, our
common happy homeland, has been the hatchery and birthplace of
artifical fish breeding for years now, and if I didn't know something
about this new nutritional factor that's so important to our national
economy, I simply wouldn't be able to show my face in the
Landsberg District beyond the Oder, least of all at my cousin Borne's
in Berneuchen."

Botho wanted to say something, but she cut him off and continued, "I know what you're going to say, that those eight novellas
are just there as a last resort. Of course, of course, you're always so
frightfully prudent. But I think that your 'last resort' simply won't
even come up. I've gotten a letter, you see, from my sister Ine, who
wrote that Anna Grävenitz has been there for a week already. You
know her, of course, Wedell, her maiden name was Rohr, charming
little blond. I was with her at Madame Zülow's Finishing School, we
were even in the same class. And I remember how we both raved over
our divine Felix Bachmann and even wrote verses to him until good
old Zülow said that she wouldn't put up with that sort of nonsense.
And Ine writes me that Elly Winterfeld is coming too. And so I tell
myself, in the company of two charming young ladies—with me as
the third, even if I'm not at all to be compared to the other two—in
such good company, I say, one really ought to be able to survive.
Isn't that right, Balafré, my dear?"

The latter bowed with a grotesque gesture, which was supposed to
express his complete agreement, with the sole exception of her
insistance that she took second place to anyone else in the world.
This notwithstanding, however, he returned to his original inter-
rogation, saying, "If I could hear just a few details, gracious lady.
Individual things, minutes, so to speak, it's they that determine our
happiness and unhappiness. And a day has so many minutes."

"Well then, I picture it like this. Every morning, correspondence.
Then the promenade concert and a stroll with my two lady friends,
preferably on some secluded avenue. Then we'll sit down and read
one another the letters, which I hope we'll be receiving, and we'll
laugh whenever he writes something that's tender and say, 'Ah, yes.'

Then comes our water cure and after the bath we attend to our toilet, naturally with the utmost care and attention, which in Schlangenbad certainly can't be any less entertaining than in Berlin. Probably just the opposite. And then we go to lunch and we'll have a general on our right and a rich industrialist on our left. I've had a passion for industrialists ever since I was a girl. And it's a passion that I'm not in the least ashamed of, because either they've invented some new armor plating, or laid an undersea telegraph, or drilled a tunnel, or put up a cog-wheeled railway. And besides, something that I by no means despise either, they're rich. And after lunch, we'll have coffee in the reading room with the venetian blinds lowered so that the shadows and light always dance about on one's newspaper. And then a stroll. And perhaps, if we're lucky, a few cavalry officers from one of the Frankfurt or Mainz regiments will have gotten lost in our vicinity and ride alongside our coach. And you know, I must tell you, gentlemen, compared to hussars, regardless of whether they're wearing red or blue, you gentlemen simply aren't in the running. From my military point of view it is and will remain a decisive mistake that they've doubled the dragoons guards and left the hussars untouched. And what's even more incomprehensible to me is that they've left them way out there. Something as special as that belongs in the capital."

Botho, who was beginning to get embarrassed because of the enormous talent his wife had for prattle, sought to check her loquacity with teasing little remarks. But his guests were considerably less critical than he, indeed, they amused themselves more than ever with the "charming little lady." Balafré, who occupied first place in the Käthe admiration society, remarked, "Rienäcker, if you say one more word against your wife, you're a dead man. Gracious lady, what does this ogre of a husband really want of you? What is he picking at? I certainly don't know. Why, when you get right down to it, I'm forced to think that he feels that his honor as a member of the heavy cavalry has been offended, and—you'll pardon the pun—that he's up in arms simply because of his arms.[3]

"Rienäcker, I beg you. If I had a wife like yours, her every whim would be my command, and if the gracious lady wanted to turn me into a hussar, why I'd become a hussar just like that and that would be the end of it! One thing I know for sure, and I'd wager my life and honor on it, if His Majesty could hear such eloquent words, those hussars out there wouldn't have another minute's peace. By tomorrow they'd be in marching quarters at Zehlendorf and day after tomorrow they'd be passing through the Brandenburg Gate. Oh, this House of Sellenthin, to which, now that I've gotten started, I'll take advantage of the opportunity and raise my glass in this our first toast of the evening, and say *vivat,* once, twice, three times over! Why don't you have any more sisters, gracious lady? Why has Fräulein Ine gotten herself engaged already? It's too soon, and in any case, she's done it just to spite me."

Käthe was delighted to receive attention of this sort and assured him that she would try to do everything that could be done, despite Ine, who, of course, was now hopelessly lost for him, even though she well knew that as an incorrigible bachelor, he was simply talking like that. In the next instant, however, she dropped her teasing with Balafré and again took up the discussion about traveling, primarily her ideas on how she envisioned her correspondence. She hoped, as she could only repeat, that she would receive a letter every day. After all, that was the duty of a loving husband. For her part, she would have to see what happened and only on the very first day was she planning to give some sign of life, as she passed from station to station. This suggestion found approbation even with Rienäcker, and was only modified to the extent that not only would she write a card at every main station as far as Cologne, through which, despite the detour, her route was to pass, but she would place all of them, as many or as few as there might be, in a common envelope. This had the advantage that she would be able to express herself completely without reservation regarding her traveling companions, without having to worry about postal clerks or letter carriers.

After dinner they took coffee outside on the balcony at which opportunity Käthe—after resisting a bit—presented herself in her traveling clothes, wearing a wide-brimmed Rembrandt hat and her duster, with a traveling bag over her shoulder. She looked charming. Balafré was more taken than ever, and begged her not to be too surprised if tomorrow she would find him timidly cowering in the corner of her compartment as her cavalier of the journey.

"Provided he gets leave," laughed Pitt.

"Or deserts," added Serge, "which would certainly be just the thing to do to top off this adulation scene of his."

In this way their chatting and teasing went on for a while. Then they all took leave from their gracious hostess, while agreeing to remain together as far as the Lützowplatz Bridge. At this point, however, they divided into two groups, and while Balafré, Osten, and Wedell ambled further along the canal, Pitt and Serge, who still wanted to go to Kroll's, headed towards the Tiergarten.

"Charming creature, that Käthe," said Serge. "Rienäcker seems rather prosaic next to her and sometimes he gets such a sour-faced smart-aleck look as if he had to apologize to the entire world for the little lady who, when you see her in the right light, is really brighter than he is."

Pitt remained silent.

"And what is she supposed to be doing in Schwalbach or Schlangenbad anyway," continued Serge. "That's not going to help. And when it does, it's usually a very peculiar sort of help."

Pitt looked at him from the side. "It seems to me, Serge, that you're becoming more and more Russianized, or to put it another way, you're getting to fit your name more and more."

"Still not enough. But all joking aside, my friend, one thing is serious in this matter. Rienäcker's getting to me. What does he have against the charming little lady? Do you know?"

"Yes."

"Well?"

"She is rather a little silly," he responded in English. "Or, if you'd rather hear it in German, '*Sie dalbert ein bißchen.*' At least, too much for him."

# 19

Even while still between Berlin and Potsdam, Käthe drew the yellow curtains of her compartment so as to gain protection from the constantly intensifying, blinding light. At the Luisenufer, however, on that same day, no curtains were let down and the morning sun shone brightly in Frau Nimptsch's window, flooding the entire room with light. Only the background lay in shadow. Here stood an old-fashioned bed, with red-and-white checkered pillows piled high, on which lay Frau Nimptsch. She sat more than she lay, for she had fluid on the chest and suffered severely from asthmatic complaints. Again and again she turned her head towards the single open window, but even more frequently towards the fireplace, in whose hearth today no fire was burning.

Lene sat next to her, holding her hand. As she noticed that the old woman glanced constantly in the same direction, she said, "Should I make a fire, Mother? I thought that since you were lying down and have the warmth from your bed, and because it's so hot that . . ."

The old woman said nothing, but it seemed to Lene as if she would like to have one. Thus she went over to the fireplace, bent down, and made a fire.

When she returned to the bed, the old woman smiled contentedly and said, "Yes, Lene, it's hot. But you know that I've always got to have it, so that I can look at it, and so whenever I don't see it, it seems to me, that everything's over and done with, there's no life left, and no spark either. And you get such a fearful feeling here . . ."

As she spoke, she pointed towards her breast and her heart.

"Oh Mother, you always think right off about dying. And yet it's passed lots of times already."

"Yes, child, it's passed lots of times, but sooner or later it comes, and when you're seventy it can come any day. You know, open up that other window too, then there'll be more air here and the fire'll burn better. Just look there, it don't really seem to want to anymore, it's smoking so much . . ."

"That comes from the sun, it's shining right on it."

"And then give me some of them green drops that Frau Dörr brought me. They always help a little bit anyway."

Lene did as she was asked and after the sick old woman had taken the drops she did really seem to feel somewhat better and more cheerful. Propping her hand against the bed, she pushed herself up somewhat higher, and after Lene had placed a pillow in the small of her back, she said, "Was Franke here already?"

"Yes, early this morning. He always asks about you before he goes to the factory."

"He's a real good man."

"Yes, that he is."

"And that sect business?"

" . . . won't be so bad. I almost think that's where he gets his good principles from. Don't you think so too?"

The old woman smiled. "No, Lene, those come from the Dear Lord. Some people got them and other people don't. I don't really believe much in studyin' and learnin' things like that. . . . Ain't he said anything yet?"

"Yes, last night."

"And what did you answer him?"

"I told him that I'd take him because I think he's an honorable and dependable man, who'd not only take care of me but would take care of you too."

The old woman nodded in agreement.

"And," continued Lene, "when I told him that, he took my hand and in a real cheerful way, he said, 'Well Lene, that's settled then!' But I shook my head and said that it wasn't so simple, because I still had something else to confess to him. And when he asked me what, I told him that I'd had an affair two times: the first time . . . well, you know about that, Mother . . . and I'd liked the first one a lot, and I had been really in love with the second one, and still longed for him in my heart. But now he's happily married and I'd never seen him again except for one single time, and I never wanted to see him again either. But I had to tell him all of that because he meant so well by us and because I never wanted to deceive anybody, least of all him . . ."

"Lordie, Lordie," whimpered the old woman intermittently.

" . . . and right afterwards he got up and went over to his apartment. But I could see real clearly that he wasn't mad. He just didn't want me to go to the door of the hallway with him, like I always do."

Frau Nimptsch was visibly overcome with anxiety and agitation, although it was not really clear whether this stemmed from what she had just heard or lack of breath. It seemed, however, to be the latter, for suddenly she said, "Lene, I ain't lying up straight enough. You'll have to put the hymnbook under me."

Lene did not contradict her, but went instead and got the hymnbook. As she brought it, however, the old woman said, "No, that ain't the one. That's the new one. I want the old one, the thick one with the two clasps." And not until Lene had returned with the thick hymnal did the old woman continue, "I had to get that for my mother too, God rest her, and I was still only halfways a child in them days and my mother not even fifty, and she had it here too, and couldn't get no air. And them big eyes, full of fear, kept on lookin' at me like that. But when I put old Porst's hymnbook under her, the one that she'd had at her confirmation, she got real quiet and just went to sleep peaceful-like. And that's what I want to do too. Oh, Lene, it ain't death . . . it's the dying. . . . There, there, ah, that helps."

Lene wept quietly to herself and since she saw clearly that the good old woman's last hour was nigh, she sent to Frau Dörr, telling her it looked bad and wouldn't she please come. The latter then responded that she would, but it was not until six o'clock that she arrived, with bugles and drums, so to speak, for being quiet even around the sick was simply not her way. She tramped through the room so that everything shook and clattered, while at the same time complaining about Dörr, who always managed to be in town just when he ought to be at home, and was always at home just when she wished he would go to the devil. As she went on, she squeezed the sick woman's hand and asked Lene if she had given her plenty of drops.

"Yes."

"How many's that?"

"Five . . . five every two hours."

That was too few, Frau Dörr straightaway assured her, and while unpacking her complete medical repertoire, added that she'd let them drops ripen in the sun for two weeks, and if a body would take them right, that water would be gone just like with a pump. Old Selke over there in the "Zoological" had been just like a barrel, and for three whole months hadn't been able to see even the corner of a bedsheet, always sittin' up in a chair, with all the windows wide open, but after he'd taken them drops for four days, why, it was just like somebody'd squeezed a hog's bladder, just like that, and everything gone and back to flappin' an' clappin'.

As she spoke, the robust Frau Dörr thrust a double dose of her foxglove on old Frau Nimptsch. As a result of this energetic assistance, Lene, overcome with redoubled and only too justifiable anxiety, reached for her shawl and got ready to go for a doctor. Frau Dörr, who was usually always against doctors, this time did no protest.

"Go ahead," she said, "she can't go on much more. Just look there," and she pointed to the sick woman's nostrils, "that's Death himself sittin' there."

Lene went. But she could scarcely have reached the square in front of St. Michael's, when the old woman, who until then had been lying in a half-slumber, straightened up and called for her: "Lene . . ."

"Lene ain't here."

"Who is it that's here then?"

"It's me, Mother Nimptsch, me, Frau Dörr."

"Ah, Frau Dörr, ain't that real nice. Over here, here on the footstool."

Frau Dörr, by no means accustomed to being ordered about, shook herself a bit, but was too good-natured not to acquiesce to the order. Thus she seated herself on the footstool.

And behold, in the very same instant the old woman began to

speak: "I want a yellow coffin and blue fittings. But not too much . . ."

"Right, Frau Nimptsch."

"And I want to be buried in the new St. James's Church cemetery, behind the Rollkrug Inn, way out towards Britz."

"Right, Frau Nimptsch."

"And I've put aside everything I need, from before, when I was still able to save somethin'. It's lying' in the top drawer there. And the gown'n the jacket, an' a pair of white stockings with *N* on them. The money's in between."

"Right, Frau Nimptsch. It'll all be done, just like you said. Anything else?"

But the old woman no longer seemed to have heard Frau Dörr's question. Without responding she merely folded her hands, looked up at the ceiling with a pious and kindly expression, and prayed, "Dear God in heaven, take her under Your protection and repay her for everything she's done for this old woman."

"Ah, she's talkin' about Lene," said Frau Dörr to herself, adding, "The good Lord'll do that, Frau Nimptsch. I know Him, and I ain't never seen anybody go wrong who was the likes of Lene, and had a heart and hands like she's got."

The old woman nodded, and a comforting picture stood visibly before her soul.

Thus the minutes passed, and when Lene returned and from the entry began to knock on the hall door, Frau Dörr was still sitting on the footstool, continuing to hold the hand of her old friend. Not until she heard the knocking outside did she release it, get up, and open the door.

Lene was still out of breath. "He'll be here right away . . . he's coming right now."

But Frau Dör merely said, "Lord, them doctors," and pointed towards the dead woman.

# 20

The first of Käthe's travel letters had been mailed in Cologne and arrived in Berlin as promised on the next morning. The address had been written by Botho himself at the time the agreement was made and now, smiling and in a good mood, he held the rather firm envelope in his hand. And in fact, three cards had been placed in the envelope, written on both sides in light pencil, all of them so difficult to read that Rienäcker stepped out on the balcony so that he could better decipher their nearly illegible scribble.

"Well, Käthe, let's have a look."

He read the following:

*Brandenburg on the Havel. 8:00 A.M.*

The train, my dear Botho, is only stopping here for three minutes, but I won't let them pass without putting them to use. If need be, I'll write while we're moving, however it works out. I'm traveling with a young and very charming banker's wife, Madame Salinger, née Saling from Vienna. When I showed some surprise at the similarity of her names, she said in that delightful Viennese way: "Ye-as, juhst imagine. Ah' juhst plain mar-reed mah own cohmparative."[1] She chatters on incessantly like that and despite a ten-year-old daughter (a blond, her mother is a brunette) is also going to Schlangenbad. By way of Cologne too and also like me, because of a visit she expects to make there. The child has a pleasant disposition but has not been brought up well. With her constant clambering around in our compartment she has already broken my parasol, which greatly embarrassed her mother.

At the station where we've just stopped, although at this very moment the train has started moving again, the whole place is swarming with soldiers, including Brandenburg Cuirassiers with a bright yellow monogram on their shoulder boards, probably Nickolaus. It's quite becoming. There were fusiliers there too, Thirty-fifth Regiment, short fellows, who seemed shorter to me than necessary, although Uncle Osten always says, the best fusilier is the one you can only make out with a telescope. But I've got to close. The child, unfortunately, is running from one window to the other in our compartment and making it hard for me to write. And at the same time she's constantly munching on cake, little pieces covered with cherries and pistachio nuts. She started on them already between Potsdam and Werder. Her mother is simply too weak. I would be more strict.

Botho put the card aside, and as well as he could, skimmed through the second. It read:

*Hanover, 12:30*

Goltz was at the station in Magdeburg and told me you had written him that I was coming. How sweet and kind of you once more. You really are the best and most attentive of husbands. Goltz is now doing surveying in the Harz mountains, i.e., he starts on July 1. Our stop here in Hanover lasted a quarter hour, which I put to use by taking a look at the square directly in front of the station. Nothing but hotels and beer halls that have been built just since we've been in control. One of them is completely in Gothic style. The Hanoverians, as one of my traveling companions has informed me, call it the 'Prussian Beer Church' out of purely Guelphic antagonism. How painful things like that are! Time will heal *a great deal* here. Amen to that![2]

The child is still nibbling away incessantly and it's beginning to concern me. What can possibly be the outcome? Her mother is really charming and has told me *everything*. She went to Dr. Scanzoni in Würzburg too and raves about him. The way she confides everything to me is almost embarrassing. Otherwise, as I can only say again, she is completely comme il faut. Just to mention one thing, you should see her traveling case! The Viennese really are tremendously ahead of us in things like that. The older culture really does show.

"Marvelous," laughed Botho. "When Käthe starts making cultural and historical observations, she outdoes herself. But all good things come in threes. Let's see."
And with that he took the third card.

*Cologne, 8:00P.M.*           **Residence of the Military Governor**

I'll have my cards posted here rather than wait until Schlangenbad, where Frau Salinger and I arrive tomorrow at noon. I'm fine. The Schroffensteins are very kind, especially the husband. Incidentally, just so that I don't forget, Frau Salinger was picked up at the station by Oppenheims' equipage.[3] Our trip, which started so delightfully, got rather arduous and unpleasant from Hamm on. The little girl was very sick and unfortunately, it was her mother's fault. "What else would you like?" she asked, just after our train had passed the station at Hamm. To which the child answered, "gumdrops." And right from that very moment on things really took a turn for the worst. Oh my dear Botho, young or old, our wishes really are constantly in need of strict and conscientious supervision. This idea has been going through my mind all the time ever since then, and maybe my running into this charming lady wasn't just a chance occurrence in my life. How often haven't I heard Kluckhohn speak in this very manner. And he's right. More tomorrow.

*Your Käthe*

Botho put all three cards back into their envelope again, remarking, "That's Käthe. What a talent for chatter! I should really be pleased that she writes the way she does. But there's something lacking. It's all so flighty, so much mere social prattle. But she'll change when she's got obligations. At least maybe she will. Anyhow, I won't give up hoping that she does."
On the following day came a short letter from Schlangenbad in

which there was much less than in the three cards. From this time on she only wrote twice a week, going on about Anna Grävenitz and Elly Winterfeld as well. Most of all, however, she wrote about Madame Salinger and her charming little Sarah. Each letter contained the same affirmations and only at the end of the third week was there a certain amount of deviation:

I now find the child more charming than her mother. The latter takes pleasure in luxurious attire which I can scarcely find appropriate, all the less since there are really no gentlemen here. I also see that she is using color. As a matter of fact, she paints her eyebrows and maybe even her lips too, they certainly are cherry red. The child, however, is very natural. Whenever she sees me she throws herself wildly at me, kissing my hand and apologizing for the hundredth time because of the gumdrops. "It was all Mama's fault," she says, and I can only agree with her. Yet on the other hand a secret compulsion for nibbling sweets must lie in Sarah's nature. I almost would have to call it something like original sin. (Do you believe in original sin? I believe in it, my dear Botho.) In any case, she can't leave her hands off sweets and is constantly buying cookies. Not the Berlin kind that taste like cream puffs, but the Karslbad kind, with sugar mixed all through them. But I'll write no more of that.

When next I see you, which may be quite soon—for I'd really like to travel together with Anna Grävenitz, one is more with one's own kind—we'll talk more about it and about lots of other things too. Oh, how much I'm looking forward to seeing you again and being able to sit on the balcony with you. Berlin really is the most beautiful place of all and when the sun is going down over Charlottenburg and Grunewald and you sit there like that dreaming and get so tired, oh how splendid that is! Isn't it so? And do you know what Frau Salinger told me yesterday? I've gotten even more blond, she said. Well, you'll see.

As always,
*Your Käthe*

Rienäcker nodded his head and smiled. "Charming little woman. Not a word about her treatment. I'll bet she's been going out for drives and hasn't even made ten visits to the baths." Following this monologue he gave several directions to his orderly who had just entered, then strolled through the Tiergarten and Brandenburg Gate, only then going down Unter den Linden towards the barracks, where duty kept him occupied until noon.

After twelve he was again at home. Having taken a bite, he was just about to make himself comfortable when his orderly reported that a gentlemen . . . a man—he was not exactly sure what title to employ—was outside and wished to speak with the Herr Baron.

"Who?"

"Gideon Franke . . . That's what he said it was."

"Franke? Strange. Never heard of him. Let him come in."

His orderly again disappeared while Botho repeated to himself, "Franke . . . Gideon Franke . . . Never heard of him. Don't know him."

An instant later and the aforementioned entered, bowing somewhat stiffly at the door. He was wearing a blackish brown jacket, buttoned to the top, immoderately shiny boots and shiny black hair that lay thick at both temples. In addition, he wore gloves and an old-fashioned high stiff collar of irreproachable whiteness.

With that courtly charm typical of him, Botho approached, asking, "Herr Franke?"

The latter nodded.

"How can I be of service? May I ask you to take a seat? . . . Here . . . Or perhaps here. Upholstered chairs are always uncomfortable."

Franke smiled in agreement, and seated himself on the cane chair to which Rienäcker had pointed.

"How can I be of service?" Rienäcker said once again.

"I've come with a question, Herr Baron."

"Which it will be a pleasure for me to answer, provided that I am able to answer it."

"Oh, nobody better than you, Herr von Rienäcker. . . . I've come about Lene Nimptsch."

Botho was taken aback.

" . . . and with your permission would like to add right off," continued Franke, "that it's not anything embarrassing which has brought me here. Everything that I have to say, or, if you'll permit me, Herr Baron, to ask, will cause neither you nor your family any embarrassment. I know that your gracious wife, the Frau Baroness, has gone away and have deliberately waited for your being alone, or, if I may be permitted, your grass widower's days."

With a sensitive ear, Botho was able to make out that the individual before him was, despite his petit bourgeois manner, a man of honesty and irreproachable convictions. That quickly assisted in helping to overcome his confusion, and he had more or less regained his bearing and composure as he asked across the table, "Are you a relative of Lene's? Forgive me, Herr Franke, if I call my old friend by this name, which is so familiar and dear to me."

Franke bowed, replying, "No, Herr Baron, not a relative. Nothing like that acts as my legitimization. But my legitimization is perhaps not inferior to that. I've known her for several years now and it is my intention to marry her. She's agreed too, but on that occasion she also told me about her previous life and in the process spoke with such great love about you, Herr Baron, that on the spot it was absolutely vital for me to ask you, openly and frankly, Herr Baron, how it really is with Lene. Lene herself reinforced me in my intent, when I told her about it, and was obviously pleased, although it's true that she immediately added, that she'd prefer I didn't do it, because you would only speak too highly of her."

Botho stared straight ahead and had difficulty in mastering his feelings. Finally, he was again in control of himself and replied, "You are a decent man, Herr Franke, who wants only Lene's happiness. That much I can see and hear, and that gives you the right to an answer. I have no doubts regarding what I have to say to you. The only thing I'm still uncertain about is as to *how*. The best thing will probably be if I tell you how it came about, how it went on, and then how it came to an end."

Franke bowed once again, an indication that he too considered this to be best.

"Well then," began Rienäcker, it's almost three years, or it's even a few months more, that on the occasion of going rowing around the Treptow Liebesinsel, I was able to be of service to two young girls by preventing their boat from capsizing. Lene was one of the girls and in the way in which she thanked me I could see immediately that she was different from others. Not a trace of insincerity about her, nor at any time later either. That's something I'd like to emphasize right from the start, because, as cheerful and sometimes almost carefree as she can be, by nature she really is thoughtful, serious and down-to-earth."

Botho mechanically pushed the tray still standing on the table to the side, smoothed out the tablecloth, and then continued. "I asked if I might be allowed to accompany her home and she accepted without a second thought, which at the time surprised me for an instant, because at that time I didn't know her. But I soon saw where it came from; from early girlhood on she had accustomed herself to act according to her own way of thinking without being much concerned about others, or in any case, without being afraid of their opinions."

Franke nodded.

"And so we walked the long way back and I accompanied her home and was enchanted by everything I saw there, the old woman, the hearth at which she sat, the garden where the house stood, and its seclusion and tranquility. I left in a quarter of an hour, and as I parted from Lene at the garden gate, I asked if I might be permitted to return. She answered my question with a straightforward 'yes.' There wasn't the slightest bit of put-on innocence, and even less any lack of womanly self-esteem. On the contrary, there was something affecting in her bearing and her voice.

Rienäcker, visibly shaken as all of this once again appeared before him, stood up and opened both wings of the balcony doors, as if it had become too warm for him in the room. Then, pacing back and forth, he continued somewhat more quickly. "I've got scarcely anything to add. That was at Easter and for one summer long we were truly happy. Shall I tell you about that? No. And then along came life, with its serious side and the demands it puts on us. And that was what took us apart."

Botho had again seated himself, and Franke, who throughout the entire interview had been occupied with brushing his hat, said quietly, "Yes, that's what she told me too."

"It couldn't be any different, Herr Franke. Because Lene—and from the bottom of my heart it makes me happy to be able to say this too—Lene never lies. She would rather bite off her tongue than lie. She's got a double sort of pride; along with making a living from the work of her own hands, she also has a way of always speaking honestly, never exaggerating, and never minimizing anything. 'I don't need to and I don't care to,' I've heard her say that many times. Yes indeed, she's got a mind of her own, maybe a bit more so than is good for her, and anybody who wants to criticize her can reproach her with being strong-willed. But she only wants what she thinks she can answer for and in reality probably can answer for. And to my mind a will like that is really more a mark of character than self-righteousness. You're nodding. I see that we're of the same opinion. That sincerely pleases me. And now just a few final words, Herr Franke. What's past is past. If you can't see your way around it, I've got to respect you for it. But if you can, then I say to you, you'll be getting an uncommonly good wife there. She's got her heart in the right place and has a strong feeling for duty and right and order."

"That's the way I've always found Lene to be and I expect that she'll be just as the Herr Baron says, an uncommonly good wife. Yea verily, man is expected to hold to the commandments, *all* of them, but verily there is a difference, according to the nature of the commandment. And he who doth not obey the one, can still be worthy, yet whosoever holdeth not to the other, be it ever so close in the catechism, he is worth naught and is cast out from the beginning and standeth outside of grace."

Botho regarded him with a look of astonishment, clearly not knowing what to make of this solemn oration. Gideon Franke, however, who was now in full swing, no longer took note of the impression produced by his wholly homegrown views, continuing therefore in a tone which became increasingly sermonizing: "And he, who in the weakness of the flesh doth offend against the sixth, unto him forgiveness may be given, if he walketh in the path of righteousness and contrition. Yet whosoever offendeth against the seventh lieth not only in the weaknesses of the flesh but in the soul of baseness, and whosoever lieth and deceiveth or giveth slander and beareth false witness, is corrupt in his very innards and hath been born in darkness, and for him there is no salvation and he is like unto a field in which lieth so many nettles, that the weeds spring up ever and anon, howsoever much good corn be sown. And by that I live and die and have learned it to be so for all my days.

"Yes indeed, Herr Baron, everything depends on decency, respectability, and honesty. And in matrimony too. After all, honesty is the best policy and a person must be as good as his word. But what's past is past, that belongs before God. And if I were to think otherwise about the matter, which I also respect, just like the Herr Baron, well then, I'd have to stay out of it and keep my affection or my love to myself entirely. I was over in the States for a long time, and even if just like over here, everything that gleams isn't gold over there either, *one* thing is true just the same: over there you learn to look at things differently and not always through the same glass. And you also learn that there are lots of roads to salvation and lots of roads to happiness.

"Yes, Herr Baron, there's lots of roads that lead to God and there's lots of roads that lead to happiness, of that I'm just as sure deep down in my heart. And the one road is a good one and the other road is good too. But every good road has got to be an open road, and a straight road, and lie in the sun and not have any morass or swamp or will-o'-the-wisps to lead you astray. It all depends on truth and on reliability and on honesty."

As he spoke these words, Franke got up, and Botho, who courteously followed him to the door, here extended his hand to him.

"Now, Herr Franke, on parting I ask you only for this one thing, give my regards to Frau Dörr for me if you see her, and their old friendship with her still goes on. And above all say 'hello' to good old Frau Nimptsch for me. Does she still have that gout and those 'bad days' of hers that she always used to complain about?"

"That's all over with now."

"What do you mean?" asked Botho.

"We buried her three weeks ago, Herr Baron. Exactly three weeks ago today."

"Buried her?" repeated Botho. "Where?"

"Out there beyond the Rollkrug in New St. James's Cemetery. A good old woman. And the way she was attached to Lene. Yes, Herr Baron, Mother Nimptsch is dead. But Frau Dörr, she's still living"— and he laughed—"*she'll* go on for a long time yet. And when she comes, it's a long way, I'll be sure to greet her for you. And I can already see how happy she'll be. You know her for sure, Herr Baron. Yes indeed, old Frau Dörr."

And Gideon Franke tipped his hat once more, and the door snapped closed.

# 21

When alone again after this meeting and especially after what he had just heard, Rienäcker was numb. Whenever in the intervening period he had thought of the little garden house and its occupants, as a matter of course he had imagined it all as it once had been. Now, everything was different and he had to come to terms with an entirely new world. Strangers were now living in the cottage, if indeed anyone lived there at all. There was no fire burning any longer in the hearth, at least no longer day in, day out, and Frau Nimptsch, who had kept the fire, was now dead and lying out there in St. James's Cemetery. All of this went around in his head, and suddenly the day on which he had half-humorously, half-solemnly promised the old woman that he would place a wreath of everlastings on her grave stood before him. In the restlessness in which he found himself, it was actually a relief for him that his vow occurred to him again and thus he decided to fulfill immediately the promise he had made at that time. "Rollkrug and noontime and burning sun—a regular trip to Central Africa. But that dear old woman's got to have her wreath."

With that he immediately got his sword and cap and set out on his way.

At the corner was a cabstand, just a small one, of course. Despite the sign—"Stopping place for three cabs"—it was really just an open spot, and only on the rarest occasions was a cab to be found at it. So it was again today, which was by no means surprising, taking the midday hour into consideration, when cabs everywhere are in the habit of disappearing as if the earth had swallowed them, not to mention the fact that this stop had been established merely out of a sense of obligation anyway. Thus Botho strode on, until, in the vicinity of the Von-der-Heydt Bridge, a rather rickety old vehicle approached him, bright green with red plush seats and a white horse in front. The nag just about crawled along, and in view of the "expedition" the poor creature was about to undertake, Rienäcker could not suppress a melancholy smile. But as far as the eye could see, nothing better was in sight, and thus he walked up to the coachman and said, "To the Rollkrug. St. James's Cemetery."

"At your service, Herr Baron."

"But we've got to stop on the way. I've got to buy a wreath."

"At your service, Herr Baron."

Botho was somewhat taken aback that his title was so promptly repeated, and as a result he asked, "Do you know me?"

"At your service, Herr Baron. Baron Rienäcker, Landgrafenstraße. Right next to the cab-stop. Driven you quite a few times."

During this exchange Botho climbed in, hoping to make himself as comfortable as possible in the plush corner seat. He soon gave up, however, for the corner was as hot as an oven.

Rienäcker had the attractive and heartwarming trait of all noblemen from the Mark of enjoying conversation with the common folk rather than with "cultured individuals" and thus, without a second thought, began to chat as they passed through the half-shadow of the young trees along the canal. "What a heat wave! That old whitey of yours probably wasn't too happy when he heard " 'Rollkrug.' "

"Oh, Rollkrug ain't so bad. He kin still make the Rollkrug on account o' the heath. When he gets through there'n smells them pines, that always cheers him up. He's from the country himself, y'know. Or, maybe it's the music. Anyways, he always perks up his ears."

"Well, well," said Botho. "He sure doesn't look much like dancing to me . . . But where will we be able to get a wreath? I really wouldn't want to go to the cemetery without a wreath."

"Oh, you got time fer that, Herr Baron. Once we get near the cemetery, past the Hallesches Tor 'n' down the whole of Pionierstraße."

"Yes, you're right; I remember now. . . ."

"An' then afterwards, right near the cemetery there's some of 'm too."

Botho smiled. "Sounds like you're from Silesia."[1]

"Yep," said the coachman. "Most of us are. But I been here a long time now and I'm really halfways a real Berliner."

"And are you making out all right?"

"Oh, I ain't sure if all right's exactly the word. Everything costs a lot'n it's always supposed to be nothin' but the best. An' oats is expensive. But that wouldn't be so bad, if only things didn't go wrong. But there's always somethin' to give ya problems. One day ya break an axle, an' the next day, yer horse collapses on ya. I still got a chestnut at home, used to be with the Fürstenwalder Uhlans. Real good horse, only it ain't got no wind left, an' prob'ly won't last much longer. An' just like that an' it's gone. . . . An' then there's the traffic police; they ain't never satisfied, no matter what ya do. Always got to paint everything over again. An' them red plush seats, they don't come fer nothin' either."

Chatting in this way as they went along the canal, they reached the Hallesches Tor. Just at this moment an infantry battalion, with band blaring, approached from the direction of Kreuzberg, and Botho, who did not wish to meet anyone, pressed for a bit more haste. Thus they quickly crossed the Belle-Alliance Bridge. On the other side, however, he ordered a halt, because right on one of the first houses he read: "Artistic and Commercial Florist." Three or four steps led up to a store. In its large window lay all sorts of wreaths.

Rienäcker got out and ascended the steps. As he entered, the door gave off a sharp ringing sound. "Would you please show me one of your nicer wreaths?"

"Funeral?"

"Yes."

The saleswoman, dressed entirely in black, perhaps in recognition of the fact that for the most part the only wreaths sold here were intended for graves, had something ridiculously reminiscent of the Parcae in her general appearance—even her scissors were not lacking. She presently returned with an evergreen wreath, into which white roses had been set. At the same time she apologized that they were merely white roses; white camellias would be more expensive. For his part Botho was satisfied. He refrained from any criticism and asked only if in addition to the fresh wreath he might not also be able to have a wreath of everlastings.

The saleswoman seemed somewhat astonished at the old-fashioned attitude implied by the question. Nevertheless, she replied affirmatively and immediately reappeared with a carton, in which lay five or six wreaths made of everlastings, yellow, red, and white.

"Which color would you advise me to take?"

The saleswoman smiled. "Everlasting wreaths are really completely out of style. At best in winter . . . and then usually just . . ."

"It's probably best if I just pick this one here." And with that Botho placed the closest yellow wreath over his arm, had the evergreen wreath with the white roses put next to it, and quickly climbed back into the cab. The two wreaths were somewhat large and stood out enough on the red plush to awaken in Botho the question as to whether it might not be better to pass them up to the coachman. But he quickly dismissed the idea. "If somebody intends to bring old Frau Nimptsch a wreath, he's also got to own up to the wreath. And anybody who's ashamed of it, really never should've promised it in the first place."

Thus he let the wreaths lie where they were, nearly forgetting the two of them completely as they soon turned into a section of street which drew him from his former reflections by its profuse and colorful scenery, which here and there bordered on the grotesque. On the right, for perhaps a distance of five hundred paces, ran a plank fence over which all sorts of booths, pavilions, and gateways decked out with lamps protruded, all covered with a variety of inscriptions. Most of them were new or of recent vintage, while at the same time a few, and especially the largest and most colorful, went back a long way, having survived from last year, even if only in a rather rain-washed condition. In the midst of these places of amusement and alternating with them, various artisans had set up their workshops, mostly sculptors and stonecutters, who because of the numerous cemeteries, were exhibiting almost nothing but crosses, pillars, and obelisks. All of this could not fail to make an impression on anyone who came this way, and Rienäcker too succumbed. With increasing curiosity, he mustered the seemingly endless and wildly contrasting slogans along with the pictures which complimented them: Fräulein Rosella, the Wonder Girl, Alive and on the Spot!; Grave Monuments at Lowest Prices; American High Speed Photography; Russian Pitchball, six throws for ten pfennig; Swedish Punch with Waffels; Figaro's Finest or the Hairstyling Salon of the World; Grave Monuments at the Lowest Prices; Swiss Shooting Gallery:

> Take your aim and then shoot well,
> Score a hit like William Tell.

Beneath the inscription stood William Tell himself, complete with crossbow, son, and apple.

Finally they reached the end of the long wall of boards and just at this point the road turned sharply towards the Hasenheide. From its shooting range one could make out the chatter of rifles in the midday quiet. Otherwise, even on this extension of the street, everything remained more or less the same. Blondin, clad only in tights and medals, stood balancing on a high wire, surrounded by fireworks. Around and next to him all sorts of smaller posters advertised balloon ascents as well as dance halls. One of them read: "A Sicilian Night. At two o'clock, Vienna Bonbon Waltz."

Botho, who had not passed this spot in years, read it all with unfeigned interest, until after crossing the heath whose shadows had for a few minutes refreshed him, he now turned beyond the latter onto the main road of a lively suburb, which continued towards Rixdorf. Wagons in rows of twos and threes moved along before him until suddenly everything backed up and the traffic came to a halt. "What are we stopping for?" But before the coachman could answer, Botho could hear cursing and scolding from the front and saw that everything had jammed up. He bent forward, looking inquisitively in every direction. Considering his inclination for popular things, the entire incident would in all probability have given him considerably more pleasure than discomfort, had not a wagon which had come to a stop directly in front of him prompted him to gloomy reflections, both through its load as well as its markings. "Broken Glass, Bought and Sold by Max Zippel in Rixdorf," stood painted in large letters on a wall-like tailboard and a whole mountain of glass fragments towered in the bed of the wagon. "Luck and

glass . . ."[2] With reluctance he stared at it, while each of his finger-
tips felt as if they were being pierced by the pieces.

Finally, however, the row of wagons not only began to move once
more but the old white nag did its best to make up for lost time.
Thus in a short time they came to a stop before a corner house built
on a gentle slope, fitted with a high roof and protruding gable. Its
ground-floor windows were placed so low to the street that they
were practically on the same level. An arm made of iron extended
from the gable, bearing a gilded key in an upright fashion.

"What's that?" asked Botho.

"The Rollkrug."

"Good. That means we're almost there. Just up the hill a bit.
Sorry about your horse, but it can't be helped."

The coachman flicked his whip and soon they were ascending the
moderately steep street. On one side lay the old St. James's cemetery,
already half-closed because of overcrowding, while on the side opposite the cemetery wall, tall tenements rose.

In front of the last house stood wandering street players, a horn
and a harp, to all appearances a man and a woman. The woman was
singing, but the wind, blowing here rather sharply, carried it all up
the hill. Not until Botho was ten or more paces beyond the pair of
poor musicians was he in a position to hear the text and melody. It
was the same song they had sung so cheerfully and happily that time
on their stroll towards Wilmersdorf. He stood up and stared back at
the pair of singers, as if they were singing to him. But they were
standing with their backs towards him and saw nothing. A pretty
servant girl, however, who was busy cleaning windows on the gable
side of the house and who perhaps ascribed to herself the glance of
the young officer looking around back, waved her leather polishing
cloth merrily from her windowsill, and cheerfully joined in the song:

> I'll remember,
> I'll be grateful all my life,
> But you, my soldier boy,
> Soldier boy, will you remember?

Pressing his hand to his brow, Botho threw himself back into the
carriage. A feeling, infinitely sweet and infinitely painful took hold

of him. Of course it was the pain which predominated, and it did not abate until the city lay behind him, and far on the horizon in the blue noonday haze the Müggelgebirge became visible.

Finally they stopped before the new St. James's Cemetery.

"Should I wait?"

"Yes, but not here. Down by the Rollkrug. And if you should still come upon those musicians . . . here, this is for the poor woman."

# 22

Entrusting himself to the guidance of an old man working just at the entrance of the cemetery, Botho found Frau Nimptsch's grave well tended. Ivy vines had been planted on it, a geranium pot in their midst and on a small iron stand already hung a wreath of everlastings. "Ah, Lene," he said to himself. "Always the same . . . I'm too late." And then he turned to the old man standing next to him and remarked, "Only a small funeral, I suppose."

"Yep, it was a little'n."

"Three or four?"

"Exactly four. An', of course, our old rector. He just said the prayers and the big middle-aged lady, around forty or so, she just kept on cryin'. An' there was a youngish'n too. She comes every week now, an' last Sunday she brought that geranium. An' she still wants a stone too, like is in style now, green polished with the name and the date on it."

With the obsequiousness characteristic of all cemetery personnel, the old man now withdrew, as Botho hung his wreath of everlastings next to the one already brought by Lene. The one of evergreen with white roses he placed around the geranium pot. Then, after he had looked for a while at the modest grave and fondly recollected dear old Frau Nimptsch, he walked back towards the cemetery entrance. The old man, who in the meantime had resumed his work on the trellises, raised his cap and looked after him, at the same time occupying himself with the question, what might actually have brought such a well-bred gentleman—about whose good breeding, considering his last handshake, he had no doubt—to the old woman's grave. "Something must be going on there. Didn't have the cab wait either." But he came to no conclusion and thus, at least to show himself as grateful as possible, he took one of the watering cans standing nearby, and went first to the iron fountain and then to Frau Nimptsch's grave to put a bit of water on the ivy which had become somewhat dried out in the burning sun.

In the meantime Botho had reached the cab, which had halted directly at the Rollkrug. He got in again and an hour later pulled up once more on Landgrafenstraße. The coachman sprang down eagerly and opened the cab door.

"Here," said Botho. "And this is extra. After all, that was halfway an excursion."

"Well, y'might even say it was whole ways."

"I see," laughed Rienäcker. "Ought to add a bit, right?"

"Sure wouldn't do no harm. . . . Thank's very much, Herr Baron."

"But see to it that you feed old whitey there better for me. That really is a shame."

He saluted and ascended the stairs.

Upstairs in his apartment everything was quiet. Even the servants were out, for they knew that at this hour he was always at his club, at least since his grass-widower's days of Käthe's absence. "Undependable bunch," he grumbled to himself, as if he were peeved. Nevertheless he was glad to be alone. He did not care to see anyone and sat down outside on the balcony to enjoy his quiet reverie. But it was stuffy under the low-hanging awning from which, to make matters worse, long blue-white strands of fringe hung down. For that reason he again arose and drew up the canvas. That was better. The current of fresh air which now ensued did him good. Breathing in deeply and stepping to the railing, he looked over forest and field as far as the dome of the Charlottenburg Palace, whose malachite green copper covering shimmered in the radiance of the afternoon sun.

"Over there lies Spandau," he said quietly to himself, "and beyond Spandau stretches a railroad bed and a line of tracks running all the way to the Rhine. And on those tracks I see a train, lots of cars and in one of those cars sits Käthe. How does she look, I wonder? Oh, fine, I'm sure. And what is she probably talking about? Well, all sorts of things, I imagine: spicy stories about what's been going on at the baths, and maybe about Frau Salinger's wardrobe and that Berlin really is the best place of all. And don't I have good reason to be glad that she's coming back? A wife, who's so pretty, so young, so happy, so cheerful? And I am glad too. But she can't come today. For God's sake, not today. And yet, that's the very sort of thing you can expect of her. She hasn't written a thing for three days and she's always been a great believer in surprises."

He pursued such thoughts a while longer. Then, however, the images changed and in place of Käthe, pictures from the distant past entered his mind: Dörr's garden, the walk to Wilmersdorf, the excursion to Hankel's Depot. That had been the last wonderful day, their last happy hour. "She said that time, that hair binds you too tightly, that's why she refused and didn't want to give me one. And I? Why did I insist on it? It's really true, there are such enigmatic forces, such sympathetic feelings from heaven or hell. And now I'm bound and can't get free. Oh, she was so dear and sweet on that afternoon, when we were still alone and didn't think anyone would disturb us. And I'll never forget the sight of how she stood there in the grass and picked those flowers right and left. Those flowers—I've still got them. But I've got to put an end to all of that. What business do I have with those dead things, things that only cause problems for me and would cost me my little bit of happiness and marital tranquility, if someone else ever caught sight of them."

He got up from his seat on the balcony and strode through the entire apartment into his study. In the morning it was always bathed in bright light, now it lay in deep shadows. Its coolness refreshed him as he approached his elegant desk, a memento of his bachelor days. Its ebony drawers were inlaid with all sorts of silver garlands. In the middle of these drawers, however, intended for the storage of valuables, stood a little Greek temple with pillars topped by a gabled panel. A secret compartment towards the back was closed by a spring. Botho pressed the release and as the compartment sprung open, he took out a small bundle of letters wrapped with a red string. On top, as if pushed in as an afterthought, lay the flowers of which he had just been speaking. He weighed the packet in his hand and, while untying the string said, "Lots of joy, lots of sorrow. Delusions, confusions. . . . The old, old song."

He was alone and had no need to concern himself with being surprised. Still not secure enough in his own mind, however, he stood up and locked the door. Only now did he take out the top letter and read it. It was the lines she had written on the day before the stroll in Wilmersdorf. He was moved as he reread it and looked once more at the pencil strokes he had made. "Stemm . . . asyle. . . . These charming mistakes make a better impression on me even today, better than all the orthography in the entire world. And how clear her handwriting is. How good, how clever what she's written there. Oh, she had the best combination of all, common sense and passion combined. Everything she said had character and depth. 'Culture,' what a pitiful thing you are, how far you stand behind something like this."

He now took out the second letter as well and wanted to read the entire correspondence through from the end to the beginning. But it caused too much pain. "Why? Why revive and resurrect what's dead and has to stay dead? I've got to clean all this out and in the process hope that along with these things that hold such memories, the memories themselves will disappear."

He was firmly resolved to do it. Swiftly getting up from his desk, he pushed the fireplace screen aside and approached the small hearth to burn the letters in it. But lo, slowly, as if he wanted to prolong the feeling of a sweet pain, he let page after page fall upon the hearth and burst into flame. The last thing he held in his hand was the tiny bouquet and as he reflected and brooded, an impulse overcame him that made it seem as if he had to look once again at each individual flower and thus untie the hair binding it together. Suddenly, however, as if a superstitious fear had taken hold of him, he threw the flowers in after the letters.

A flare-up and in an instant everything was gone, reduced to ashes.

"Am I free now? Do I really want to be? No, I *don't*. Ashes, all of it. But *still* I'm bound."

# 23

B otho peered into the ashes. "How little, and yet how much."
And then he again placed the elegant fireplace screen with the
reproduction of a Pompeian wall-figure at its center before them. A
hundred times his eye had passed over it without taking note of what
it actually was. Today he saw it and said, "Minerva with shield and
spear. But with her spear at her foot. Perhaps that means peace. If
only that were so." Then he stood up, closed the secret compartment
which had become poorer by its most precious treasure, and returned to the front of the house.

On the way, passing through the long but narrow corridor, he
encountered the cook and housemaid, who had just returned from
their stroll in the Tiergarten. Seeing the two of them standing there
embarrassed and timid, he was overwhelmed with a feeling of
human sympathy. Nevertheless he suppressed it, telling himself,
although with a touch of irony, that an example would have to be
finally set around here. Thus, as well as he could, he pretended to
play the role of a thundering Zeus. Just where had they been hiding?
he wanted to know. Did they consider that orderliness, or the right
sort of behavior? He had no desire to present her ladyship, when she
got home—perhaps even today already—with a household that had
completely gotten out of hand. And the orderly? "Fine, don't say a
word. I don't even want to hear a thing, least of all excuses." Having
said this, he walked on, smiling, mostly at himself. "How easy it is
to preach, and how difficult to act accordingly. What a pathetic
soapbox hero! Haven't I gotten completely out of hand myself?

Haven't I been acting contrary to order and the right sort of behavior? That such a situation has existed might be excusable, but that it keeps going on, that's the awful thing about it."

With that he again took his place on the balcony and rang. Now his orderly also appeared, almost more embarrassed and apprehensive than the maids. But it was no longer necessary, the storm had passed. "Tell the cook I want to eat something. Well, why are you still standing there? Ah, I see," and he laughed, "nothing in the house. Everything's turning out just splendidly. . . . Well then, tea. Bring me some tea—certainly there's some of that around. And have a few sandwiches made. Damn! I'm hungry. . . . Are the evening newspapers here yet?"

"As ordered, Herr Rittmeister."

It was not long before the tea service was set up outside on the balcony and even a bite to eat had been scraped together. Botho sat leaning back in his rocking chair, staring thoughtfully into the blue flame of the teakettle. He reached first for his wife's *Moniteur,* then the *Fremdenblatt,* and finally picked up the *Kreuzzeitung,* while turning to the last page. "Good Lord, how happy Käthe will be to be able to study this last page right at the source again, in other words, twelve hours earlier than in Schlangenbad. And isn't she right? 'Adalbert von Lichterloh, Government Official junior rank, 2nd Lieutenant of the Reserves, and Hildegard von Lichterloh, née Holtze, are honored to announce their marriage, which was sanctified today.' Wonderful. And to tell the truth, just to see how living and loving go on in this world is really marvelous. Weddings and christenings! And a few deaths in between. Oh well, you really don't have to read about them. Käthe doesn't and neither do I, just when the *Vandals* have lost one of their 'old boys' and you see their fraternity insignia right in the middle of the obituaries. I always read those. Never fail to give me a kick. It seems as if the old geezer had been specially invited to Valhalla for a bit of *Hofbräu. Spatenbräu* would even be more appropriate."[1]

He put the paper aside. The bell had rung. "Would she really . . ." No, it was nothing. Nothing but a soup list for charity sent up by the landlord, on which only fifty pfennig had been subscribed so far. Nevertheless he remained in a state of excitement throughout the entire evening, because the possibility of a surprise constantly hovered before him. Every time he saw a cab with a trunk in the front and a lady's traveling hat in the back turn the corner onto Landgrafenstraße, he exclaimed to himself, "There she is. She loves something like this. I can already hear her saying, 'I thought it would be so funny, Botho.' "

Käthe had not come. Instead a letter came next morning announcing her arrival in three days. She planned to travel with Frau Salinger again, who, all in all, was really a charming lady, always in a good mood, very fashionable, and equipped to travel in style.

Botho laid the letter down and in that instant was sincerely pleased at the prospect of seeing his pretty young wife within three days. "There's room for all sorts of contradictions in our hearts. She's a bit silly, it's true, but a silly young wife is always better than none at all."

He then called the entire staff together and informed them that the mistress would be back in three days. Everything was to be made ready and all the doorknobs polished. And not a single flyspeck on the large mirror.

Having completed these preparations, he went off to duty at the barracks. "If anyone asks, I'll be home after five."

His program for the intervening time was so arranged that he would remain at the squadron yard until noon, followed by a few hours of riding after which he planned to eat at the club. If he did not meet anyone else there, he would definitely find Balafré, which was the same as saying a game of whist *en deux* and a host of court rumors, true and false. The fact was that Balafré, as reliable as he was, nevertheless put aside one hour per day for boasting and gossip. In fact, this activity, for him a sort of intellectual sport, occupied first place among his pleasures.

The program was carried out exactly as planned. The courtyard clock at the barracks was just striking twelve as he swung himself up into his saddle. After passing Unter den Linden and Luisenstraße, he immediately turned onto a path which ran along the canal further on towards Plötzensee. As he rode, the day on which he had also ridden in this area to gain courage for his parting from Lene came back to him, that parting which had been so difficult and yet had to be. That was three years ago now. How much lay in between?

A good deal of happiness, of course. But then again, it had not been real happiness. A bit of candy, a bonbon, not much more. And who can live on sweets?

He was still pursuing such thoughts as he saw two comrades coming towards him on the riding path which led from the Jungfernheide to the canal. As their clearly recognizable flat-topped helmets revealed even at a distance, they were uhlans. But who were they? Of course the doubt about that could not long prevail, and before they had approached to within six hundred paces, Botho saw that it was the Rexins, who were both cousins in the same regiment.

"Ah, Rienäcker," said the older of the two. "Where to?"

"As far as the sky is blue."

"That's a bit far for me."

"Well then, as far as Saatwinkel."

"That's better. I'll ride along with you, provided I'm not disturbing you. . . Kurt," and as he spoke he turned to his younger companion, "*Pardon!* But I've got to talk with Rienäcker. And under certain circumstances . . ."

"Two's company and three's a crowd. Just as you wish, Bozel." With that, Kurt von Rexin saluted and rode off. His cousin, who had just been addressed as Bozel, turned his horse and took the left side next to Rienäcker, who stood far ahead of him on the ranking list, saying, "Well then, Saatwinkel it is. I don't suppose we'll ride into the line of fire out at Tegel."

"At least, I'll try to avoid it," responded Rienäcker, "firstly for my sake and secondly for yours. And third and last for Henriette's sake. What would dark-haired Henriette say if her Bogislaw were to be shot dead—and by friendly fire to boot?"

"That would certainly cut her pretty deeply," replied Rexin, "and put quite a damper on things for both of us."

"What kind of things?"

"That's the very point I wanted to talk to you about, Rienäcker."

"To me? About what point?"

"You really ought to be able to guess, it certainly isn't difficult. Naturally, I'm talking about an affair, *my* affair."

"Affair!" laughed Botho. "Well, I'm at your service, Rexin. But frankly, I'm not quite certain what it is that makes you want to place your confidence especially in me. I'm no source of wisdom in anything, least of all in that direction. We've got quite different authorities for that sort of thing and one of them you know quite well. Moreover, he's a special friend of yours and your cousin."

"Balafré?"

"Right."

Rexin sensed an attitude of reserve and rejection in Botho's remarks, and somewhat put out, became silent. That was more than Botho had intended, for which reason he immediately became more conciliatory. "Affairs, *pardon*, Rexin, they come in so many varieties."

"Of course. But as many as there may be, they're all different."

Botho shrugged his shoulders and smiled. Rexin, however, obviously not willing to let himself be put off a second time by oversensitivity, merely repeated in an indifferent tone, "Yes, as many as there may be, they're all different as well. And I'm surprised, Rienäcker, that you of all people would shrug your shoulders. I sort of thought . . ."

"Well then, out with it."

"All right."

After a while Rexin continued, "I've been through the school of hard knocks twice over you might say, once with the uhlans and before that—you know I didn't enter the service until rather late—at the university in Bonn and Göttingen. When it comes to the usual sort of thing, I don't need any instructions or advice. But when I really ask myself in all honesty about it in this case, it's not really the usual sort of thing, but an exception instead."

"That's what everybody thinks."

"Short and sweet, I feel that I'm bound, no, even more than that, I love Henriette, or to really give you an idea of my feelings, I'm in love with my little dark-haired Jettie. It's true, a suggestive and trivial sounding name like that, one that's even got the ring of the canteen about it, fits best for me, because I'd prefer to avoid any sort of solemn airs in the matter. I'm quite serious enough about it just as it is, and because I really am serious about it, I don't need anything that smacks of solemnity or fancy sentiments. That just cheapens it all."

Botho nodded in agreement, more and more casting off any hint of mockery or superiority, which he had, in fact, up to now shown.

"Jettie," continued Rexin, "hasn't got any line of angels for ancestors and she's not one herself either. But where are you going to find the likes of her? In our circles? Don't make me laugh. All of these 'distinctions' are nothing but sham and the biggest shams of all are in the realm of virtue. Naturally, there really are such things as virtue and other niceties like that, but innocence and virtue are like Bismarck and Moltke, in other words, rare. I've come around to views of this kind completely; I consider them to be valid and intend to act according to them as far as possible. Listen, Rienäcker, if instead of along this boring canal, which is just as boring and straight as the conventions and formalities of our society, if, I say, instead of next to this miserable ditch, we were riding along the Sacramento, and instead of the Tegel firing range, we had the 'diggings' in front of us, I'd simply up and marry Jettie. I've completely fallen for her, and I can't live without her. Her naturalness and genuineness and her real love all mean more to me than a pack of countesses. But I can't. I can't do it to my parents and I don't want to have to leave the service at twenty-seven to become a cowboy in Texas or a waiter on some Mississippi steamboat. Well then, the middle course . . ."

"What do you mean by that?"

"A union without sanction."

"You mean marriage without marriage."

"If that's the way you want to put it, yes. Words don't mean anything to me, any more than the actual legalization, or sanctification or whatever other terms they use for these things. I've got a streak of the nihilist in me and really don't put much faith in any pastoral blessings. But, to make it short, because I can't be any different, I am for monogamy; not on moral grounds but because of my own inborn nature. I abhor all of those affairs where beginning and breaking-off take place in the same hour, so to speak, and if a minute ago I said I was a nihilist, I can say that I'm a Philistine with even greater justification. I yearn for the simple things, for a quiet, natural way of life, where one heart speaks to another, and where one has the best thing that one can ever have, honesty, love, freedom."

"Freedom," repeated Botho.

"That's right, Rienäcker. But because I well know that there are dangers lurking behind it and that the happiness that goes with freedom, maybe all freedom in general, is a two-edged sword that can cut you without you're knowing how, that's why I wanted to ask you."

"And I'll give you an answer," said Rienäcker, who with every passing minute had become more earnest and for whom as he listened to these intimate revelations his own life, past as well as present, again stood before him. "Yes, Rexin, I'll give you an answer, as well as I can. And I think that I can give you one. And for that reason, I beg you, stay away from it. In situations such as you've got in mind, there are always only two things possible, and the one is just as bad as the other. If you take the part of loyalty and stead-fastness towards her, or in other words, if you break from the very roots with class, tradition, and convention, sooner or later, if you don't fall apart, you'll become a horror and a burden to yourself. But if things work out differently and as usually happens, some years down the line you make your peace with society and family, then comes the real misery. Then you've got to sever something that has become intertwined and interwoven through all kinds of diffi-culties and worries, through good times and—my God, what's even more important—hard times as well. And that hurts."

Rexin seemed to want to answer but Botho did not notice and went on, "My dear Rexin, a few moments ago in a real masterpiece of discreet phrasing you spoke of affairs, where 'beginning and breaking-off take place in the same hour.' But those affairs, which really aren't affairs at all, they're not the worst kind. The worst are the ones which, to quote you again, take the 'middle course.' I warn you, keep away from this middle course. Look out for such halfway measures. What seems to you like a winning hand really leads to losing everything, what looks like a port in a storm really turns out to be a shipwreck. It *never* leads to anything good, even if outwardly everything seems to go smoothly and no one disinherits anybody and scarcely a silent reproach even gets made.

"And it can't be any different. Because everything has its inevitable consequences; we've got to keep that in mind. Nothing can be made not to have happened, and an image that's been etched into our soul doesn't ever completely fade away, never just completely disappears. Memories stay with us and comparisons come too. And so, I'll say it again, friend, don't go through with your intent—or else your life will come under a cloud and you'll never be able to fight your way through into clarity and daylight again. There are lots of things that one can do, but not that, in matters of one's innermost being, you can't get hearts involved, even if it were only your own."

# 24

On the third day a telegram arrived, clearly sent at the last minute: "Coming tonight. K."

And she really came. Botho was at the Anhalt Station and was introduced to Frau Salinger, who wouldn't hear a thing about gratitude for being good company on the trip, repeating instead in her heavy Viennese accent that it was *she* who was the lucky one, but especially how lucky *he* must be to have such a charming young wife. "Wha jus' look, Herr Baron, if Ah were as lucky as thet, an' Ah were the husban', wha Ah certainly wouldn' bay apaht frum such a wahf for eyvun thray days." To this she then proceeded to append lamentations and complaints about the entire male world, while in the same moment also adding an urgent invitation to Vienna. "We got a nahce littl howse, real close ta Viehnna, an' a pair a' rahdn' horses an' a kitchn. In Prussha you got yoah schools, an' in Viehnna we got owah kichns. An Ah jus' don' know which Ah prayfer."

"I know," said Käthe, "and I think Botho does too."

Following that they went their separate ways. Our young pair climbed into an open carriage after orders had been given that the baggage should follow.

Käthe threw herself back and placed her little feet against the back seat on which lay a traveling bouquet, the last homage of the Schlangenbad hostess who had been completely enchanted by the charming young lady from Berlin. Käthe herself took Botho's arm and nestled close to him, but only for a few seconds. Straightening herself up again, while using her parasol to prop up the bouquet which continuously kept toppling over, she said, "It really is charming here, all these people and so many Spree barges, all so jammed up that they don't know which way to go. And so little dust. It's a real blessing that they're spraying now and keeping everything down with water. Of course, you can't wear long dresses when they do. And just look at that bread wagon with the dog in harness. It's just too funny. Only the canal . . . I don't know, it's still always so . . ."

"Yes," laughed Botho, "it still always is. Four weeks of July heat haven't been able to do much to improve it."

They rode along under the young trees. Käthe tore off a linden leaf, placed it in the hollow of her hand and struck it so that there was a bang. "That's what we always did at home. And when we didn't have anything to do in Schlangenbad, we did the very same thing. We took up all the old games and tricks from when we were children again. Can you imagine, I still hang on to such foolishness quite seriously, even though I really am an old woman and I've done with all that."

"On now Käthe . . ."

"Oh yes, oh yes, a matron. You'll see. Oh, but just look at that, Botho, there's that stockade fence and that old beer garden with the funny name that's a bit off-color, that we always used to laugh at so frightfully at finishing school. I thought that place had long since gone out of business. But the Berliners won't let something like that be taken away from them. A thing like that endures. Everything just has to have some kind of comical name they can make fun of."[1]

Botho vacillated between feelings of happiness and a touch of irritation. "I see you haven't changed a bit, Käthe."

"Certainly I haven't. And why should I have changed, anyway? I certainly wasn't packed off to Schlangenbad to change, at least not as far as my character goes, or my conversation. And as to whether I've changed otherwise? Well, *cher ami, nous verrons.*"

"A matron?"

She put her finger to his mouth and pushed back the traveling veil that had half fallen over her face. In the next moment they passed under the Potsdam railroad viaduct just as an express train roared over its iron framework. A trembling and thundering ensued, both at the same time, and once they had the bridge behind them, she said, "It's always unpleasant for me to be right under it."

"But the ones on top don't have it any better."

"Perhaps not. It all has to do with how one imagines it. One's ideas of things are so powerful in general. Don't you think so too?" She sighed as if suddenly something frightening that penetrated deeply into her life had occurred to her. Then, however, she went on, "In England, as Mr. Armstrong, one of my acquaintances from the baths, about whom I've got to tell you in more detail—married to an Alvensleben, by the way—in England, he said, the dead are buried fifteen feet deep. Well, fifteen feet isn't any worse than five, but as he told me about it, I actually felt how the 'clay'—that's the real English word, incidentally—lay like a ton on my breast. In England they've got heavy clay soil, you know."

"Armstrong you say. . . . There was an Armstrong in the Baden Dragoons."

"A cousin of his. They're all cousins, just like we are here. I'm really looking forward to describing him to you with all of his idiosyncrasies. A perfect 'cavalier' with an upturned mustache. Actually, he overdid it a bit there. It really looked funny, those skinny little tips that he always kept on twisting."

Ten minutes later the carriage halted before their apartment and Botho, extending his arm to her, led her up the steps. A garland stretched across the vestibule door and a sign with the inscription *Willkommen,* on which unfortunately one *l* was missing, hung somewhat crookedly below the garland. Käthe looked up at it and laughed.

"*Willkommen!* But with just one *l.* That seems to mean, just halfway. Well, well. And *l* is the letter of love in the bargain. Well, you'll just have to get everything halfway then too."

Thus she went through the door into the entryway, where the cook and the housemaid already stood waiting to kiss her hand.

"Hello, Bertha, hello, Minette. Well, girls, here I am again. Well, how do I look? Do I look like I've recovered?" But before the girls could answer, something that wasn't expected anyway, she continued, "My, my, *you've* certainly gotten healthy looking. Especially you, Minette, why you've really put on quite a bit."

Minette stared straight ahead with an embarrassed look, for which reason Käthe good-naturedly added, "Just here around your chin and neck, I mean."

In the meantime the orderly also appeared. "Well now, Orth, I was really worried about you. Thank God, no need, still in fine shape, just a bit pale. But it's the heat that does that. And still the same old freckles."

"Yes, your ladyship, they stick."

"Well, that's just fine. Just the right touch of color."

Chatting in this manner, she reached her bedroom, followed by Botho and Minette, while the two others withdrew into their culinary realm.

"Well, Minette, help me. First this coat. Now take this hat, but be careful, or else we'll never be able to save ourselves from all this dust. And now go and tell Orth to set the table out front on the balcony, I haven't had a bite all day because I wanted to have it taste all the better here with all of you. And now go on, my dear, go on, Minette."

Minette hurried out while Käthe stood before the tall full-length mirror rearranging her hair, which had become somewhat disorderly. At the same time she looked in the mirror at Botho, who was standing next to her, carefully studying his pretty young wife.

"Well, Botho," she said mischievously and coquettishly, without turning to look at him.

And that charming coquettishness of hers was calculated to perfection; he embraced her, while she abandoned herself to his caresses. Then, with his arms around her waist, he lifted her up. "Käthe, my doll, my dearest little doll."

"Doll, your dearest little doll. I really ought to hold that against you, Botho. People play with dolls, you know. But I don't hold it against you. Not at all. Dolls get loved the most and treated the best. And that's what interests me."

# 25

It was a glorious morning with a partly cloudy sky. In the gentle westerly breeze, the young couple sat on their balcony. As Minette cleared the coffee things from the table, they looked over at the zoo and its elephant houses, whose colored domes lay in the morning light.

"I really don't know a thing yet," said Botho. "You fell right off to sleep and sleep is something I hold sacred. But now I want to know absolutely everything. Tell me."

"Well now, tell you. What should I tell you? I did write you so many letters, of course, and by now you must know Anna Grävenitz and Frau Salinger as well as I, or really better, because now and then I wrote more than I knew."

"Fine. But just as often, you said, 'I'll tell you the rest later.' Well, the moment has finally come. Or else I'll think you want to keep something from me. I really don't know a thing about those excursions of yours, and after all, you did go to Wiesbaden. They say, of course, that there's nothing but colonels and old generals in Wiesbaden, but there are Englishmen there too, I understand. And speaking of Englishmen, that Scotsman of yours just popped back into my head, the one you wanted to tell me about. What did you say was his name?"

"Armstrong. Mr. Armstrong. Yes, he was a delightful man. And I really never did understand his wife—an Alvensleben, as I think I told you—who was constantly getting embarrassed whenever he said something. And he really was a perfect 'gentleman,' always very proper, even when he let himself go and became a bit casual. 'Gentlemen' are always best at showing their good qualities in moments like that. Don't you think so too? He wore a blue tie and a yellow summer suit and looked as if he'd been sewn right into it, which was why Anna Grävenitz always said, 'Here comes the pencase.' And he always went around with this great big opened parasol, something he'd gotten accustomed to in India. He was an officer in a Scottish regiment, you know, stationed in Madras or Bombay, or maybe it was Delhi. It's all the same, anyway. The things *he'd* gone through! His conversation was charming, even if now and then you didn't quite know how to take it."

"You mean he was forward? Insolent?"

"Really, Botho, the things you say! A man like that, *cavalier comme il faut.* Well, I'll give you an example of his way of speaking. We were sitting across from old Frau General von Wedell and Anna Grävenitz asked her—I think it was the day of the anniversary of Königgrätz[1]—if it was true that thirty-three Wedells had fallen in the Seven Years War.[2]

"The old Frau General said it was true and added that it had been actually even a few more. Everybody who was sitting there was astonished at the large number, except for Mr. Armstrong, and when I jokingly called him to account because of his indifference, he said that he couldn't get excited about such little numbers. 'Little numbers,' I said, and by way of refuting me, he just laughed and said that one hundred thirty-three of the Armstrongs had been killed in the various feuds of his clan. And when the old Frau General, who at first couldn't believe it, finally out of curiosity asked Mr. Armstrong, who kept sticking to it, if all one hundred thirty-three had really 'fallen in battle,' he said, 'No, gracious lady, not actually in battle. Most of them were hung for horse stealing by the English, who were our enemies in those days.' And when everybody was horrified at this rather unbefitting, well, you could even probably say, embarrassing hanging business, he swore we were wrong in finding it in the least bit improper. Times and ways of looking at things change, he said, and as far as his family goes, which is, after all, the one most intimately involved, they all look back on these heroic ancestors of theirs with pride, because for three hundred years the Scottish way of waging war had consisted of stealing cattle and horses. That was the custom in their country and he couldn't seem to find much difference between stealing cattle and stealing countries."

"A Guelph in disguise," said Botho. "But he's got something there."

"Of course. And I was always on his side, whenever he indulged in such remarks. Oh, you could laugh yourself to death over him. He said, one shouldn't take anything too seriously, it's not worth the trouble, and that the only serious occupation is fishing. Sometimes he goes fishing for two whole weeks in Loch Ness or Loch Lochy—just think, they really have such funny names in Scotland—and then he just sleeps in his boat and at sundown gets up again, and when the two weeks are over, he peels himself, and all of that loose skin comes off, and he's got skin like a baby's. And he does it all out of vanity, because a smooth, even skin is really the best thing you can have. And he always looked at me in such a way that I wasn't able to come up right away with an answer. Oh, you men! But it's true. I had a regular attachment to him from the beginning and never got upset at his way of speaking, which now and then did lean toward long orations, although he really much more preferred to jump constantly from one thing to another. One of his favorite sayings was, 'I can't stand it, when a single dish stays on the table for an hour. Anything but the same old thing. I always find it more pleasant when they change courses quickly.' And so, he just hopped around from one thing to another."

"Well, you two must really have been kindred souls," laughed Botho.

"We were too. And we're going to write one another, in the very same style as we talked to one another. We agreed to that just as we parted. Our men, your friends included, are always so thorough. And you're the most thorough of all, which sometimes really depresses me and tries my patience. And you've got to promise me to be like Mr. Armstrong, and chat in a more simple and uncomplicated way, and a bit more quickly too, without always sticking to the same thing."

Botho promised that he would reform, after which Käthe, who loved superlatives, following the presentation of a phenomenally rich American, an absolutely albino Swede with rabbitlike pink eyes, and a fascinatingly beautiful Spanish lady, finally rounded things off with an afternoon excursion to Limburg, Oranienstein, and Nassau, while alternately describing the crypt, the cadet academy, and the hydropathic institute to her husband.

Suddenly she pointed towards the cupola of the Charlottenburg Palace and said, "You know, Botho, we've got to go out there today, or to Westend or Halensee. The air in Berlin is really a bit stuffy and doesn't have a trace of God's own divine breath such as you get when you're out in the open and which the poets are so right in praising the way they do. And when you've just come back from the bosom of nature, like I have, you've regained an affection for what, I suppose, I might want to call innocence and purity. Oh Botho, what a treasure a pure heart really is. I've firmly resolved always to keep my heart pure. And you've got to help me. Yes, you really must. Promise me you will. No, not like that. You've got to kiss me on the brow three times. Chastely. I don't want any tenderness, I want a kiss of consecration. . . . And if we can be satisfied with just a 'lunch,' something warm naturally, we can be in the country by three."

And in fact, they did go for a drive out into the country, and although the Charlottenburg air was even further from God's own divine breath than the air in Berlin, Käthe was nevertheless firmly resolved to stay in the Palace Park and forget about Halensee. Westend, she maintained, was such a bore, and Halensee would be another trip halfway around the world, almost as far as Schlangenbad, but in the palace grounds you could see the mausoleum, where the bluish light always had such a strange effect on you, in fact she could almost say, as if a piece of heaven had fallen right into your soul.[3] That put you in a religious mood and inspired pious thoughts. And even if there weren't any mausoleum, there would be the Carp Bridge, with the little bell on it, and whenever one of the old, moss-covered carp swam over in answer to the bell, it always seemed to her as if a crocodile were coming. And perhaps there would also be a woman there with biscuits and wafers, from whom you could buy something and in your own modest way perform a good work. She was saying "good work" intentionally, avoiding the word *Christian* because Frau Salinger had always given too.

And everything went according to the program; after the carp were fed, both strolled further into the park until they approached the Belvedere with its rococo figures and historical associations. Käthe knew nothing of the latter, and Botho therefore took the opportunity to tell her about the ghosts of deceased emperors and electoral princes that General von Bischofswerder[4] had conjured up on this very spot to rouse King Frederick William II from his lethargic condition or, what amounted to the same thing, from the hands of his mistress, and lead him back to the path of virtue.

"And did it do any good?" asked Käthe.

"No."

"Too bad. Things like that always touch me really painfully. And when I think that that unfortunate prince—he *must* have been unfortunate for sure—was the father-in-law of Queen Louise,[5] my heart just bleeds. How *she* must have suffered! I can't really ever quite imagine things like that in this Prussia of ours. And Bischofswerder, you say, was the name of the general who conjured up those ghosts?"

"Yes. At court they called him the 'Tree Frog.' "

"Because he could change the weather?"[6]

"No, because he wore a green coat."

"Oh, that is too funny. . . . The 'Tree Frog.' "

# 26

By sundown both were home again and Käthe, after she had given her hat and coat to Minette and ordered tea, followed Botho to his room, wishing to have the awareness and satisfaction of having spent the first day after her trip completely at his side.

Botho was content with this and, because she had taken a chill, placed a cushion under her feet, while at the same time covering her with a blanket. Shortly thereafter he was called away, however, to dispose of some military matters in need of immediate action.

Minutes passed. Since the cushion and blanket did not seem to help in producing the desired warmth, Käthe pulled on the bell cord, telling the servant who appeared, that he should bring a few pieces of wood, because she was so cold.

At the same time she got up to push the screen aside, and having done so, noticed the little pile of ashes that still lay on the iron plate.

Botho entered in the same moment, and gave a start at the sight he encountered. He immediately controlled himself, however, as Käthe, pointing at the ashes, remarked in her most jocular tone, "What does this mean, Botho? See, I've caught you again. Well then, out with it. Love letters? Yes or no?"

"You'll just believe what you want anyway."

"Yes or no?"

"Very well then, yes."

"*That* was good. Now I can put my mind to rest. Love letters, too funny. Why don't we just burn them up twice over; first to ashes and then to smoke. Perhaps that will work."

Skillfully she piled the pieces of wood together which the servant had brought and with a few matches sought to ignite them. She succeeded; in no time the fire flamed up brightly. As she pushed the footstool towards the flames, and stretched her feet right up to the iron bars to warm them comfortably, she said, "And now I'll finish telling you the story of that Russian woman, who naturally wasn't Russian at all. But she was a very clever type. She had almond-shaped eyes—all of those types have almond-shaped eyes—and made out that she was taking the cure in Schlangenbad. Well, we all know about that sort of thing. She didn't have a doctor, at least not a regular one, but every day she was over in Frankfurt or in Wiesbaden or even in Darmstadt and always on somebody's arm. And some people even said it wasn't always the same man. And you should have seen, what a wardrobe! What conceit! She would scarcely even say 'hello' to anybody when she came to the table d'hôte with her 'lady-in-waiting.' But of course, she had a 'lady-in-waiting,' that's always the first thing with women of that sort. And we called her 'Madame Pompadour,' the Russian woman, I mean, and she was well aware that we called her that too.[1]

"And old Frau General Wedell, who was entirely on our side and quite annoyed about this dubious type—that she was a 'dubious type' there was no doubt whatsoever—old Wedell said quite loudly right across the entire table, 'Yes indeed, ladies, fashions change in everything, in pocketbooks and handbags too, why, even in evening bags and purses. When I was still young we still had Pompadours, but these days there aren't any Pompadours any more. Don't you agree? There aren't any Pompadours any more.' And when she said that we all laughed and looked straight at Madame Pompadour. But that frightful creature nevertheless carried the day against us and said in a loud and sharp voice—because old Wedell didn't hear well, 'Yes indeed, Frau General, it's just as you say. Only it's strange, isn't it, when the Pompadours were replaced, the *réticules* came in, and people started calling them *ridicules*. And *ridicules* like that are with us still.'[2] And as she said it she looked straight at good old Frau Wedell, who, since she couldn't answer, got up from the table and left the room. Now I ask you, Botho, what do you say to that? What do you think of such impertinence? . . . But Botho, you're not saying a thing, you're not even listening."

"Oh, of course I am, Käthe."

Three weeks later there was a wedding in the Church of St. James. Its cloisterlike forecourt was also on that day occupied by a dense and inquisitive crowd of people, mostly working-class women, some with their children on their arms. At the same time schoolboys and street urchins had found their way among them as well. All sorts of coaches drove up, and from one of the very first alighted a couple who, as long as they remained in the view of those present, were accompanied by laughter and whispering.

"What a waistline," said one of the closest women.

"Waistline?"

"Well then, those hips."

"Looks more like whale ribs to me."

"*That's* for sure."

Without a doubt this conversation would have continued had not the bridal coach driven up in the very same instant. The coachman, leaping from his seat, hastened to open the door, but the groom, a gaunt man in a tall hat and pointed old-fashioned stiff collar, got there first and extended his hand to his bride. She was an extremely pretty young woman, who incidentally, as is usually the case with brides, was admired less for her good looks than for her white satin dress. The two of them then ascended the few somewhat-worn carpeted stone steps, entering first the cloister and immediately passing through the portal of the church. Everyone's eyes followed them.

"Ain't she got no wreath neither?" said the same woman in whose eyes Frau Dörr's waistline had also failed so badly shortly before.

"Wreath? . . . Wreath? . . . Don't you know about it then? . . . Ain't you heard the talk?"

"Oh, yeah. Sure I have. But, my dear Kornatzki, if everything went according to the talk you hear, they wouldn't need any wreaths any more at all, an' Schmidt on Friedrichstraße could just up an' close right off."

"Yep," laughed Frau Kornatzki, "he sure could. An' to pick such an old'n in the bargain. I'll bet he's got a good fifty years on'm at least, an' he really looks like he's all set to celebrate his silver anniversary already."

"Yeah. He sure looked that way. An' did you see that collar of his? It's outa' this world."

"He kin use it ta kill 'er with, if them stories ever start over."

"Yeah, he sure can."

And so it went on for a time, while from the church the organ prelude could already be heard.

Next morning Rienäcker and Käthe sat at breakfast. This time they were in Botho's study. Its two windows stood wide open to admit fresh air and light. Swallows nesting in the courtyard chattered as they flew about, and Botho, who was in the habit of strewing a few crumbs for them every morning, was again today just reaching for the breakfast basket as the unrestrained laughter of his wife, who had been deeply immersed in her favorite newspaper for the last five minutes, caused him to put it down again.

"Well Käthe, what's up? You look like you've found something especially nice."

"Oh, indeed I have. . . . It really is just too funny. The names you come across. And it's always in the marriage and engagement notices. Just listen to this."

"I'm all ears."

"Notice is hereby respectfully given of their marriage, which took place today: '*Gideon Franke*, Factory Foreman, *Magdalene Franke*, née *Nimptsch*' . . . Nimptsch. Can you imagine anything funnier? And then, Gideon!"

Botho took the paper, actually only because he wished to hide his embarrassment behind it. Then he returned it to her, and in the most casual tone he could possibly muster, said, "What have you got against Gideon, Käthe? Gideon is better than Botho."

*Translated by William L. Zwiebel*

# THE
# POGGENPUHL
# FAMILY

# 1

The Poggenpuhl family consisted of Major von Poggenpuhl's widow and her three daughters—Therese, Sophie, and Manon. Since they had moved to Berlin from Pommersch-Stargard seven years ago they had lived in a corner house in the Grossgörschenstrasse, a new building only just completed and still damp in the walls when they arrived. It belonged to August Nottebohm, a decent, portly fellow who was a retired builder's foreman. The Poggenpuhls had chosen the Grossgörschenstrasse not least because its name commemorated an event in military history, but also because of its so-called magnificent view. The front windows looked out on the monuments and family tombs of Saint Matthew's churchyard, and the rear windows gave on to the backs of several houses belonging to the Kulmstrasse, one of which bore the legend "Schulze's Sweets" in huge letters of alternate red and blue. It is possible, even probable, that not everyone would have appreciated these two views. But Frau von Poggenpuhl, née Pütter (she came from a poor but highly respected family of clergymen) was equally well pleased with both. The view from the front appealed to her because she was rather sentimental and fond of talking about death; and the view from the back, because she suffered from a perpetual cough and lived almost entirely on barley sugar and cough pastilles, despite her efforts to economize. So whenever visitors came it was the custom to speak of the tremendous advantages of this apartment, whose only real advantage was that it was very cheap and that Herr Nottebohm had promised never to put up the rent for the major's widow. "No,

no, Frau von Poggenpuhl," was more or less what he had said on
that occasion, "as far as that's concerned, you have no need to worry,
nor the young ladies either. My, my, when I think back on it all! You
will pardon me, Frau von Poggenpuhl, but little Manon was only a
little bit of a thing when you moved in that Michaelmas . . . and
when you came down on New Year's Day with our first rent pay-
ment and all the other apartments were still empty because of the
walls being damp—which was nonsense, of course—I said to my
wife, because that was before we had any money at all, 'Line,' I said,
'that's our first takings and it'll bring us luck.' And so it did; because
from that quarter on we've never had an empty apartment and
always respectable people, that I must say. . . . And then, Frau von
Poggenpuhl, you'd be the last person I'd start on—putting up the
rent, I mean. After all, I was out there too; my word, that really was
a hellish business. I've still got a bullet in here. But the doctor says
it'll drop out one day, and then I'll have a souvenir."

And that was the end of Nottebohm's speech, the longest he had
ever made. He could not have had a more sympathetic listener. The
"hellish business" referred to the battle of Gravelotte, where Major
von Poggenpuhl had died an honorable death late in the evening
when the Pomeranian Division had been sent in. He had led the
battalion in which Nottebohm had served. He—the major, that is—
left nothing but his fine old name and three bright coronation talers.
They were found in his purse and later given to his widow. These
three coronation talers were the family's inheritance and therefore,
naturally, their pride as well. Sixteen years later when the youngest
daughter Manon (born a few months after her father's death) was to
be confirmed, the three talers, whose preservation during all those
years had been no mean feat, were made into three brooches, one
for each of the daughters, in memory of this confirmation day. All
this was done with the participation and help of the clergy; for
Superintendent-General Schwarz loved the family, and in the evening
after the confirmation he had joined a few old comrades and friends
in the Poggenpuhl apartment and raised the presentation of the
brooches to the level, if not of a religious ceremony, then at least of a
solemn celebration. It had impressed even Nebelung the porter, a
rather crude fellow full of prejudice against "that aristocratic gang."
If he was not exactly converted to the more benign views held by his

landlord and employer Nottebohm, he was at least brought a little closer to them.

It goes without saying that the arrangement of the Poggenpuhl apartment also reflected the circumstances in which, for better or for worse, the family now found itself. There was no plush-covered upholstery, and the only carpet was a small Schmiedeberg rug with a somewhat fuzzy black woolen fringe. It lay in front of the sofa in the parlor, which was the room nearest the passage and therefore served as the reception room. The narrow curtains with darns here and there were in keeping with the rug. But everything was very clean and well kept. A long mirror with a strip of gilt beading on its white frame had recently been bought at an auction; it probably came from some old patrician family home in the Mark. Although the otherwise meager furnishings appeared to have been scraped together (or perhaps because of that appearance) the mirror invested them with an aura of expiring grandeur—expiring, but nevertheless bearing witness to past glories.

Above the parlor sofa there hung a large, knee-length portrait in oils of a Major von Poggenpuhl in the Sohr Hussars. In 1813 at the battle of Grossgörschen he had broken through the enemy formation and had been awarded the order Pour le Mérite. He was the only Poggenpuhl ever to have served in the cavalry. The major's face, half-martial and half-benign, looked down upon a shallow glass bowl filled with primulas and a circle of forget-me-nots in summer and with visiting cards in winter. Directly facing the major, against the opposite wall, stood a bureau with a shelf. To enable the family to show some sort of hospitality to visitors, half a bottle of Cape sherry was enthroned here, surrounded by a number of small liqueur glasses; all these stood on a gold-rimmed plate which never stopped rattling.

Next to this parlor was the living room with a single window, and, behind that, the so-called Berlin room, which was really just a passage, though spacious. Three beds stood along one of the longer walls—three only, although they were a family of four. The fourth couch was of a somewhat more peripatetic character and consisted of a sofa frame strung with cane; the two younger sisters took turns to ensconce themselves on this piece of furniture.

Behind the Berlin room (Nottebohm had drawn up the ground

plans himself) there was a kitchen and an attic for hanging out the washing. This was where the old servant Friederike had her being. She was a faithful soul who had known the "master" and had been Frau von Poggenpuhl's confidante through all the family's ups and downs, including the move from Stargard to Berlin.

That was how the Poggenpuhls lived and how they proved to the world at large that, with the right outlook and, of course, the necessary skills, it was possible to exist contentedly and very nearly according to one's station in life even in the humblest circumstances. This was admitted even by the porter Nebelung, albeit with reluctance and much head shaking. All the Poggenpuhls—the mother possibly to a lesser degree than the rest—possessed the happy gift of never complaining, of making the best of life as well as being good reckoners, though there was never anything unpleasantly calculating about their calculations.

In this the three sisters were all alike, but in other ways they were very different from one another in character.

Therese, already thirty, might seem somewhat unpractical at first sight, and that is what she was often taken to be. The only art she appeared to have learned was that of reclining gracefully in a rocking chair. But she was really just as capable as her two younger sisters; it was only that she labored in a different vineyard. Because of her particular character, she was convinced that the task of holding high the Poggenpuhl banner had fallen to her, and it was her duty to take her place more deliberately than her sisters cared to in the world to which they rightfully belonged. So she was at home in the families of generals and ministers of state in the Behren- and Wilhelmstrasse; their tea tables never failed to resound with approval and applause when she gave one of her maliciously humorous accounts of her younger sisters and their adventures in the "would-be aristocracy." Even the old commander who had ceased to be particularly impressed by any earthly matter would cheer up and be quite merry and agreeable; and the under secretary of state who lived diagonally across from the general's family and was on friendly terms with them would always be quite carried away by the delicate satire of the young lady who was so poor but so properly conscious of her class, although—or perhaps because—he himself belonged to the very newest aristocracy. A further consequence of Therese's triumphs in society was that if anything needed to be asked for, she could afford to ask for it; but it must be noted that she never asked for anything for herself; or if she did, then she took care to choose something that could be granted effortlessly—and which therefore gave particular satisfaction to her benefactor.

Such was Therese von Poggenpuhl.

The two younger sisters were quite different; they had adapted themselves to their condition and to the modern world, and they worked more or less as a team.

Sophie, the second, was the family's prop and stay because she possessed something that hitherto had not distinguished the Poggenpuhl family, namely, talents. It is possible that under more favorable economic conditions these talents would have been regarded somewhat dubiously and would have been considered unbecoming to someone of her station in life; but in the Poggenpuhl's straitened circumstances her natural gifts were a daily blessing for the family. In her calmer moments even Therese would admit that. Sophie— who was physically unlike her sisters as well, having an amiable poodle face framed in little curls—was good at almost everything: she was musical, she drew, she painted, she wrote verse for birthdays and nuptial eves, and she knew how to lard a hare; but all this, much as it was, would not have been half as significant for them all if it had not been for Manon, the baby of the family.

In contrast to Sophie, Manon—now seventeen—had no gifts at all except the gift of making herself universally popular, especially in bankers' families. She preferred the non-Christian ones, and her favorite was the highly esteemed house of Bartenstein. Most of these families were prolific, so that there was never any lack of girls in their early teens who needed to be instructed in the rudiments of some branch of art or learning. Any conversation, whether short or long, about the various disciplines would regularly end with Manon's nonchalantly proffered remark: "I think my sister might possibly be able to help out there." This remark was perfectly justified, because in fact there was nothing Sophie was afraid to take on, from physics to spectrum analysis.

So that was the distribution of roles in the Poggenpuhl family. As has already been indicated, it brought with it certain financial advantages, and sometimes these advantages considerably exceeded the tiny pension that formed their basic income. None of the three young ladies lost any part of her dignity thereby. On the contrary, they were all (but especially the two younger ones) as carefree as they were grateful; they tactfully avoided any kind of exaggerated compliments, let alone flattery, and everyone respected and thought well of them because everything they did—and that was the important point—was done absolutely unselfishly. Their wants were few, especially with respect to dress (though this did not preclude a pleasing appearance; they knew how to manage on a minimum). All their thoughts and hopes centered on the "two boys," their brothers Wendelin and Leo. The elder was already a first lieutenant of over thirty, the younger still a mere cub, barely twenty-two. It goes without saying that both had joined the East Pomeranian regiment (now, incidentally, stationed in East Prussia) in which their father's career had begun—and ended, with honor and renown, on that memorable eighteenth of August.

To increase the family renown as much as lay in their power was the object for which the trio of sisters strove with all their might.

As far as Wendelin was concerned, he cooperated with his sisters' efforts in every way, especially as he knew how to economize; there was hardly a doubt that he would achieve the highest goals. He was clever, ambitious, and level-headed. By keeping her ear to the ground in the houses of their military excellencies, Therese had gleaned that it was really just a matter of whether Wendelin's next posting would be to the War Office or to the General Staff. Things were not as happy in the case of Leo, who was less talented than his older brother and whose only aim in life was to cut a proper dash. Two duels, in one of which a junior legal counsel had suffered a shot through both cheeks and the loss of several front teeth, bore witness to the fact that Leo was rapidly approaching his ideal of what a proper dash should be; and there was no reason why his career should not have justified hopes as great as those placed on Wendelin's talents, had it not been for the specter of dismissal that stalked beside it: Leo was in perpetual danger of being cashiered because of his steadily mounting debts. He was everyone's favorite, but at the same time he was everyone's problem child; and everything the family thought and did was directed toward helping him avert another catastrophe. No sacrifice seemed too great, and although their mother sometimes shook her head, the daughters never doubted that, "if only it were possible to keep him going for the necessary length of time," the next great battle against the Russians, the Zorndorf of the future, would be won through Leo's intervention.

"But he's not even in the Guards," said their Mama.

"No. But that's neither here nor there. The next battle of Zorndorf will be won by the infantry."

# 2

It was a winter day, the third of January.

Friederike was just returning from her regular morning shopping expedition, a basket of rolls for breakfast in one hand and a jug of milk in the other. Both rolls and milk came from the basement shop across the street. In spite of Friederike's woolen gloves, the cold had numbed her fingers, and as soon as she came into the kitchen she took the teakettle from its hole in the stove and warmed herself at the glow. But not for long; she had fallen back to sleep before dawn, and so she was half an hour behind with her work—and of course she intended to make up the time.

So she took the coffee mill down from its shelf and went briskly to work. When she had ground the coffee beans, she tipped them into the filter bag so that they would be ready later for her to pour on the water; finally she put the kettle back on the fire, picked up the basket of firewood (the bottom of which, incidentally, threatened to drop out at any moment), and went off to the front part of the apartment to light the fire in the living room with the single window. She knelt before the stove and piled up wood and briquettes so skillfully that she managed to light the whole structure with a single match, which she applied to a wad of neatly twisted newspaper.

Scarcely half a minute had gone by before she heard the fire popping and crackling inside the stove, and as soon as she was sure it would burn, she rose from her place before it to apply herself to the second task of the morning, which was dusting. Whatever effort she made, the three young ladies were never quite satisfied with the result; and so, conscientious though she normally was, she went about it rather superficially and contented herself with putting a moderate amount of shine on the row of pictures hanging over the sofa. Although they were all contemporary portraits, Leo always called them "the house of Poggenpuhl's gallery of ancestors." Three or four were cabinet-sized photographs; but the older ones belonged to the days of the daguerreotype and had faded so much that their artistic merit could be assessed only under exceptionally favorable lighting conditions.

But the "ancestors" did not have the whole wall to themselves. Immediately above them hung a fairly large oil painting, artistically of the third or even fourth degree of merit. It depicted the most important historical moment in the life of the family. Most of the canvas was covered with gunsmoke, but in the middle it was possible to discern fairly clearly a church with a desperate nocturnal battle raging in the churchyard.

It was the assault on Hochkirch; the Austrians were admirably "kitted out," but the poor Prussians' clothing was in a lamentable condition. The immediate foreground was occupied by an elderly officer in his underclothes and waistcoat; there was no question of boots, but he held a gun in his hand. This old gentleman was Major Balthasar von Poggenpuhl, who had held the churchyard for half an hour until he too joined the corpses on the ground. This picture— probably on account of its sentimental value to the family—was set in a broad, handsome baroque frame, while the glazed photographs and daguerreotypes had to be content with simple gilt borders.

All the members of the family—even Leo, who was something of a skeptic in artistic matters—extended their reverence for "the Hochkirch major" (as this officer was called to distinguish him from the many other majors in the family) to include the pictorial representation of his glorious act; only Friederike, in spite of her complete adherence to the family cult, was on a kind of war footing with the half-clad old hero. The reason was simply that it was her duty, at least every third day, to run her ancient, cobweb-thin dust cloth over the highly irregular baroque frame—with the very frequent, if not absolutely regular, result that the picture slid down from the wall and fell across the backrest onto the sofa. It was always put aside until after breakfast, when it was hammered back into place; but that did not do much good and could not be expected to, for the whole expanse of wall had been damaged too often, and quite soon the newly inserted nail would come out again and the picture would slide onto the sofa.

"Lord," said Friederike, "he probably stood there like that all right, it was a good thing he did. But to put him in a picture like that . . . it just won't stay in place, it just won't."

After this monologue she screwed the stove door tightly shut. That was always the last thing she did. Then she put her dustpan and dust cloth back into the firewood basket and softly began her retreat through the long bedroom into the kitchen. But there was no need to be so careful, because all four ladies were already awake, and Manon had even half opened a window into the courtyard, proceeding on the assumption that a temperature of several degrees below freezing was still preferable to air in which four people had slept through the night.

A bare quarter of an hour, and coffee was served. The ladies were already in the warm living room, the major's widow on the sofa, Therese in her rocking chair, and Manon with a toolbox, hunting for a longer nail for the old Hochkirch major who had fallen down again.

"Friederike," said the major's widow, "you really ought to be more careful with that picture."

"Oh, ma'am, I am, I barely touch him; but he's always so wobbly. . . . Lord, Manon dear, if you could find a really long one; or better still, if you could knock in a proper hook. Lord, it isn't as though I didn't remember all the time, but when he suddenly starts sliding, it always gives me a turn. And sometimes I wonder whether perhaps he's not properly at rest."

"Oh, Friederike, don't talk such nonsense," said Therese, a little sharply, "*Him*, of all people. As though he could fail to be at rest! Whatever do you mean? I tell you, *he's* at rest all right. I only wish everyone could be at rest as he is. A clear conscience is the best pillow. You ought to know that. And as for a clear conscience, well, he's certainly got that. . . . But wherever did you get these rolls again? They look as though someone had given them a fright, worse than the one you had. I don't like shop rolls. Why don't you go to young Karchow? He's a proper baker."

This difference of opinion occurred every third day between the maid and the young lady. Friederike enjoyed complete freedom of speech, and she would not have remained silent now and would have stoutly defended her dictum that "one must keep in with the base-ment shop people" if it had not been for a sudden knock on the front door. "The postman!" the three sisters cried altogether; and a moment later Friederike reappeared with the mail: a newspaper in a wrapper, an advertisement for firewood and peat, and a real letter. The advertisement went straight into the stove; the paper probably contained a review of a recent exhibition of Sophie's watercolors and was pushed aside; only the letter caused a general rejoicing. "From Leo," cried the sisters, and handed the letter to their mother. But she gave it back to Therese. "You read it. He's such a good boy. But he always gives me a fright. He always wants something. And now we've just had Christmas and the New Year and the rent. . ."

"Oh Mother, you always start to worry right away. It's obvious you're not a soldier's daughter."

"No. Certainly not. And a good thing too. Who else would hold together what little we've got?"

"We would."

"Oh, you. . . ! But now read the letter, Therese. My heart's positively thumping."

*Dear Mama,*
Christmas was hopeless. I might have got leave from the regiment, but the fare! There's all this talk about cheap fares nowadays, but I think they're much too high, quite unnaturally high! And Wendelin also said, "Leo, it can't be done," and so it couldn't; and so, as you know, I went down to my landlord Funke the butcher, and watched their family celebrations. Everyone was deeply emotional, even Funke. It seems quite incredible, because especially over Christmas they never stopped slaughtering, and sometimes I simply couldn't stand the sound of the poor brutes squealing any more, and Funke always supervised it himself. Incidentally, the freshly made sausages and the pig's head brawn were quite excellent. As far as food is concerned, one couldn't do better than here in Thorn. But the mind starves and so does the heart. All in all, starvation seems to be my lot. Oh Mother, why weren't you born a Bleichröder?[1]

"Monstrous," said Therese, interrupting her reading. "There's Manon with her everlasting Bartensteins, and now Leo's starting too."

"Having the Bartensteins is not at all a bad thing for us. Why don't you go on?"

. . . Well, so Christmas was no good. However, there are other important days in the year. And the most important is the fourth of January, the birthday of our dear old mother, née Pütter. And that's the day after tomorrow, and I shall report booted & spurred to deliver my good wishes personally.

"It's not possible! No money for Christmas, and after the New Year, just when all the bills come in, he intends to make such an expensive journey!"

"I expect there'll be an explanation, Mama," said Manon. "Probably in the letter. Just go on listening."

. . . because signs and wonders still happen, and sometimes I feel as though atheism and all the other disagreeable phenomena of our times were on the way out. Even the aristocracy will rise again, and the *poor* aristocracy will go to the very top, and that means the Poggenpuhls, of course. Because there is absolutely no doubt that in that sphere we represent a kind of perfection, the pure breed, as you might say. But back to our subject, as they say in parliament. So now lend me your ears and hear: on New Year's Eve I was a beggar (albeit a happy one, because we got through seven bowls of punch at the mess, outsize ones!); and on the morning of January first, I was a god, a Croesus. Because Croesus is always tops, or what is called the climax. It was only ten o'clock when there was a knock on the door. I dragged myself from my morning dreams and felt a certain leaden condition, but not for long. For who stood before me? Oktavio? No, not Oktavio. For today we shall call him Wendelin. And what he said was as follows: "Leo," he said, "you're in luck. Our ship has come home. With money."

"For me?" I asked.

"No, not for you. At least not directly. But for me. The Military Weekly sent me my check this morning."

"Is it a lot?" I interrupted in the highest excitement.

"The Military Weekly always sends a lot," he replied quietly and laid three twenty-mark notes before me. Dazzled, as though they were not notes but the purest gold, I was about to rush at him blinded with gratitude; but he restrained me with noble reticence and said, "All yours, Leo. But not for swigging. Tomorrow morning you're off to Berlin . . . .

"Kind Wendelin! He's sending him because he knows he's your favorite," Manon interrupted at this point, and she stroked her mother's hands. But Therese continued:

. . . You are to arrive at four in the afternoon, behave nicely, and next morning you're to help celebrate her birthday. Next to the emperor's birthday, Mother's birthday is the most important date in the calendar. That's in the Poggenpuhl catechism. And now get dressed and take an hour's walk. You look like Saint Sylvester when his last hour had come." And with these words he left me like a prince. And I shall do as he commanded and arrive on Tuesday afternoon. Four o'clock. *Tout à vous, ma Reine Mère.*

Your happy, crazy,
well beloved
*Leo I*

The two younger sisters clapped their hands; even Therese, much as she deplored their boisterousness, was pleased about the visit. Only their mother said, "Oh dear, and I'm supposed to feel happy. But how can I? I suppose he'll just about get here with the money, but while he's here we'll have to give him a treat for a few days, and even if he doesn't ask much, he'll have to go back on the third day, and we'll have to pay."

"Don't always keep on about that," said Therese.

"Yes, Therese, you always imagine a liveried servant will come and bring you a money box with the inscription: To the valiant House of Poggenpuhl; but those are all fairy tales, and the man at the ticket office who sells the tickets is an inexorable reality."

"Oh Mama," said Sophie, "you mustn't spoil the pleasure of looking forward to it. There are still signs and wonders—he said so.

And if they don't happen, then I'll get an advance on my last lot of pictures, and if that doesn't work. . ."

"Well, then we've still got the sugar caster," Manon interposed.

"Yes, that's always going to get us through. But one day it will be gone."

"Which wouldn't matter either," Manon continued consolingly. "The Bartensteins will give us another. Only the other day Frau Bartenstein said to me, 'Dear Manon, is there really nothing that you want?' Yes, Mama, that's how it is, and I'm only sorry that just when Leo arrives this evening I shall have to go to the wedding eve rehearsal. But perhaps I could take him along. I've thought about it for some time, and I'm sure Flora would be really pleased."

"You keep forgetting that he wears the emperor's uniform."

"Oh Therese, that's petty and old-fashioned and totally out of date. Our crown prince is the crown prince and he wears the emperor's uniform too, and if he hasn't been to the Bartensteins, then he's been to other people just like them."

"Well, we shall see," said Therese; her attitude to the Bartensteins was critical, but she was nevertheless glad of their existence.

# 3

The next day came, and late in the afternoon, when it was beginning to grow dark, a cab stopped at the house, and mother and daughters saw Friederike and Leo merrily exchanging greetings; then Friederike took the officer's little case from the driver's box and walked toward the door, past Agnes Nebelung, who had stationed herself by the sidewalk because she wanted to see the lieutenant. Leo followed. Kisses were exchanged on the stairs, where the sisters were standing one step above the other. Their mother stood at the top. "Hello, old thing," and another kiss. Confused and disjointed sentences flew about, and then Leo went through the parlor into the living room with its single window. Here he threw off his greatcoat and sword; his tunic had ridden up, and he tugged it into place in front of the looking glass. Then he performed a smart about-turn and said, "Well, my dears, here I am again. How do I look?"

"Oh, superb."

"Thank you. That sort of remark always does one good, even if it's not true. One might almost say it refreshes. But apropos of refreshment: inspite of the fresh air, I'm colossally thirsty. For seven hours I've had nothing but an anchovy roll. You wouldn't have a glass of beer?"

"Of course, of course. Friederike can go and fetch a tankard of real beer . . ."

"No, no. Nobody's to fetch anything. Why should they? Water

will do just as well." Manon handed him a glass of water and he swallowed it all in one gulp. "Brrr. But it's good."

"You're in such a hurry," said Manon. "It's not good for you. I think you should have a cup of coffee now. It's half past four and at seven we'll have something to eat."

"Excellent, Manon, excellent. Only perhaps we could change the order of events. I've just put down that water. If I have coffee right on top of it, that'll be too much fluid—an unnecessary dilation of the stomach, tantamount to a weakening effect. And I need my strength. Or, let us say, my country needs it."

"So you think . . ."

"Permit me to think along the following lines: a reversal of the accepted order. First a bite to eat, then coffee. For if my thirst was great, my hunger is almost equally great. Seven hours . . ."

"You've already said that."

"I know. Truth will out. Come on—what have you got?"

"A duck."

"Splendid."

"But it's still hanging up by the attic window and hasn't been plucked or drawn. So it'll be about two hours . . ."

"Rather a long time."

". . . But I think I've got the solution. We'll take out the liver, and in a quarter of an hour it can be fried and on your plate. Would you like it with apple or with onion?"

"Both. Never refuse anything, unless decency absolutely demands it."

"Oh, so you think such cases exist?" said Therese.

"Of course I do, of course. But now, dear old Mama, tell me how you are. Have you still got a pain round here?"

"Yes, Leo. Every night."

"Heaven knows, those doctor fellows are absolutely useless. Look at my forefinger. I twisted it the other day—actually about three months ago—and I've still got the same weakness in it. I may have to ask for my discharge."

"Oh, don't talk like that," said Therese. "Poggenpuhls don't ask for their discharge."

"But they get it."

"No, they don't. He (and she pointed to the Hochkirch major) will never be forgotten, nor will the Sohr major, nor Papa either. The emperor knows our worth."

"Yes, Therese. And what *is* our worth?"

"Our principles and the certainty that we'll be loyal to the last drop in our veins."

"Oh well, I suppose so. . . . But listen, Mother, have you tried healing?"

"Healing?"

"Yes. Faith healing. They puff and blow on you and mutter things, it's sort of sympathetic medicine. It always works. We've got an old Polish woman up there, and as soon as she starts puffing and blowing everything gets better. . . . Apropos, is the Christmas market still on?"

"I think so; some of it, anyway."

"There's bound to be a few stalls left, and we absolutely must go, girls. 'Count, just *one* three pfennig piece.' It's time I heard a classic remark like that again. And then we'll go to Helms and have a grog or hot chocolate with whipped cream and then off to the Reichshallen."[1]

"Oh, what a splendid idea," said Manon. "Don't you think so, Sophie? You're so quiet. . . . Why don't you say something too. . . ? I don't expect it would do for Therese, the Reichshallen are too common for her. But two sisters should be enough, and I'm really looking forward to it. Only you must arrange it so that we get to the Bartensteins at nine o'clock or not much later. Yes, Leo, you'll have to take us as far as the Vossstrasse."

"Certainly. But why? What goes on there?"

"Wedding eve rehearsal. Seraphine Schweriner, a cousin of Flora's, is getting married in a fortnight, and we've been rehearsing ever since Christmas. I've got a part—two, actually: first a girl with a baton, and then a Slovak mousetrap seller. They say I look charming."

"Of course."

"And Sophie's painted a transparency and written the prologue. But she won't recite it."

"Perhaps you'll have to do that too."

"Possibly. But I don't want to. Prologues are such a bore. People are always glad when they're over. But whether I do it or not is something we can discuss on the way—that is, if any kind of conversation is possible on the way. You really have to watch out now; it's always so foggy in the evenings. Altogether, the Berlin air . . ."

"Oh don't talk nonsense, Manon. Berlin has the best air in the world. I can tell you, I'm glad to have a chance of sniffing about a bit in it once more. Fog! Fog's no problem. Fog's just an external, and externals don't mean a thing. It's the inner life that counts, that's where the creative force is—fresh, happy, and free; I'll leave out the 'devout' bit, if you'll excuse me, Therese. . . . Good God, our little hole up there, it has the purest air, there's always an East wind or whatever, and if you've got a weak chest" (and he thumped his own) "you catch pneumonia before you know where you are. All right, so it has the purest air, no question about it. All the same, I tell you, everything there is stuffy, narrow, small. If the colonel sneezes, the sentry hears him and presents arms. Horrible. If it weren't for the odd spot of gambling and the Jew girls . . ."

"But Leo . . ."

"Or one of the two or three Christian girls. But the Jewish ones are prettier."

"But you must have some intellectual activity?"

"Heavens, I should hope not. There's no time. But every now and then I work out my debts, and I sit there adding and subtracting, adding and subtracting, to see how I can get by. That's my only intellectual activity. It's quite serious—you might almost say scientific."

"Oh dear, Leo," said his mother with an anxious look at him. "I'm sure that's the only reason you came. Is it a lot this time?"

"A lot, Mother? It's never a lot. How can it be? No one's as silly as that. A lot—that would be the last straw. But it is a little. And although it's very lucky that it is so little, in a way that's just what makes it so annoying—the most annoying thing about it, really. Because you say to yourself, 'Good God, it's so little, how could you have had any fun on so little?' And you haven't really had any. And then the other trouble begins; even though it is so little, you just can't pay it. And no one to help, not a soul! And when I look at the others! Every one of them has an uncle . . ."

"Oh, we have an uncle too!" Sophie interrupted. "And Uncle Eberhard is a man of honor . . ."

"Granted. But kind as he is, Uncle Eberhard does nothing to prove he's an uncle; or anyway, not enough. And then, my dears, the ones that haven't got uncles, well, at least they've got a grandfather, or a godparent, or a canoness.[2] Canonesses are best of all: they believe any story you tell them, and even if they haven't got much themselves, they'll give you everything, down to their last penny."

"Oh Leo, don't talk such nonsense. How can they give everything away?"

"Everything, I say. A proper canoness can give everything away because she doesn't need anything at all. She has a roof over her head, and fish, and game, and turkeys run about the courtyard, and pigeons sit on the roof, and there's a huge vegetable garden which they look after themselves of course, because they have nothing else to do, and there's always a turnip to be found or a carrot; and there's always a fire in the kitchen because they get their firewood free. And that's why—yes, I must say it again—that's why they can give everything away; because they need nothing and what they need they've got."

"But they have to have clothes."

"Clothes? Good heavens, no. They don't have clothes. They have one dress and it lasts them thirty years. Of course they wear something; they're not the type to go about like Eve in the Garden of Eden. . . . Ah, there's the liver—it smells delicious, exquisite. And now, my dears, we'll divide it up; Mother has the middle bit because its the tenderest, Therese the right end and me the left end, and Sophie and Manon . . ."

"Oh Leo, don't put on an act. You know quite well you're having it all. That's how you've always been: you want to make nice—as long as no one takes you at your word."

"Don't make revelations about my character, Sophie. You had better give me a roll instead, to eat with my liver, or else it'll be too rich. And I'm right all the same about our relatives; not a kinswoman, not an aunt, hardly a female cousin, at least, not a proper one—it's enough to drive a man crazy, as Mephisto said somewhere. Mother, do you know Mephisto?"

"Of course I know him. You Poggenpuhls always think you're the only ones with any wisdom or knowledge, and all acquired through inspiration. Because it's not as though you got it at school. And you of all people, Leo! When I think of your teachers' reports! Wendelin was another matter. You know why? Because he takes after the Pütters."

"Oh Mother, you really are the tops. What would we do without you? And I'm almost ready to believe that the Pütters really are superior. But in one respect they're just like us; they haven't a penny and that's my misfortune. Oh Mama, no money anywhere, no cover—and that for a young fellow and a lieutenant! It's a devilish situation. And there I was inviting you to go to Helms and the Reichshallen!"

"He's incorrigible," laughed Sophie. "Whatever next! First of all, you're our guest, and your only duty is to do the honors. And surely, you'll feel able to act as our escort?"

"Goodness, you're good girls, all of you. And so broadminded; and you understand that this is how it has to be; and still you go on giving me your love and respect. At least I hope you do, otherwise I shouldn't accept. And now I think we should go. You're coming, Mama, aren't you?"

"No, Leo. Every extra person makes a difference. And then my coat—if we're going to a café, it's too shabby."

"Oh, that doesn't matter."

"And then I get rheumatism so easily—just here—and you never know where you're going to find a table, and it might be in a draft. And if I sit in a draft I always get my rheumatism, and then I have to go to bed. Or if I don't get my rheumatism, I get my colic, and that's even more miserable."

# 4

Leo really did go to the Christmas market and to Helms and the Reichshallen with his two younger sisters. Then he accompanied them to the Bartensteins, took his leave of them, and arrived home a little after nine. It was his plan to have a long chat with his mother and Therese, and to tell them all about his impressions of Berlin, for he was one of those fortunate people who only have to set foot in the street to have an adventure—or to imagine they have. But things turned out differently from what he had expected; for Therese had gone into town to buy a few extra trifles for their mother's birthday, and Mama herself, so Friederike told him as soon as he entered the passage, had already gone to bed. "Hm," he grumbled; and, having no other choice, he was just about to settle down to a little quiet meditation in a corner of the sofa when his mother sent for him to come and talk to her at her bedside. That was a great deal preferable to "contemplating his inner life," as he put it, while waiting for Therese.

"Are you feeling unwell, Mama?"

"No, Leo, not really. I just lay down because I wanted to build up my strength a bit for tomorrow. Get a chair and bring it close and then fetch the lamp so that I can look at you. Because you've got a nice Poggenpuhl face, and if there's something that isn't as it should be, I can always tell by looking at you, and get an idea of what's going on."

"Oh, Mama, you always think I'm fibbing. I'm not as bad as all

191

that. I'm not even very talented in that line—all I do is exaggerate a bit."

"Never mind. And you were always my favorite, and the others have never begrudged it. But you are irresponsible, and you always think 'something will turn up.' And you see, that's what worries me. Turn up! How can anything turn up, where is it to come from? It's really a miracle that we've managed to scrape along so far."

"But, Mother, that's just it; that's where our hope lies, I might almost say, our certainty. If a miracle could happen yesterday, why shouldn't it happen today or tomorrow or the day after tomorrow?"

"That sounds quite good, but it's not right. If we take miracles and grace for granted, then we vex Him from Whom all grace comes, and in the end He won't send us any more. God doesn't want us just to accept everything and thank Him (and sometimes we do that very perfunctorily); He wants us to deserve His grace, or at least to show that we are worthy of it, and He wants us to keep our eyes fixed not on what *might* happen through a miracle, but on what *must* happen according to reason and calculation and probability. That kind of calculation has His blessing upon it."

"Oh, Mama, I never stop calculating."

"Yes, you never stop calculating, quite true; but you calculate afterward, not before. You start calculating when it's too late, when you're in trouble right up to your neck, and then you try to calculate your way out, and all you do is to calculate yourself further in. You don't and won't see what you don't like; and when something seems flattering or pleasing to you, then you turn it into a probability. People have done so much for us—for you too—and now, I think, the time has come for us to say, 'We must help ourselves!' If we keep on saying, 'But we're the Poggenpuhls' we shall make a nuisance of ourselves and in the end we'll turn into whiners, which is something I should not like to see."

"We're far from that, Mama."

"Not as far as you think. Uncle Eberhard is a very fine and generous man. I really must say it: he's a true nobleman; but even he is gradually beginning to cool off a bit and grow impatient. He doesn't say so right out, just because he *is* generous, but you can read it between the lines."

"Oh, Uncle! The old bone of contention! Look, Mama, I ask you:

he really does do too little, and what he does is all just for the sake of God. What he ought to think is: 'I've had my time, and now it's someone else's turn!' It's true he gives us something every now and again, but his sacrifices on the altar of the family are not in proportion either to his income or to his sermons. He ought to write less and give more. After all, he had a colossal stroke of luck and now he's been living in clover for twelve years and more, or sitting pretty, as some people call it."

"How is it that nothing can make you change your mind and that you simply will not see how things really are with Uncle. He married a rich widow and lives in a *Schloss,*[1] and when his wife wants to invite Prince Albrecht or one of the Carolaths, there's a great to-do and half the nobility of Lower Silesia comes to dinner too, and it looks as though Uncle Eberhard were giving the party. But he's not the one giving it, *she* is; he only lends his name to it, and hardly even that, because lots of people call her by her first husband's name when they talk about her behind her back. He was a Silesian, and of a very distinguished family, much more distinguished than the Poggenpuhls—you've all got to face the fact that there *are* more distinguished families. . . . I tell you, kind as she is, she still keeps him short, and he hasn't got much more than his general's pension, and out of that he still has his old debts to pay off . . ."

"Old debts? You see, Mama, now you're the one saying it! So he has old debts too. And he was made a general just the same and now he's got a rich wife . . ."

"He still has his old debts to pay off," his mother repeated, taking no notice of the interruption. "And so what he has left is just pocket money."

"But a tidy sum . . ."

"Possibly, or let's say, certainly. And if he's careful with it nevertheless, it may well be because he doesn't trust you, or, if he does, then his wife doesn't, and she influences him."

"That's just it, that's what's so galling—the indignity of petticoat influence! And then, Mama, I won't even talk about myself—perhaps I'm an *enfant perdu;* that may be so. But Wendelin, that model of a boy, if I may call my respected brother by such a name—surely he must be pleased with *him,* and even Madam Aunt should be. It just shows how stingy they are. It's obvious."

"Is that what Wendelin says too?"

"No. Not him. He doesn't need to. Wendelin has the gift of feeling king of infinite space on a pitcher of water. Wendelin will get on anyhow. But even for him there's a difference. There's a difference between getting on effortlessly and getting on through perpetual abstinence. People who go in for abstinence usually have a screw loose—they become famous, or at least they *may* become famous, but even when they *are* famous, they usually behave like little schoolmasters. Possibly Wendelin may be an exception."

"But do you really believe—with any kind of certainty—that he'll get to the top?"

"Certainly, Mother. In less than six months he'll be on the General Staff. The stuff he wrote about Skobeleff made everyone sit up. And a year or two after that they'll send him to Saint Petersburg, and there he'll marry—at least that's what I'm assuming for the moment—a Yousoupov or a Dolgoruzka; they all have at least ten thousand serfs and diamond mines as well. What do you think? Not a bad forecast? Come on, admit it! But if Uncle were different—or Aunt, if you prefer; though we can't expect much from her—she's only a relative by marriage and she was from the petty bourgeoisie, which is always bad; at least *you're* middle class—well, then he'd be there already. He'd be in Saint Petersburg, and I'd be posted there, and I'd go with him to the Caucasus or to Merv or Samarkand—and none of that will happen, or at any rate it's being cruelly delayed, only because we haven't the wherewithal, the filthy lucre."

"Goodness, Leo, one would think, to listen to you, that everything would fall into your lap if only the wind changed. Dreams! Plans! You were like that even as a little boy!"

"Yes, Mother, and that's the way to be—for people like us, that is. If you've got something, well, then you can take life as it really is, you can be what they call a realist nowadays. But if you've got nothing, if you live in the Sahara, then you simply can't exist without a mirage of palm trees and odalisques and suchlike. A mirage, I say. And even if there's nothing there when you get up close, at least you've lived for an hour, and hoped, and got your courage back, and then you can go on wading through the sand quite happily. And so the visions that lead us on, however deceptive and unreal they may be, are really a mercy after all."

"Yes, the young can live like that, and perhaps they have a right to. And I'll grant you another thing: hope is sometimes better than fulfillment, and people who can go on hoping, at least they've had their share of happiness. But all the same: you hope too much and work too little."

"I don't work much, that's true, and I won't boast about it. But I'm cheerful by nature, and in the end that's better than any amount of work. Cheerfulness attracts people, it's like a magnet; so I think in the end there'll be something for me too."

"Well, I hope there may. And now go into the kitchen and tell Friederike to give you some supper."

# 5

Leo made no objection; he really was hungry. The duck liver at lunch had not been much, and the cup of chocolate at Helms even less.

So he went out and found Friederike. She was sitting by the kitchen lamp with an inkwell close beside her, doing her bookkeeping. She sat pondering, pen poised between thumb and forefinger. It was a new, wooden pen (probably a Christmas present) with an eagle—or it might have been a dove—carved on the end. As far as could be ascertained in the semidarkness that reigned in the kitchen, everything there was tidy and clean, if not exactly gleaming. The only gleaming object was the teakettle standing in its hole in the stove; its lid rattled perpetually. Never to be without boiling water was a luxury peculiar to the Poggenpuhl family. It was a carefully calculated luxury, because it enabled them to dispense modest hospitality at any time. This hospitality could take various forms, but at the top of the list—almost a specialty of the house—was a clear soup with a French name that could be quickly concocted with the help of a few slices of toast and a pinch of nutmeg. Every single member of the family excelled in its preparation to such a degree that even Flora would ask for it when she dropped in for an hour's chat in the evening, having first charmingly declined offers of "cold meats" and suchlike; and she was wise to do so.

"Well, Friederike," Leo now said as he pulled up a kitchen chair and leaned over the back, "Mama sent me along, and she even spoke

196

of supper. What's the supper situation? I'm hungry and I'd be grateful to God for anything. And to you too."

"Well, Master Leo, there isn't much."

"But what is there?"

"Well, a meatball left over from lunch yesterday, and a few pickled herrings with dill and sliced gherkins. And then there's an Edam cheese. But there's not much of that left. And then perhaps I could make you a cup of tea. The water's still bubbling."

"No, Friederike, not tea. What's the good of that? But the rest sounds good, and I might as well stay here and have it in the kitchen. Mama is tired and worn out. And then you can tell me a bit about the girls. They're always writing to me. Manon always writes four pages, but there's never much in the letters. How are things?"

"Well, Master Leo, how should they be? Miss Therese, well, you know what she's like . . . but, mind you, I haven't said a thing. And then little Sophie. Little Sophie, she's a marvel. And little Manon's always bright and cheerful, there's no denying that."

"And she's in with the rich bankers, and that's very wise and sensible of her. Bankers are really the only people one should know; only it's a pity they nearly all belong to the Old Dispensation."

"Yes, Master Leo, that's how it is, and I've spoken to her about it; but she says: 'Friederike, if you want somthing, you mustn't be choosy, you've got to take what comes.' "

"Very sensible; a wise girl; I like that, and I've no objections. Because I'm in with them a bit too, I've started a little flirtation in the same direction. Fine, black-haired figure of a gal, with a waist like *that,* and eyes—well, Friederike, I tell you, her eyes . . . real almond eyes, and actually everything about her reminds you a bit of a harem. Ever heard of harems?"

"Course I've heard of harems. They're what the Turks keep their wives in, no windows, just tiny little holes, so they can only peek out now and then."

"Right. And mine looks just like one of those Turkish women, or anyway, very nearly."

"But will it be possible, Master Leo? Will the family give their consent?"

"Which? Mine or hers?"

"Oh, I mean the Poggenpuhls."

"I don't care, Friederike. And then . . . look, the Poggenpuhls aren't all that dumb either, and if it's really a lot, they'll be quite happy to consent to anything."

"Is it a lot then?"

"Ah, I'm not sure myself yet. Those Orientals are so horribly careful, always making marriage contracts that don't give you a thing unless you manage to produce half a dozen straight off. And it can't always be done as quickly as that."

"Oh, Leo, dear, you'll surely . . ."

"Yes, Friederike, so you may say. But nature plays strange games with us; and then when they *are* born (charming little angels, because when they're quite small they're always little angels) then they go and die; and look: there you are, back where you started, and all that trouble has been for nothing."

"Yes, yes, such things do happen. But have you come to an understanding, then, the two of you?"

"God forbid, and I haven't said a word to her, and I'm only talking like this because one's always got a knife at one's throat, and then one starts building castles in the air and then one feels a bit better and thinks, 'Well, one day I suppose I'll find a way out of this misery . . .' But Friederike, I think you might make me some tea after all, that is, if you've got a drop of rum left."

"No, Leo, dear. Rum there isn't. Only a Gilka."

"Hm, that's not really a very good mixture. Still, after all, why not? I can't pour it in, of course, but it would be quite acceptable to drink on the side. And that herring has made me a bit thirsty. And apropos of what I told you about the beautiful Jewess with the black hair: you must keep your mouth shut about that, and you mustn't mention it—not to Mother and not to my sisters either—anyway, not to Therese. It wouldn't matter so much telling Manon, since she's practically in it too with her everlasting Bartensteins, and she's always trying to get me to go to their place with her. The old man there is supposed to be very rich too, incidentally, and I haven't made up my mind yet what I'm going to do. Then one's troubles would all be over at one go, and that's the main thing. But if nothing comes of it, well, then, Friederike, then it'll have to be blacks, real, genuine blacks, because then I'll have to go to Africa."

"Oh Lord, Leo, dear! And I've just been reading about that. Oh, my goodness me, but they kill everybody there and cut poor Christian folks' throats."

"They do that here too. It's the same everywhere."

"And all those wild animals. Snakes and crocodiles, so even though it's so hot, you can never go for a swim."

"Yes, that's true. Still, you get everything free, and if you shoot an elephant you've got as much ivory as you want, and then you can get them to make you a billiard cue. And believe me, to be free like that has its advantages too. Have you ever heard of people being arrested for debt? Of course you have. Well, you see, there's nothing like that there, because they don't have debts or IOUs or interest or usury, and when I'm in Bukoba—that's a middling kind of place, sort of like Postdam—well, when I'm there, the equator—which you've probably heard of and which is a good thousand miles long—well, this equator might run right through my body."

"For Heaven's sake . . ."

"And that sort of thing is quite impossible here, and that's why I want to go there, unless something turns up here really soon."

"Oh Lord, Master Leo, then it would be better to . . ."

"Exactly, Friederike, much better. And all that Poggenpuhl stuff, that Therese's always making such a fuss about. . . . Heaven's, that reminds me: wherever has Therese got to? You said she was just going into town to buy something for Mama's birthday. . . . Oh God, birthday! I say, Friederike, I suppose I'll have to get something or other for the old lady too, otherwise she'll think I never think of anybody but myself. What do you think I could give her, what does she need?"

"Lord, Master Leo, come to that, Frau von Poggenpuhl needs everything!"

"Everything? That's too much, that's impossible, that's above my means. After all, I've got to get back again, and I haven't enough money for that as it is. . . . But you mentioned some Edam cheese just now. Is there any left?"

"Of course there is."

"Oh, good. But first we must get this birthday present business settled. Though I've got to get back—that's the first consideration."

"Well, Master Leo, how much do you want to invest?"

"Want to? A million! But how much can I, Friederike, how much can I? That's the trouble, there's the rub. More than . . . more than . . . well, I'd prefer not to mention any figures. But it's got to be something nice, something imaginative."

"Well, I'd say a primula."

"Good. A primula. A primula fits the bill exactly. Primula—or *primula veris,* because that's the Latin name—more or less means the beginning of spring. And mother will be fifty-seven. And you see, that's exactly what I'd call imaginative."

"And then, Master Leo, perhaps a bag of ginger nuts as well: she really loves those. But they must be crisp, and not sticky and tough as old boots."

"Very well. A primula and ginger nuts, good and crisp and all white with sugar on the outside. But it's so late now, I doubt if they'll have any left."

"No, not today. But I'll get them tomorrow morning early. She won't have her presents before nine, because first the place must be warmed up, and tidied up a bit too."

As she spoke Friederike began to clear the plates and glasses from the table, and in their place she put half an Edam cheese, which was not really much more than a red rind. But that did not matter. Leo had already taken out his little pocket knife because that was the handiest, and was scraping out the good bits with dexterity; as he did so, he kept declaring that finding something where nothing was really to be found was preferable to anything else, and that there was something imaginative about it too. "Yes, Friederike, that's the way to live. Pick up the small joys until the great stroke of luck comes along."

"Ah, as long as it does come along . . ."

"And if it doesn't, then at least one's had the small strokes."

And with that he placed the hollow cheese on his left forefinger and spun it around, first slowly and then faster and faster, like a little half-globe.

"Look, up here, that's the Northern Hemisphere. And down here, where there's nothing, that's where Africa is."

# 6

Leo had had his bed made in the parlor, where he slept uncomfortably but soundly on the small cane sofa that normally had its place in the bedroom. He only woke for a moment when Friederike came through to light the stove, but quickly fell back into a quiet morning slumber when he heard the wood crackling and, a moment later, the stove door rattling in the single-windowed living room next door.

It was already half past eight when Manon came to wake him. "Up, Leo; it's high time. We can't keep Mama in bed any longer." Then he leaped up, and accomplished his morning ablutions with soldierly speed. The long mirror over the console table was quite impressive enough for the purpose; everything else was all the more primitive: a kitchen chair held a wash basin, towel, glass, and water jug; all the other requisites came out of his suitcase.

"Good morning, ladies"; and with these words he went in to his sisters and gave each of them a kiss. It was already agreeably warm in the little room. The presents for Mama still lay higgledy-piggledy on an old piano, because naturally they were not going to be set out here but in the parlor, which still needed to be put in order. When this had been duly accomplished, a proper survey became possible: there was a morning cap, two pairs of cotton gloves, and a pair of felt slippers. Friederike had contributed a pot of heather, and Leo's primula stood between the two felt slippers, together with the paper bag. Leo himself quickly tore a page from his notebook, wrote a few lines, and inserted it between the two pale mauve flowers of the primula. "A picture of my fate," he said to Sophie who was standing beside him. "Two blossoms, and pale mauve." Their mother had been growing impatient in the bedroom, from which she was now released and led to the table with the birthday presents. Leo and the two younger sisters kissed her hand, while Therese contented herself with a kiss on the cheek. "Goodness, children, such a lot of things!" said the dear old lady. "And everything so well chosen. Yes, the felt slippers are just what I needed; I'm always so cold. And the primula—and with a message too!" She took the piece of paper and read, " 'A primula from your . . .' Yes, yes, Leo, it's you. You didn't finish the last word, but it wasn't necessary. Well, God loves us all, and perhaps he'll come to your aid too one day."

"Of course, Mother," said Therese. "You mustn't depress him like that. He must keep his self-esteem and tell himself that a Pomeranian nobleman will always find his place in the world. I am full of confidence."

"And will you go surety on it?"

"No, that you must do yourself. And if you do it properly, as befits a Poggenpuhl—and there you can follow Wendelin's example— things will go well for you. We have a star in our crest."

"I wish I had one on my epaulettes."

"All in good time. And now take Mama's arm and take her in to breakfast."

They must have sat an hour over their coffee. Leo had to tell them about his life at Thorn, especially about his visits in the country around, to the German as well as the Polish aristocracy.

"And do you win any moral victories over them?" asked Therese, referring to the latter. "Are you gaining ground?"

"Ground? Honestly, Therese, we're quite satisfied if we beat them at skat. But there are ways of doing that. Those Poles, I can tell you, they're damned crafty fellows, artful dodgers, the whole boiling . . ."

"You use such a lot of Berlinisms, Leo."

"I do; and because one can never get enough of them, I suggest we set off as soon as possible and go into town to see if we can find a few more. If you have eyes and ears, you can always pick up something. I feel like looking at a Litfass column[1] again. 'Save three hundred marks!' or 'Golden Number 100'; or 'Tapeworm cure.' I simply adore reading that kind of stuff. Who's coming with me? Who has time and feels like coming along?"

Therese silently turned aside.

"Hm. Therese is abandoning me, and Sophie has her household chores. But I think I can rely on Manon. And then we shall go and see the Rezonville panorama (the French are really good at that kind of thing) and at twelve we'll be on Unter den Linden and watch them change the guard with the full band playing, and if we're lucky the old emperor will be at his window and wave to us. Or at least we can imagine he's waved."

With these words Leo and Manon got to their feet.

"Don't be late; two o'clock!" warned Sophie; and they promised.

Leo and Manon returned on time, and punctually at two they went in to lunch. The table had been set in the parlor. There was a cake in the middle flanked by the heather on the right and the primula on the left. The Sohr major looked down from his frame and smiled.

Immediately after the soup the glass plate with the little bottle of wine for visitors was taken down from the desk and placed before Leo; with great dignity he said, "If this is for *me*, I must decline; but if it's because of Mama's birthday so that we can drink her health, then it can stay."

And while they were still arguing about it and overcoming Leo's resistance, Friederike appeared with the duck.

"Which bit would you like?" asked Sophie.

"Drumstick, please. I think asking for the drumstick is always the best policy. First of all it makes a good impression because it sounds modest, and secondly the top joint tends to come along with it. And then the question of the actual quantity is not to be taken lightly either."

So he did himself proud; everyone was ready to humor him. Then he proposed a toast to their mother's health. She had to take a sip, but the girls only touched the knuckles of their forefingers to one another's glasses.

"It's absolutely true, everything tastes better at home. There's no maternal duck like this in the whole of Thorn. And the stuffing—

two kinds, even, chestnuts this end and currant stuffing the other. My dears, I almost believe it's all pretense: I think you've got something hidden away somewhere, you're not as poor as all that."

"Oh Leo, don't say things like that, don't talk like that. It always frightens me. You're quite capable of imagining that it's really true . . ."

"No, no. I know perfectly well how things really are. I just happened to think of something I once read in a newspaper, a story about an old woman who had sewn a whole fortune into—well, I won't say what she'd sewn it into. And then I also thought of Uncle Eberhard, our uncle the general, and that he could really . . ."

At that moment the door bell rang and Friederike came to announce the general.

"Lupus in fabula." But before Leo could utter the words, their uncle stood in the doorway bringing his fingers to his temple in a semimilitary salute. "My respects, sister-in-law."

The girls hurried toward him. Leo naturally following; but when the old lady tried to rise, her strength failed her, she was so touched by the kindness of her brother-in-law for whom she had always had a special love and admiration.

"Stay put, my dear Albertine. That's what comes of too much youthful exercise. And I bring you greetings from my wife too. . . . And fancy finding Leo here. Gracious, boy, you look terrific, and exceedingly well nourished. Ah, I see, I see . . ." and he pointed to the duck.

"You must join us," said Manon.

And their uncle fell in between them. Tucking his napkin round his neck (which he himself described as an old-fashioned habit), he began to gnaw at a wing with much relish. "Exquisite. And by the way, it's a well-known fact that really delicious food is only to be found in small households. I'll tell you why. Because in a small household people still cook with love. Yes, my dear Albertine, with love. And that is what counts, after all."

"You're always so kind, Eberhard, always just the same. And if you like it. . . . But tell me first of all, what brings you here? To Berlin in winter?"

"Ah, Albertine, what brings me here? I might say your birthday. But perhaps you wouldn't believe me, so I'd better come out with the truth at once. Business brings me here, mortgages, things to write off, and this and that at the bank. Boring, really. And on the other hand quite interesting."

"Oh, very, very," sighed Leo, and he was about to elaborate. But Therese raised her finger to stop him.

". . . and," their uncle the general continued, "since the journey had to be made, of course I chose the fourth of January so as to be able to wish happy returns to my dear sister-in-law."

"You'll stay with us," said the major's widow. "We haven't much to offer, but we do have a view of Saint Matthew's."

"I know, Albertine," said the general. "It's very nice here. But to be quite honest, I prefer the Potsdamer Platz, because there's lots of life there. And lots of life is the best thing a big city has to offer. That's what we miss in Adamsdorf. So I've put up at the Fürstenhof as usual; they know me there and, honestly, it looked as though they were all really pleased to see me arrive."

"I expect they were."

"And when I lean out of my window in the morning with a sofa cushion under each elbow and the fresh winter air blows from the Hall'sches Tor (and I can afford to do that because I'm used to fresh air: there's quite another wind blowing from our old Koppe at home), and I can see the Café Bellevue and Josty, where they all sit reading their papers in that glass projection from early morning on, and the horse trams and omnibuses all coming from different sides as though they were all going to collide at any moment, and the flower girls (only they're not really flower girls—they're men with wooden legs), and then in all that noise and confusion they suddenly start calling out late extras, the way they used to call out fire alarms in the old days, and in such croaky voices that it sounds as though the end of the world were nigh, to say the very least—yes, my dears, when I have that scene before me, then I know I'm among human beings once more, and I don't want to miss that."

Leo gave a silent nod.

"So forgive me, Albertine, if I refuse. The Fürstenhof is more conveniently located too. But let's all do something together all the same. It's three o'clock now. What shall we do today? Kroll![2] Good, that's an idea. There's bound to be a Christmas show on there, Snow White or Cinderella. Cinderella would be better. With Snow White you get the glass coffin. And on the whole I'm not keen on coffins. I'm more in favor of cheerfulness."

"Well, Uncle," said Leo, "then perhaps a theater would be best. They're doing *The Quitzows*[3] in two places today, the real ones at the Royal Theater, and a parody at the Moritzplatz. What do you think of going to the Moritzplatz Quitzows?"

"No, Leo, that won't do, fond as I am of that kind of thing. But we owe something to our name. Look, the Poggenpuhls were more or less the same kind of thing in Pomerania as the Quitzows were in the Mark, and so I think that from esprit de corps we shouldn't sit there cheerfully watching a parody of the whole affair."

Therese rose in order to give her uncle a kiss. "It always gives me great satisfaction, Uncle, to meet with such sentiments. Leo gets more shallow every day. You know why? Because he's chasing after the Golden Calf."

"Yes," said Leo. "I am. I only wish it would get me somewhere."

"It will," Manon consoled him; her thoughts immediately turned to Flora.

"But what are we talking about?" Leo continued. "It's all beside the point. We're still on the Quitzows, the real and the false. The false ones have been turned down, so . . ."

". . . the real ones, then," the general concluded. "The real ones at the Royal Theater. That's where we'll go. And afterward we'llo somewhere where we can have a chat and try and establish what the play was really all about. It's supposed to be a good play, if only because it does justice to both sides, which is always a difficult thing to do. But I've heard this much: Dietrich von Quitzow is supposed to be more interesting than the Elector Frederic. Of course. Bound to be. A man who thumps the table with an iron mail fist is always more interesting than a chap who just preaches an afternoon sermon. You never get anywhere like that. I imagine Dietrich like Götz von Berlichingen, who wasn't afraid of the emperor and made fun of Heilbronn Council. That's always been my favorite scene. I suppose we'll get tickets all right—I don't mind if we have to pay a bit extra. If your name is Poggenpuhl, you have to show some feeling for an old comrade."

"It's a good thing, Eberhard," said the major's widow, "that the walls have no ear. You aristocrats are all alike. And you Poggenpuhls . . . yes, of course, I know, you're among the best of them. But even you! The Hohenzollerns gave you everything, and as soon as the question of the estates comes up, you stand up against them."

"Quite right, Albertine. That's how we are. But it's not as serious as all that. When it comes to the crunch, you'll always find us ready. There's the Hochkirch major next door, still without his coat on, and that's to his credit and I should almost be prepared to say it suits him; and here (and he pointed to the picture over the sofa) we have the Sohr major, and your dear father, my brother Alfred, buried at Gravelotte. Those are our deeds, and they speak. But when times are quiet, like now, then we get a bit restive, and we like to think back to the old days when there was no War Ministry and no blue letters[4] and a man went to war off his own bat. I suppose I shouldn't say so, and I'm only talking off the top of my head, but I think it must have been more fun in those days. The commoners brewed Bernau and Cottbus beer, and we drank it. And that's how everything was. There was more go and gaiety to life—for commoners too, when you come to think of it. No competition yet, in those days. True, Leo?"

"And how. Much more dash in those days. Perhaps one day it'll come back."

"That's what I think. But not for us. It'll never be our turn again. It may seem like it now—but that's just the last flicker. . . . But now our plan of campaign for tonight. First of all I'm going to the Fürstenhof to write a few lines to my wife, and at half past six you come and meet me there. You too, sister-in-law."

"No, Eberhard. That sort of thing's not for me any more. I've got rheumatism and I'd rather stay home. When you've all gone, I shall first of all read the newspaper and then the evening blessing. Or else Friederike can read it. She's beginning to wonder why we've been living like the heathen since New Year's Eve."

# 7

They managed to get seats, good ones in the fourth row of the stall. Mitterwurzer, who happened to be giving a quest performance in Berline, played Dietrich von Quitzow. The scene with Wend von Ilenburg in the second act made a tremendous impact. The interval came soon after, and the general, who had been growing increasingly agitated, turned to Therese on his right and said, "Strange—just like Bismarck. And both of them—there's coincidence for you—born practically next door to one another. I believe you can shoot from Schönhausen to Quitzöwel with an air gun, or a country postman can walk it in a morning. Marvelous part of the world, that. Lombard country. Ah well, you've either got what it takes or you haven't. What do you think, Leo?"

Leo would have liked to reply, but, uninhibited though he normally was, he now felt somewhat embarrassed, because he could see, in the rows in front and behind his party, people putting their heads together and whispering. His uncle saw it too. But he did not take it amiss and merely thought, "I know their sort. Berlin fusspots."

The performance finished shortly before ten, and after a brief consultation on a rather draughty corner they agreed to remain as close by as possible and to have supper in a theater restaurant in the Charlottenstrasse. The place was almost full, but they managed to find a table. Glancing briefly at the menu, they came to a rapid decision. Everyone chose sole, except for Therese, who declared herself in favor of macaroni with tomatoes. An instant later five pint mugs of beer were planted before them as though this were a matter of course, and it was only when the mugs were half-empty that their order made its appearance; whereupon the general, who had grown somewhat edgy, regained his equilibrium. He drew his plate a little closer and squeezed lemon juice over the crisp coating of bread-crumbs. Savoring the first bite as a connoisseur, he said, "Yes, Berlin is becoming a world city. And what's more, it's becoming a port. They're beginning to talk of building a big one somewhere near Tegel—and I must really say this sole tastes as though we'd already got one, or at least as though we were sitting in Wilkens' Cellar in Hamburg. That's one of my memories of forty-eight, when I was a very young lieutenant like Leo now, only with less pay."

"I can hardly imagine that, Uncle."

"Well, we'll drop the subject. It can easily become personal, and when things get personal there's always a risk of squabbling. But art—art you can discuss; art is always peaceful. And my dears, what about the Berlin dialect in that play? It started off as soon as the Straussberg people came on when the watcher was on the lookout for them. And that was supposed to be around 1411!"

"I imagine," said Therese, "that the author—a man of good family—must have studied the subject. Perhaps he found the turns of speech and the expressions that surprised you in old legal documents."

"Oh, my dear child, the Berlin slang they spoke just now isn't a hundred years old, some of it isn't even twenty. But I suppose it's difficult. The one I like best was the Polish countess, Barbara, I think she was called, a beauty—no doubt about that. On the program it said, 'Natural daughter to King Jagellos of Poland.' I can well believe it. She'd really got something. Eyes like coals. And that Dietrich, damn it all, what a spoiled fellow he must have been to jilt a Polish king's daughter like her just like that! I don't now of many similar cases, perhaps Charles XII and Aurora von Königsmarck. But that wasn't really a similar case. Because the Charles XII business was different, there was a snag there . . ."

"A snag? What snag, Uncle?"

"Oh, Manon, dear, that's not for young ladies to hear. And in such a public place . . ."

"Then whisper it in my ear."

"Can't be done. You see, these kind of things are tricky; you have to wait till you pick something up by chance—let's say on an old piece of wrapping paper, or in an old newspaper—the column with the court cases or miscellaneous historical items. For in my experience what we call wastepaper contains quite an important body of history, more than many history books. I might call on Leo to support me, but he's busy staring at that elegant young man over there through his monocle—there, at the second table from ours. And now he's even nodding to him."

Indeed, Leo had been somewhat inattentive for the last few minutes, and now he rose from his seat and went toward the young man of whom his uncle had just spoken. It was not difficult to see that each was equally surprised to find the other there, and after exchanging—so it seemed—a few questions to orient themselves, Leo led his unexpectedly rediscovered friend to the Poggenpuhl table and said, "My dear Uncle, allow me to present Herr von Klessentin. An old comrade of mine from the cadet school . . . My three sisters . . ."

Herr von Klessentin had graceful, easy manners and the bearing of a typical lieutenant; he bowed to the general and to the young ladies, and then remarked that he well remembered the general's coming out to Lichterfelde on a visit.

"Quite right, von Klessentin. I used to go out there quite often—after all, I had to keep an eye on things from time to time." And with that he pointed at Leo. "Not that it did much good. But won't you join us? This is the best table, a bit away from the rest and no drafts."

Klessentin bowed, fetched his beer mug, and took a seat between the general and Therese.

"We've struck root here," the general continued, "because it's so near the theater. . . . Were you there too?"

"Yes, sir."

". . . and I could almost swear I saw you in the orchestra stalls on the left—in row six or seven."

"Sorry, sir. I was considerably closer to the field of action."

"Further forward?"

"Yes, sir. On the stage itself."

Everyone, including Leo, gave a start of curiosity but also of shock, and they were glad when their uncle continued in a cheerful tone, "Ah, then we must congratulate you, von Klessentin. Behind the scenes: *à la bonne heure*, not everyone is so fortunate. But on the other hand—excuse me—I can't help being surprised that such a thing is even possible under the present regime, which—so far as I know—is very strict in matters of morality. Or have you personal relations with Count Hochberg's family?"

"Unfortunately not, sir. And it's not a matter of special personal relations. I'm simply a member of the company. Dietrich Schwalbe—you may remember him in the last act: it says standard-bearer in the program, but foster brother to the Quitzows would have been more correct; only delicacy probably prevented them from using that term—anyway, that Dietrich Schwalbe is me."

Therese recoiled slightly toward the right, while the two younger girls listened even more attentively than before and looked at their brother's newly rediscovered friend with rapidly growing interest. Leo himself still seemed a little uncertain, and he was glad when his uncle continued with great joviality, "Glad to hear it, von Klessentin. One can serve one's king anywhere. It's the loyalty of the service that counts . . ."

Klessentin bowed.

"But you surprise me, because I studied the program at least three times, and I didn't notice your name. . ."

"It's not there, sir. On the program I'm simply Herr Manfred—my Christian name. It's the custom. Manfred is my nom de guerre."

"Nom de guerre," the old man laughed. "Excellent. A Klessentin leaves the army and goes on the stage, and at the very moment he relinquishes the profession of arms, he acquires a nom de guerre. What a bit of luck you had such a pretty Christian name. But pretty as it is, I should like to inquire whether a poetical—a historical Christian name like that couldn't lead to complications. Manfred in particular, couldn't that get you into an awkward situation?"

"I wouldn't go so far as to deny the possibility, sir. But when I think of all the vast number of plays and parts that there are, I can think of a possible complication in my case only if I had to play Lord Byron's Manfred. Then, it's true, the program would have to read, 'Manfred . . . Herr Manfred'; and that, I admit, might startle the public a little and cause momentary confusion."

"I see, I see. Confusion which you would nevertheless be able to overcome."

"I think I can say yes to that, always supposing that I ever find myself in such a position. But that's almost out of the question, because it's right outside my sphere."

"Are you sure of that?"

"Absolutely, sir. Byron's Manfred . . ."

"And then, excuse me, von Klessentin, the elder brother in *The Bride of Messina* . . . the one, if I remember rightly, who isn't quite so guilty . . ."

". . . Yes, sir. But—forgive me—actually, he's Don Manuel."

"Oh, quite right, quite right. Don Manuel. Don Manfred or even just Manfred, I got it mixed up. . . . And so you think this Manfred, and probably this Manuel as well, are both parts quite outside your sphere?"

"Absolutely, sir. Byron's Manfred is a colossus of a part, lofty, great—like Lord Byron himself; I myself, on the other hand, I'm still a beginner."

"That will change. That's the same everywhere. A cadet today and a general forty years later. All in good time."

"I wish to God that that's how it was. But it isn't. I've started on a stage career now and I must stick to it; if you keep chopping and changing it makes a bad impression. But since I've been at it, I've come to realize that Herr Manfred is never going to be a great stage name. . . . It is possible—or at least very desirable—that sooner or later I shall make a good match; after which event I wouldn't hesitate for one moment to retire from the boards. I really like acting, I could almost say I love it; but all the same—a house in the Tiergarten with a dolphin fountain playing continuously and watering the lawn. . ."

"A house like that is what you would prefer, my dear Klessentin. I should call that a healthy reaction. May God grant you His blessing on it. Yes, a park with deer and a waterfall and old plane trees, golden yellow in autumn—that's what I fell for too. But while you're still at it, can't you ever get promotion?"

"Unlikely, sir."

"And if not—please forgive my curiosity, but I'm interested in all such things—well, if not, what kind of roles should we look for you in? When I'm back on my estate and I pick up the morning paper and I read: 'Tomorrow, Wednesday, *Wilhelm Tell*, then, having had the pleasure of your acquaintance—because I'm enormously taken with you, Herr von Klessentin: forgive me for saying so right out—then I'd like to know which slot in *Tell* I'm to find you in; you're too young for Attinghaus, and not demonic enough for Gessler; Rudenz, perhaps?"

"You are still several degrees too high. There are, of course, a few exceptional cases, like this evening, when I was Quitzow's standard-bearer and therefore slightly distinguished from the crowd; but on the whole, sir, you will have to look for me in groups or categories: first citizen, second murderer, third Pappenheimer: that's my fate. Especially in *Tell*, of course, I'm up on the Rütli with the others, close up against the moon rainbow and afterward against the sunrise. All the same—so far I've always only played Meier von Sarnen, and just once I was Auf der Mauer, and my ambition doesn't stretch beyond Rösselmann. It's a slow climb. But—and I'll hide nothing from you—even a very modest advancement such as that upsets other interests. And I don't care that much about it."

"Bravo, bravo. That's exactly how I've always felt. Never push, never go forward over dead bodies."

"And then, sir, it's said that even little men have their great moments, and that's especially true on the stage. There's hardly one among my humbler colleagues who doesn't say to himself: 'Yes, Matkowsky! Matkowsky plays Mortimer and the Prince in Calderon's *Life Is a Dream,* and he plays both of them well, very well; but Friesshardt (excuse me, but he's the soldier who stands watch over Gessler), or Devereux, who knocks Wallenstein down with his pike, or the witch in *Faust*—please excuse me, ladies, I seem to be drawing all my examples from this sphere—or the Third Witch in *Macbeth*—those are parts that *I* play, and I play them better than Matkowsky' . . . well, I've had moments of happiness like that myself."

"Very, very interesting, Herr von Klessentin. And now you must go one further and tell me: apart from Meier von Sarnen, of whom, to be quite honest, I have only the dimmest conception—apart from this Meier von Sarnen, then, you must tell me the names of your other parade horses, large or small, because one can go on parade perfectly well on a pony."

"I'm flattered that you take such a friendly interest in me, and I'll gladly tell you all, only I hope that my disclosures won't make me forfeit that friendly interest. Strangely enough, my talent—if one can even speak of talent—leans toward the grotesque. And so I might say that so far my little triumphs have been in the *Midsummer Night's Dream,* and especially in Shakespeare's *Henry IV, Part II.* By a fluke—lucky or unlucky—I have had to play the whole lot of Falstaff's recruits in turn—the so-called cannon fodder. With the exception of Feeble, that is. Once His Majesty even distinguished me by applauding—which naturally made me very happy. But so far, the public has appreciated me most in the role of Bullcalf."

Therese reacted to this word with a haughty movement of her head which was not lost upon Klessentin. So he quickly added, "Once you start to confess—and here I must apologize all over again to the ladies—things are inclined to come out which may seem more or less offensive. And especially when it comes to Shakespeare. This very *Henry IV* contains persons and names—Mistress Quickly, for instance—well, Mistress Quickly herself might pass, but there's a blonde called Doll who practices her profession there, a girl with a surname . . ."

"Oh, I know, I know!" laughed Manon.

"You do *not* know," said Therese with all the severity of an elder sister watching over the education and upbringing of a younger sister for whom she has assumed responsibility.

"Yes, I do, I do, and Leo will bear me out. In fact, he'll have to, otherwise the poor fellow will never have another chance to open his mouth again. He's been entirely wrapped in admiration, a silent listener, and I bet that all this time he's been wondering which parts would suit *him* best."

Sophie put her finger to her lips. But Manon either did not see her or did not want to, and she continued, "And we shall see the day when, after the example of Manfred. . . Herr Manfred, we shall read Leo . . . Herr Leo on a program. But of course the part must be a pope—I'll not be satisfied with less. Yes, Leo, I mean it. And maybe I'd really like to see you on the stage. . . . Why not? I think the important thing is to be famous, never mind in what field."

Therese interrupted, "That was the principle adopted by the man who became famous for setting fire to the temple at Corinth . . ."

"Ephesus," Leo corrected her. "Corinth is where the cranes were . . ."

"It's all the same. A temple is a temple. And by the way, Uncle, I hope you'll forgive me for encroaching on your prerogative, but it's time we left. Herr von Klessentin will forgive me too; but our dear Mama . . ."

"Of course, of course. And especially today, on her birthday . . . Leo" (and with these words Uncle Eberhard drew a banknote from his wallet), "please capture the waiter and clarify things with him. Von Klessentin, perhaps you'll walk along with us a little way?"

"It would be an honor, sir. But at the same time I hope you'll forgive me if I take my leave when we get to the corner of the Friedrichsstrasse. An appointment—two fellow officers from my old regiment. I would try," and he turned to the young ladies, "to suborn your brother, because once a man's in Berlin he wants to enjoy the Berlin air; but I doubt whether his chivalrous principles will permit him to desert the flag . . ."

"I am afraid it will be impossible, Herr von Klessentin," Therese said with a meaningful smile. "And as far as the Berlin air is concerned, I think it is purer in our Grossgörschenstrasse than in the Friedrichstrasse . . ."

"Purer, but not more authentic, my dear young lady."

Meanwhile Leo had paid the bill and joined them, and they left in a body—the general with Therese, Leo with Manon, and Klessentin with Sophie, who had spoken least but whose expression had shown particular interest all evening.

During the ensuing conversation with her escort, she asked him about Fräulein Conrad, of whose engagement she had heard recently. "Her fiancé," she said, "is supposed to be a very stern critic. I think it must be hard always having a critic at your side. It takes the wind out of your sails."

"Not always. If you're a sailor, nothing will stop you from sailing."

"I'm so glad to hear you say that."

With these words they reached the corner of the Leipziger and Friedrichsstrasse, and Klessentin took his leave; the Poggenpuhls walked on toward the Potsdam Gate and the Fürstenhof. Leo had not only presented an exact account of his financial transaction, but also—much to his uncle's amusement—tried to return the change. "Until tomorrow, then," and with those words they parted.

# 8

It was nearly midnight when the brother and sisters arrived outside their house. Sophie had the key and unlocked the door. They were all somewhat excited, so that their voices were raised as they came up the stairs, with the fortunate result that Friederike—already a little anxious at their long absence—came to meet them on the second floor and brought a light.

"Is Mama still up?" asked Leo.

"No, Master Leo. The mistress went to bed just after nine. She said she was so cold. But she's just lying there. She's not asleep."

During this short exchange Leo had taken off his greatcoat and the young ladies their wraps. Together they went into the large bedroom to wish their mother good-night. Friederike retired to her kitchen.

The major's widow was more sitting than lying in bed, and she seemed more cheerful than usual. "But children, how late you are . . . time for decent folk to be in bed. I was beginning to think something had happened to you . . ."

"And it did, Mother."

"Well, that's bound to be bad news. Perhaps you've lost your fortune. But I'll hear about that soon enough. Come, Manon, give me your hand and look at me. And now pull up your chairs and tell me all about it. And you, Leo, you can sit on the foot of my bed. It's not as hard as being sentenced to the slates.[1] That still used to happen when I was young. You've been gone nearly six hours. It's lucky I've got Friederike to have a good chat with."

"I expect you've had a thoroughly good one. You're always so familiar with her, far more than one should be with a servant."

"Is that what you think?" said the major's widow, sitting up even straighter in her bed. "My blue-blooded Therese, what a lot you think and know. But now I will tell you what *I* think. I think that simple loyalty like that is the most beautiful thing in the world, for the giver as much as for the receiver. Children's love for their parents—even if they are good children—that doesn't last. They think of themselves, and it's not for me to blame them, and I wouldn't want it otherwise; but an old piece of household furniture like Friederike, all she wants is to help and be a support to you, and all she asks is an occasional 'thank you.' And I tell you, Therese, there's a good deal of Christianity in that."

"Yes, that's what you always think, Mother."

"No, I don't think it, I know it. Let's leave it at that. I'd rather Leo told me all about your evening."

"Well, Mama, if I'm to tell you about it, I can only do it by dividing it into three parts, like a sermon."

"Please, Leo . . ."

"All right then, simply in three parts, without any attributes or comparisons. Part 1: Uncle and the Quitzows. Part 2: Uncle and Herr Manfred (Manfred is my friend Klessentin from the cadet school). And part 3: Uncle and . . . but that comes later. I'm not going to play my best trump right away by putting it in the heading."

"Oh Leo, that's just another bit of nonsense. In the end there'll be nothing to it."

"On the contrary. As you will soon see. But now, attention please! First of all: Uncle and the Quitzows."

"Dear Uncle. Of course he'll have been enchanted by all those high-flown speeches."

"Not at all, Mother. On the contrary, I should say that although he admired Dietrich von Quitzow, it wasn't really his kind of thing. But it's a moot point. All I can say is that when the Straussberg people came on with bag and baggage, he began to talk—rather loud, or anyway loud enough to be embarrassing—about Mühlendamm and flea markets. What he seems to have liked best was a pretty countess, a certain Barbara, who was on very good terms—

to put it mildly—with the dukes of Pomerania, and was then prepared to take on our Dietrich von Quitzow as well. But there she had her comeuppance. Even in those days the Mark represented the higher morality, the very same to which she owes her subsequent greatness."

"Don't be sarcastic."

"And here too Uncle showed his Pomeranian descent: he was fired with ardor at once. And when we met Manfred Klessentin in the theater restaurant after the performance, he immediately wanted to know who the countess really was. I mean the actress who played the countess."

"A fine story . . ."

"And here we have the perfect bridge passage to part 3 under the imposing heading: Uncle Eberhard and the hundred-mark note. And, what's more, a brand-new one. Yes, Mama, that was a big moment. True, it no longer exists as a whole—I mean the bank note, of course—but still, there are very respectable remnants. Here they are. As you can imagine, I resisted for quite a while, but when I saw it would upset him . . ."

"Leo, you've never lied like this. . . ."

"Self-mockery isn't lying, Mama. But it just shows how wrong you are to be so everlastingly worried. 'Even at the graveside he raises the banner of hope'[2]—the poet's great words were not spoken in vain and should never be forgotten. I gladly admit that I felt a certain anxiety all evening about the return ticket, because I think I may say that I prefer to give than to receive . . ."

The girls laughed.

". . . However, God never forsakes a German, least of all a Poggen-puhl, and it's always darkest before dawn. I have always found it so. And so I'm back on top of the world, happy as a clam, and that, God willing, is how it'll be for some time to come. Because the return journey won't eat up much, even if I travel first class."

"But Leo . . ."

"Calm down, my dears. I am *not* going first-class, it just makes me happy to think—just for once—that I could. It's all just make-believe and chimeras. But now this *is* serious; I want to know how much of my fortune I'm to leave behind: any sum you name, and I don't want it paid back and no interest. I just want to enjoy this state of affairs unalloyed and to the hilt, just once I want to trump Wendelin. But why don't you say something? You too, Mama?"

"Well, I'll take the thought for the deed, Leo. And now go into the front room and take Manon with you; she can help you pack. But don't be too long about it. I know you always start chattering, and then you don't know how to stop. And now good-night, and we'll say good-bye at the same time. Don't come in to me tomorrow morning, and give my love to Wendelin, and tell him it was nice of him to let you have the trip. Tell him he's the best of the whole family, not a bit like . . ."

"Leo . . ."

"Yes, not a bit. But you can stay as you are. All old mothers are alike: they always love the good-for-nothings best, as long as their hearts are in the right place. And yours is. You're no good, but you're a dear. And now good-night, my boy."

He stroked her and gave her a kiss; and then he and the youngest sister, his special confidante, went into the next room to prepare everything for his departure next morning.

When they had finished packing, Manon took Leo's hand and said: "Sit in the corner of the sofa. I've got something to say to you."

"Brrr. It sounds terribly serious. Is it?"

"Yes, it is a bit. Though hardly as you see things. And now listen very carefully. The thing is, I'm a bit worried that because of your everlasting debts you are taking the wrong step. And in Thorn too. Please, don't rush into anything! You've dropped a few hints recently, first in your letters, and now while you've been here too—last night, for instance, on the way home. You know I don't think like Therese on these delicate matters. She thinks the Poggenpuhls are the pillars of society, the bulwark of the state, and of course that's ridiculous. But you lean in the opposite direction: you set too little store by our ancient name, or—which is the same thing—by the *reputation* of our ancient name. But names and reputations mean a lot."

"I'm prepared to agree with you there, Manon; but who doesn't have a name, nowadays? And look what *makes* names! Pears' Soap, Blooker's Cocoa, Johann Hoff's Extract of Malt! Chivalry and heroism are nowhere by comparison! Take Maréchal Niel, for instance. I believe he took Sebastopol, and if I'm not mistaken he was a genius at military engineering; a military celebrity, anyway. And yet if there weren't a rose named after him, no one would remember he'd ever existed. Let's take something much nearer home; let's take the great name of Hildebrand. I believe there were three famous painters of that name—or perhaps the third was a sculptor, it makes no difference. But when people speak of Hildebrand, especially around Christmas, nobody thinks of paintings or busts, but only of little dark blue packages with a picture of a ginger snap, tied up with a bit of string. I tell you, Manon, I have my Poggenpuhl pride just as much as you and nearly as much as Therese; but if I'm to enjoy it, then, in addition to my Poggenpuhl name, which for all its fame unfortunately only runs into single figures, I need at least four zeros. Or maybe five, really."

"I don't mind your calculating like that, Leo. I'm not too fussy myself on that point. Yes, I admit it, you've *got* to think along those lines. But I'm afraid you're not on the right ones. There are the Bartensteins, there's Flora. . . . Yes, that really would be something. Flora Bartenstein is an intelligent and beautiful girl, and on top of that she's my friend. And she's certainly rich. Now there's something that *would* be worth considering. But in Thorn—that business you're always writing and talking about—though only mysteriously and in hints. I ask you, Leo, what's it all about? In Thorn . . .! What's her name, for a start?"

"Esther."

"Well, that would do. Lots of English girls are called Esther. And her surname?"

"Blumenthal."

"Ah, that's not so good. But maybe even that would pass, because it's a dual-purpose name, you can use it *à deux mains,* so to speak, and when you are a staff officer (which is still in the distant future, I'm afraid), at Court or in whatever other circles you move in they'll say, "Major or Colonel von Poggenpuhl's wife is a Blumenthal," and they'll think she's the Field Marshal's granddaughter. When a Poggenpuhl marries a Blumenthal, the least of the advantages he can expect from his ancient name is surely to move straight to the right wing of all the available possibilities."

"Bravo, Manon. I see your objections are melting away."

"Not entirely; I can't concede that much. I'm simply trying to make the best of Esther and Blumenthal. Besides, I understand your position, I can feel the pressure you're under, and I'm glad you want to escape. But if it's at all possible, stick to your own stamping ground: don't let it be on the Vistula, and not Esther. Whatever she's like, she can't be a patch on Flora. Besides, the whole Bartenstein family—there are three brothers, two in the Vossstrasse—are especially well thought of. The one whose family I know is a man of honor, and incidentally a humorist too, and I'm quite sure he'll get a title when the government floats its next loan. Not that it means anything to me; on the contrary, it's almost a disadvantage from my point of view, because I hate all halfway measures, which is what it comes to in the end. But in the eyes of the world . . ."

"I'll think about it, Manon. For the moment I find it entrancing to have the choice, as you might say: or at least I can pretend I have. What I'd really prefer is to remain as I am for a while; there's nothing better than being a bachelor. Only a widower with his perspective into the past and the future could conceivably stand higher in my eyes. But that takes time. And now good-night. Mama will be wondering what we've been up to together."

And with these words they parted.

But Manon went to her mother's bed to see if she was asleep.

"You've been crying, Mama."

"Yes, my dear. But they were happy tears. They did me good."

# 9

Manon was up early to lend her brother a hand with his departure, but the other two sisters contented themselves with stretching an arm out to Leo through the crack of the door as he passed down the corridor.

"I can recognize you just the same," said Leo. "The fat arm belongs to Sophie." This diagnosis was correct but painful to Therese, and so the moment of departure was clouded by a touch of ill-humor. Friederike, of course, had also risen, and she carried the suitcase to the nearest cab rank. Leo chose a cab, settled into it, and called out "Friedrichsstrasse!" to the driver; then he pressed something into Friederike's hand. Little opportunity as she had had with the Poggenpuhls of developing a fine feeling for the value of tips received in the half-light, she recognized it immediately as a Prussian taler. Her shock was almost as great as her joy.

"Goodness, Master Leo . . ."

"Yes, Friederike, not all days are alike, and if I had any say in the matter . . ."

"No, no . . ."

". . . and if I had any say in the matter, I'd take that hollow Edam cheese, which you've probably still got, and fill it right up with gold pieces. Well now, with God's grace, let's be off." And he gave her his hand once more before the cab set off at a reckless but soon diminishing pace.

As Friederike walked home from the corner of the Potsdamerstrasse, a number of thoughts passed through her mind. "It really does go to your heart," she said. "And when I think of the rich folks I used to work for, they never treated me like a human being. And when you compare them with the Poggenpuhls! They really don't have a penny, and sometimes I feel really bad when I have to say: 'Well, ma'am, we really do need a new floorcloth.' But there's something about them all, even Therese: she's a bit high and mighty at times, but in the end she's really not so bad. And as for little Leo! He's a good-for-nothing and a fibber, the poor old lady's quite right there, and he has his faults, they all have, except for Frau von Poggenpuhl . . . ah, she's had to struggle too hard, that knocks it out of you. . . . But they treat you like a human being, and that's true of the whole lot. I'm glad I've got this situation. It isn't as though I was starved, and when things are a bit short sometimes, they just take a mouthful and leave it for me. But then I don't want it either; when I see how they go on, it sticks in my throat and won't go down. Oh dear, oh dear, money. . . . And a taler! Where can he have got that? Uncle must have really forked out. . . ."

When Friederike got back to the apartment, she found both the elder girls already at the breakfast table and Manon kneeling before the stove to light the fire. As soon as she had got it going, their mother entered and took her usual place on the sofa.

"Well, did he get off all right?"

"Yes, Mama," said Manon. "And he asked me to give you a kiss for him and to tell you you were the best person in the world, even though you're not a real Poggenpuhl."

"No, that I'm not. Heavens, children, if I were, we'd never make ends meet at all . . ."

"Oh, never mind that. We're all right anyway. Courage, that's all. I'd just made up my mind to speak to Flora, and then all of a sudden Uncle turned up . . ."

"Yes, he's come to our aid again. But we mustn't imagine it will always be like that . . ."

"Not always, Mama. But nearly always."

"Yes, you're a harebrained creature, just like your brother. And I expect young Klessentin was just the same. There you see what comes of it. So now he's called Herr Manfred. And if a miracle doesn't happen soon—and you've said something of the sort yourselves—we shall read 'Herr Leo' on a theater program too one day.

How did you like young Klessentin? How did Uncle get on with him or he with Uncle? It must have been quite awkward."

"No, Mama," said Sophie. "Why should it? You have to look at it the right way. I'm a noblewoman too, and a Poggenpuhl, and I paint plates and cups and give singing and piano lessons too. He acts on the stage. It's really the same thing."

"Not quite, Sophie. It's doing it in public. That's the difference."

"Oh, what does 'public' mean? When they have dancing at the Bartensteins and I play my three dances because it would be disobliging to refuse, that's in public too. As soon as we leave our rooms we are in public and playing our parts."

"All right, all right, Sophie. You win; I believe you. But young Klessentin—what sort of things does he act? I've never read about him."

"He gets only very small parts, and he told us what some of them were. But—and this is what's comforting—he added straightaway that there isn't really any difference, and that small parts are sometimes just as important as big ones. And everything he said sounded so charming and so contented and good-humoured that Uncle Eberhard was quite taken with him and congratulated him."

"Yes, I can quite believe that. Dear Uncle is a darling, and he can't bear stuck-up people who give themselves airs; and anyone who says, 'I'm for the small things in life' wins his heart at once. He doesn't like it when people puff themselves up and behave as though they couldn't live without brocade on the walls. He has practically no personal wants and is content with whatever he's offered, and that's why I am going to ask him to take pot luck with us for lunch. Because I expect he will drop in again. What could we give him? It's your week, Sophie; what do you think?"

"Well, pale ale soup with sago, I think; he loved that last time. And then we've still got a small dish of baby parsnips left, and we could have some slices of smoked goose with that."

"No, I don't think that would do," said Therese. "The smoked goose is from Adamsdorf; it was a present from Aunt."

"Never mind. One smoked goose is just like another. And if he does notice, it will be a little compliment. And then as a third course we could have cream meringues from the Eschke patisserie across the street. And then bread and butter and cheese."

Their mother regarded the whole thing in the nature of a symbolic act, as she knew very well that Uncle Eberhard would have a snack before coming; so she was content with the menu and only asked her daughters to return punctually by two o'clock: for they still had New Year's calls to pay in town. Otherwise it would get too late; but she would hold onto their uncle until then.

And when everything had been settled in this manner, the breakfast table was cleared, and they withdrew to the back room in order to dress for their calls.

All three sisters left the apartment simultaneously to catch the horse tram at the stop by the Botanical Gardens. They were very familiar with the tariff. When they had all gone, the major's widow set about "doing herself up," and she had scarcely finished when she heard a genial and somewhat noisy conversation out in the hall: there was no doubt that her brother-in-law the general had arrived.

"Good morning, Albertine. Forgive me for coming a bit early; though, as I see, I am not *too* early. Everything spick and span already, everyone in 'full dress' (he used the English expression), "if you can say that about a lady. Because 'full dress' is probably masculine and I think it means white tie or tails. Tails is what we used to say in the old days."

"Oh, Eberhard, you mean well and you always have a kind word to say, and you've even noticed that I've got on my very best party cap with a new ribbon. But my dancing days are over."

"Oh, no, they're not, Albertine. You're still a good-looking woman. And you're not even sixty yet. And even if you were, what is age? Nothing at all. Look at me. Just now I met a battalion of your railway regiment—I call it yours because you've got it on your street—and I can tell you: as soon as I heard the first bang on the kettle drum, it went right through me and my old bones felt young and spry again. The cards are in our own hands, and we're as young as we want to be. But you shut yourself up too much; you'll be an antique fit for the Egyptian Museum before you know where you are. Look at yesterday, for instance. Why didn't you come along?"

"My dear Eberhard—the theater—I'm past that kind of thing."

"Absolutely wrong. That's what everyone thinks. But once you're back in the firing line, you find you enjoy it as much as ever. I tell you, Albertine, if you'd seen this Quitzow, this Dietrich von Quitzow, a study after Bismarck, but compared to him Bismarck's a newborn babe. Eyebrows like a boothbrush, he had. What fellows they must have been! And his brother is supposed to have looked even wilder, because he only had one eye. Polyphemus. Wasn't he called Polyphemus?"

"I think so, Eberhard. At least, there was someone called that."

"And then after the theater. In the pub. Well, the children will have told you about it, and about this Herr Manfred, this Klessentin. Charming young fellow, dashing, fresh, with a touch of humor. Oh Albertine, sometimes I feel as though everything were just prejudice. Well, *we* don't have to get rid of it; but if other people have a bash, quite honestly, I can't see much objection. There are two sides to everything. Noble birth is all right, Klessentin is all right, but Herr Manfred is all right too. In fact, everything's all right, and when you think of it, everyone's an actor."

"Oh, not me, Eberhard dear."

"No, not you, Albertine. You've had it knocked out of you. But me—I'm an actor. Look, I play the easygoing, good-natured old buffer, and I wouldn't even say that the part was unsuitable for a general. There have been quite other types who all play-acted too, emperors and kings among them. Nero played and sang and made them set fire to Rome. And now you can see it in the panopticon for fifty pennies. Just think, how cheap everything is now! And I've just remembered that ten years ago they were even showing *Nero's Torches*—a huge painting. I was still in the service in those days, and I can still see that great canvas in my mind's eye. Perhaps you saw it too."

"No, Eberhard. I've never seen anything like that. I have to deny myself such things. You know why."

"Don't talk about denying yourself. I can't stand that expression. No one should deny themselves, and if they don't want to, they don't need to. Well, see here: it was a picture as big as the sail on a Spree barge, or even bigger, actually; and at the side, on the right, there was what the pundits call 'Nero's torches,' and some of them were already burning, and the others were being lit. And what do you suppose, Albertine, what do you suppose those torches really were? Christian folk, they were, Christian folk bandaged up in rags soaked in pitch, and they looked like mummies or like big babies in swaddling clothes, and this Nero, who had organized all these horrors, he was lying quite peacefully on a golden chariot drawn by two golden lions, and a third lion lay beside him, and he was scratching its mane as though it were a poodle. And now look: this very same Nero, who could afford to do a thing like that, and who ruled the whole world—right up to our area here around Berlin, I believe—this Nero sang and played too, just like that Herr von Klessentin; and so I ask myself, 'Well, why shouldn't he, that young fellow? If an emperor can play, why not Klessentin? A blameless young man who's probably never lit a torch at all, let alone a torch like that.' "

The major's widow stretched out her hand to her brother-in-law and said, "Eberhard, you're just as you always were. And Leo's going to be the same. Your brother Alfred was always serious, a bit too serious—which may have been due to our circumstances."

"Don't talk about circumstances, Albertine. Circumstances—I can't stand that word."

"And it's funny the way children often have the same character as their collateral relations. And I can only hope that his life—I mean Leo's—will turn out like yours; the same luck . . ."

"Don't talk about luck, Albertine. That's another word I can't stand. A man should stand on his own feet. But no, forget I said that. . . . Just call it luck. . . . You're quite right. . . . I've been lucky. First in the service. Of course I always did what was expected of me, but after all, I wasn't exactly a Moltke. . . . Thank God, by the way, there aren't many of those, they'd eat each other up, and when things came to the crunch there'd be none left. . . . Just one is best, then there can be no competition and no envy. But now let's leave Klessentin and Nero and Moltke and talk about something else. Where are the girls?"

"They've run out. But I promised to make their excuses to their kind uncle. They had to make some calls they'd put off—it was high time. But you'll see them. I'm counting on your staying and being our guest—whatever we have ourselves . . ."

"Ah, ah, ah. I can't stand that. Whatever we have ourselves. What does that mean? A plate of soup . . ."

"Sophie was talking about pale ale soup with sago . . ."

"Excellent. Almost enough to upset my program. But I've still got various things to do and get. All nonsense, actually. Nothing that couldn't be done better by sending a postcard. But my wife wishes it. And a woman's wish is an order, otherwise it's war. And we military are always beaten: the more dashing we are, the greater the defeat. So I must be off. And much as I should have liked to see all three girls again, it rather suits me not to have them here. Because I want to take one of them back to Adamsdorf with me—my wife expressed the wish—and the only question is (assuming you agree), which one?"

"And you think that question can be settled more easily between you and me?"

"Yes, Albertine."

"Well, then I think Therese. She went to Pyrmont last summer with your wife, and she knows all about everything and has more or less got used to her."

"All quite true. All the same, a change might be indicated. Let me speak openly to you. Therese is an excellent girl and a lady. But she's more of a lady than my wife likes. My wife comes from the middle class, like you, and she has simple habits and opinions, all of which I can only approve of. And Therese—you must forgive my saying so—has a rather marked tendency to emphasize her Poggenpuhlishness. I don't want to criticize, and I personally have no objection. But my wife thinks it's a bit exaggerated, and there have been a few arguments about it between them."

"I understand, Eberhard. And your wife is right. I have the same trouble with her here. She has a sense of responsibility and she takes her ideas about nobility and its obligations rather seriously. But it's very difficult in circumstances . . ."

"No, no, no . . ."

". . . when one lives as modestly as we do. It always leads to differences of opinion and quarrels. But if not Therese, who then? I shouldn't like to lose Manon."

"No need to, Albertine. Manon is your baby, and you must keep her. My wife—with your agreement, I repeat—has decided on Sophie. She liked her very much when she saw her here, and she liked her letters, including the ones she wrote to Therese. All very sensible. And my wife has a predilection for sensibleness—no fiddle-faddle or pilot phrases and pomposity. And as for false pretenses, she really hates those."

"Thank goodness Sophie has none of that. Her life has always been work, and she holds things together when they're falling apart . . ."

"They mustn't. They mustn't. Nothing must fall apart. All right then: Sophie. Because my wife wants all sorts of new things, and what she particularly wants is a new set of plates with our crest on them. At first, I admit, that surprised me considerably. But she explained it to me. 'I am a Poggenpuhl now,' she said to me the other day, 'and so it's not proper that all our things should have the Leysewitz crest. I think people are talking about it, and we must avoid that.' Sophie paints so well: she can paint the Poggenpuhl crest for us, and that will keep her happy and she will be glad to use her gifts in the service of the family. And then she's so musical. I'm looking forward to hearing a Schubert song played as dusk falls; it will clear up the house, which is too quiet now, and we can invite people to come and listen."

"And when do you think she should start?"

"Now, today. With me. She's to be at the hotel at three with her trunk. By herself would be best. Farewells are disturbing, and kissing is ridiculous. The train leaves at four, and we'll be in Adamsdorf by eleven."

And with that he rose, sent his best wishes to Therese and Manon, and took his leave.

# 10

D*ear Mama,*

    We arrived here safely just after eleven last night. Right at the end, on the way from Hirschberg to here, I was enchanted by the drive in the open carriage although it was cloudy, and the mountains I had so looked forward to seeing were invisible. But there was still life in the villages, and through the mist you could see the lights of the factory at Erdmannsdorf where they work all night. It all looked medieval and romantic as though an ancient Piast family[1] lived there. Here in Adamsdorf everything was quite still, except for a dog barking in the distance and another dog answering him. The court-yard was absolutely quiet too, and for a moment I felt afraid; but that feeling dropped away as soon as I got into the drawing room, where Aunt greeted me in the friendliest manner. A marvelous woman, I can't understand why Therese never really got on with her. Perhaps I'll discover some snags too, but I hardly think so. If only, my dear old Mama, life had been as kind to you as it has to her! I mentioned the drawing room. Well, it *was* the drawing room, but it is really more of a hall. Adamsdorf was originally a Benedic-tine abbey, and the previous owner incorporated a lot of the old buildings when he rebuilt it. This hall was once the refectory. It has three Gothic pillars down the middle, and there was a fire burning in the hearth and every time the flames flickered up the light was reflected on the vaulted ceiling. Apart from Aunt there was only a cat, a big, beautiful creature which walked round me purring all the time and then jumped up on my lap. It gave me a fright; but Aunt reassured me and said that it was a demonstration of affection, and that Bob (I suppose it is a tom) was normally rather sparing of those; he has a suspicious and jealous nature. We were frozen, so Uncle asked for an eggnog: they make it with Hungarian wine and egg yolks here. It was quite delicious. And what was more important, I slept marvelously after it, and when I got up quite early and raised the blinds, the whole long line of mountains lay before me all covered in snow. During the next few days we are to make an excursion to the Heinrich Cabin, and then to come down the mountains on sledges. They say it is absolutely beautiful, but I'm a little frightened. Keep well. Love and kisses to you all, and to the boys in Thorn when you write to them.

> With my fondest love,
> *Your Sophie*

*Schloss Adamsdorf, January 16*

Dear Mama,

I am completely settled here. Aunt goes on being kindness itself; I don't need to reassure you about Uncle; and even Bob remains faithful to his attachment. He goes a bit far, because his shows of affection are always a bit like an assault. Suddenly he jumps at me— you can see the tiger in him. The trip to the Heinrich Cabin has been put off because we are to wait for another fresh fall of snow, because they say that the thicker the snow the better the run down into the valley, and it's less dangerous too; in the thick snow the sledge flies over the rocks as though they were molehills.

Our life is rather quiet, there are few visitors. Except for the Adamsdorf parson, who calls occasionally, we see only other clergymen from the neighborhood, and an old colonel from the town; and then a district court judge and his wife. I always enjoy these visits very much, but even without them I have plenty of entertainment, because Aunt likes to talk about her life, especially her childhood, which was spent in poverty. In addition to all that we have a curious picture gallery here; the basic stock consists of various paintings from when the house was an abbey: some saints (not many), and then portraits of abbots and priors, and even a

Prince Bishop of Breslau. Mixed up with them there are all sorts of specifically Prussian things: Frederick the Great (three times), Prince Henry, General Tauentzien, and at the end of a dozen portraits from the family of Aunt's first husband. All Leysewitzes. No Poggenpuhls at all, not even a portrait of Uncle. A few days ago I seized an opportunity to remark on this, and he laughed and said, "Yes, Fiechen[2] (that's what he always calls me), no Poggenpuhls at all, but that's a good thing: it's a terrific jumble already, and if we had to cope with the Hochkirch major and the Sohr major as well, there'd be total confusion." Uncle has so much good sense: he has absolutely no desire to see members of his own family competing with the old Silesian nobility. And it's probably because of that that no more has been heard on the subject of crested plates. I think Uncle Eberhard must have been against it from the start, and finally gave in—I won't say gladly but at least without a long struggle. But a new task awaits me which makes me very proud and happy. But I'll tell you about that in my next letter.

If you get any letters from Leo or Wendelin, please send them on—first of all for my sake, of course, but for Uncle's too; he is genuinely interested in them both, and expects both of them to do well—Wendelin of course, but Leo too. Only today he said that Leo was born lucky, and that that was the best thing that could happen to a person. Aunt got quite solemn and disagreed, but she calmed down when he said—very charmingly and with a courtly gesture, "Did I deserve you or was it luck?" She gave him a kiss, which I found touching, because it wasn't an amorous kiss (I don't like to see older people doing that), but just genuine affection and gratitude. And quite right too. Because as sure as this marriage has made him happy, it's made her happy too.

From all this you can see how happy I am here, though occasionally I feel homesick for you and wish I could stroke your hands. Don't worry too much. Everything will turn out all right. Uncle specially asked me to tell you that from him too. Today he told me there was a motto which went, "Take care, but not too much: everything will be as God wills." And he said you broke this injunction more often than was right and proper. And by the way, if you imagine I agreed, you are mistaken; on the contrary, I said, "Only the person who feels the pain can know how much it hurts." And then he gave me a kiss too. He is a wonderful man, and I can't make up my mind who is better, he or she. But now farewell.

*Your Sophie*

*Schloss Adamsdorf, January 19*

Only a card today, dear Mama. Yesterday it snowed: it's all piled up round the house like a wall. But since this morning there is a clear blue sky, a light frost, and divine weather. One day soon we are going to drive or walk to the top of the ridge and then toboggan down. The parson and an assistant judge from the town are coming along. I am looking forward to it immeasurably. Keep well, all of you.

*Your Sophie*

*Heinrich Cabin, January 22*

Only a card again, but with a picture (the Heinrich Cabin) this time. Because this is where we are, and we shall probably stay another day, we shall *have* to. And it's my fault. What happened was this: almost as soon as I had got my sledge and was whizzing down, I lost the way and would certainly have plunged into a crater—they call it the 'little pond' because there's water at the bottom—when another sledge which was going the right way saw me and deliberately ran into me from the side. The crash (a lucky one for me because it saved my life) flung me off my toboggan, and as I couldn't walk because of a slight injury, they had to carry me back up here. We are waiting for the doctor to come from Krummhübel (the nearest large village) in a few hours. Don't worry about me. But I am never going to go in for tobogganing again. My rescuer was a young assistant judge (titled) and already engaged to be married. As always.

*Your Sophie*

*Schloss Adamsdorf, January 25*

Two telegrams from Uncle will have reassured you about my condition. There's no question of any danger any more. I've broken my thigh. In four weeks—six at the most—I'll be dancing again. The doctor is excellent and very tactful. He's a weaver's son from the neighborhood (Therese please note). My rescue, as I think I told you, was entirely due to the assistant judge; he's a lieutenant in the reserve, of course, and if there's a war he intends to stay in the army. He hates paperwork, and his chief, the district court judge, smilingly acknowledged the truth of this declaration. I should find it trying to lie still for so many weeks if the doctor had not given me permission to move my arms as much as I want. Aunt immediately had an easel set up for me so that I can write and draw comfortably. I am making copious use of it and producing sketch upon sketch. And so the time has probably come, my dear old thing, to tell you about the new project I hinted at briefly just after my arrival a few weeks ago. Instead of painting crests on plates—now listen and marvel—I am to be entrusted with decorating the interior of the Protestant church (as in nearly every village round here, there is a Catholic one as well). The idea is to have biblical scenes painted on panels going all around the lower edge of the gallery. Each panel is to be about the size of a folded card table—rather an odd way to describe size and measurements in the case of a church, when you come to think about it. Of course it won't be a great work of art—there's no fear of that—but it won't be despicable either, and what makes me happiest of all is that I shall try to solve the problem in a completely fresh way. So: Joseph Sold into Egypt, Judith and Holofernes, Samson and Delilah are all out. Instead I am going to find stories where the landscape is the most important element, and at the moment I am searching through the Bible for scenes and material with suitable settings. When I find something I try and hold it down with a few strokes as best I can in my present position.

You can tell from the length of this letter that in spite of everything I am very well. Manon may disagree and point out that as letters are written by hand, no conclusions can be drawn as to the condition of one's leg. But she is wrong. If your big toe hurts—really hurts—you can't write any better than if your thumb hurts.

Write to me with every detail of how you all are. And ask Friederike to write too; letters from servants are always so charming, quite different from educated letters. Educated people don't write so well because they're less natural; anyway, that's how it usually is. The heart is what counts. True, is it not, my dear old thing? You know that better than anyone. And Therese is to describe the soirée at the Bronsarts, and whether they had tableaux vivants, and if so, what they were. And Manon must write about the Bartensteins and their ball and whether she danced and who with. And what she wore. Manon knows how to make a fairy dress with a bit of net and a pink ribbon. And now farewell. Aunt wants to add a few lines (perhaps to report on my progress).

> As always,
> Your very loving daughter,
> *Sophie*

# 11

During the weeks of this correspondence between Berlin and Schloss Adamsdorf there was also a correspondence between Berlin and Thorn. Leo began it with a postcard to Manon, which, after writing it, he wisely slipped into an envelope.

*Thorn, January 8*

Got back three days ago. Copernicus still stands. The whole town smells of fish stewed in beer, though actually that isn't quite true because here they cook their carp with gingerbread and Hungarian wine. In these matters we are superior to you, though I must say it's carried a bit far.

Wendelin met me at the station, fearfully polite, but very gracious as well. He overdid it: a patronizing air, General Staff all over. And he isn't even on it yet. But of course he will be one day. The state couldn't possibly let so many virtues go to waste. Forgive these catty remarks, but when one feels so invisibly small, one is driven to such malice in order to hold up one's head before oneself and others. The worm turns. I'll write again tomorrow, perhaps today if drilling recruits doesn't deprive me of the breath of life. "Dobry, dobry" and every now and then "fathead!"

A thousand good wishes,
*Your Leo*

236

A postscript was scribbled along the edge of the card:

Just had an invitation for tonight: innermost circle. I need hardly say where. Incidentally, I saw Esther at her window this morning, very grand, pomposissima almost, which is a bit frightening. Because she's only eighteen. What will it lead to?

Three days later Manon replied.

*Berlin, January 12*

*My dear Leo,*

Thank you for your lines, which gave me much pleasure because they were so exactly like you. Your card (fortunately inside an envelope) arrived by the same post as a letter from Sophie. You could tell the difference at once. Sophie always writes, as it were, with the palette in her hand: always as the artist, always full of feeling and gratitude. The latter quality especially is something no one could reproach *you* with. Your elder (and better) brother makes a fuss of you, and you make fun of him. Come, come! Such behavior is certainly not Poggenpuhlish. The Poggenpuhls are full of reverential feeling. I believe you must have caught your tendency to mock and sneer from somewhere; it's the influence of your environment, or—which comes to the same thing—the tone you find in the home of the very grand Esther, your Pomposissima, as you call her. I know that tone from the Bartensteins, although they themselves don't use it and get embarrassed when it raises its head. But even the Bartensteins can't quite prevent it happening; given the peculiar composition of their society, things aren't entirely in their own hands. To give just one example: their relatives who gather together there every Sunday always belong to two quite different worlds: one uncle may have spent thirty years in London or Paris, and the other in Schrimm. And there's no denying that it makes a difference. I mentioned the influence of environment: it exists. I feel its power myself, and when I look at Therese, I see the same power from another direction, like a perfect textbook example. Because Therese—even if one might prefer her to be different in other ways—

always knows what is right and proper, and she owes that to the air of the Wilhelmsstrasse, which, for better or for worse, is the air she breathes. I don't know what street Esther lives in (perhaps it's a Wilhelmsstrasse too), but I do know that in our Wilhelmsstrasse there are no Pomposissimas. Here I must stop. I just heard the bell, and from Friederike's conversation in the passage I can tell that Flora has arrived and gone in to Mama. I expect she wants to invite me over. More about the other subject next time. Your whole future—it becomes clearer to me every day—is contained in the question: Esther or Flora. Flora is blonde, thank goodness, a pale, reddish blonde, in fact. Farewell.

> With unchanging love,
> *Your Manon*

*Dear Leo:*

You replied to my first letter at once, without waiting for the second, which was meant to complete it. That was very nice of you, but unfortunately also a bit worrying; the very promptness of your answer was disturbing to me, and several of the remarks you made in your letter even more so. I hope the invitation for the evening of the eighth which you mentioned on your card did not turn out to be fateful. I know that dark complexions have always been your downfall. And Esther! It is strange how some names seem to carry a mystic power, a sort of spiritual fluid which works in a mysterious way. Pull yourself together, be stronger than Ahasverus was (I mean the Persian king): he succumbed to an Esther too. I have just glanced through your letter again, and again I got the impression that you had already given your word. If it is so, I know it won't be the end of the world, but it will be the end of your career. Because in the provinces, and especially in yours, religious feeling (or, as the Bartensteins always say, denominational considerations—they are fond of using curious convoluted expressions like that) is much more stubborn, and her parents will simply forbid her conversion. In that case it would have to be a civil ceremony for you, and, broadminded as I am, I find that a positively horrifying idea. Such a step would exclude you not only from the army, but also, even more important, from society as well; you would have to roam the world as a stranger, rejected and with no resting place. Then we'd have the other Ahasverus. Don't do such a thing to us. Therese would not survive it.

*Your Manon*

*Berlin, January 18*

*My dear Leo,*
Thank God! Now everything may still turn out all right. I can't tell you how relieved I feel that this storm has blown over—for us all, but not least for you. You make fun of my scruples and tease me, and ask what—if it really had happened—the difference would have been between the despised Blumenthals and the enthusiastically recommended Bartensteins. Yes, you add that Blumenthal has been a Commercial Councillor for years, and you say that such a sign of approval from the state, which is, after all, a Christian authority, even though it may not actually be baptism, is almost as good, and that therefore the house of Blumenthal is really a step ahead of the house of Bartenstein. Oh Leo, it sounds quite good and I'll gladly accept it as a joke; but the true state of affairs is quite other, after all. The Bartensteins have received the Crown Prince, Bartenstein is the Romanian Consul, which is higher than a Commercial Councillor, and Droysen and Mommsen have been to their house (yes, and just before he passed away, Leopold von Ranke was there too); they have several paintings by Menzel in their gallery, one is a court ball, I think, and the other a sketch for a coronation scene. Well, my dear Leo, who else has things like that? Frau Melanie (that is Frau Bartenstein's first name) has sat on a ladies' committee for the Magdalenum[1] for several years, Drysander[2] is always singling her out on every possible occasion. . . . And then Esther and Flora themselves! There is a difference, there *must* be. And I implore: think it over! But above all—and I cannot emphasize this enough— above all do not deceive yourself into thinking (just because I secretly wish it so very very much) that they are waiting for you here with impatience and anxiety! There is no doubt that both her parents' wishes, and Flora's too, are directed toward the nobility; but they are very choosy, and if, for instance, it fell to Frau Melanie

to decide, I know for certain that she would not be very pleased with less than an Arnim or a Bülow. So you can work out the Poggenpuhl chances for yourself. In spite of Therese they are not exactly overwhelming, and in the end your personal charm would be far, far more decisive than our historical importance. All the same, that too is a factor to be taken into account, especially as far as Flora is concerned: unlike both her parents, she has a distinctly romantic turn of mind, and only the day before yesterday she assured me once again that when she saw the grenadier caps of the first regiment of guards in Potsdam the other day, it brought tears to her eyes. Altogether, Leo, you still have no clear conception of what or how much is at stake: in spite of my good relations—I might say my very intimate relations with them—there is still a lot of trouble and effort ahead before you can hope to win the bride. So don't be proud and don't turn down the proposal I am about to make to you: that would be a folly from which I hope your good sense and your financial difficulties would equally protect you.

But here comes Flora to take me "shopping" (she likes to use English expressions), and so I must stop without having told you the details of my plan, which is, oh listen and marvel, that *you* should write a family history of the Poggenpuhls. Only this much: Wendelin will have to do most of it, and then Uncle Eberhard, of course. Think about it! But above all—courage and silence! Flora knows nothing, suspects nothing. As always,

*Your Manon*

Leo replied by return of post.

*Thorn, January 19*

*My dear Manon,*

I feel quite shamed by your love and concern. An excellent plan, positively stupendous. But, but. . . . Alas, this only puts me into a rather melancholy frame of mind. Wendelin—who, after all, is the one who's got to do it—Wendelin doesn't want to. He thinks it's simply ridiculous. Because in his honest opinion the Poggenpuhls don't begin with the Crusades, but simply with Wendelin von

Poggenpuhl. All the deeds that were done for hundreds of years by people like the Sohr and Hochkirch majors he considers very run-of-the-mill stuff; to stand out in front and shout hurrah means very little to him; strategic thinking is what counts. Anyhow, he puts himself before the family. It's true he always helps me and in many ways he's an excellent fellow, but he always has to appear to his own advantage and glory in the eyes of the world; as soon as he thinks he might upset one of his high-up chiefs or, worse still, appear in a questionable light, then all his family feeling and his readiness to stand by us evaporates. His name is Poggenpuhl, but he isn't a Poggenpuhl; or, if he is, then it's in his own way, which is quite different from ours. But not a word to Mama; she's quite capable of putting it in a letter to him, and then I shall be in the stocks. As it is, I always feel uneasy when he comes into my room. He's got such a damned superior smile and I'm supposed to knuckle under. Altogether—and that's what's so rotten about one's whole career—one's continually having to knuckle under. But enough of this confession, and let's get back to the main topic, which is the pamphlet about our glory that we're supposed to be writing. Wendelin, as I said, won't do it, and I can't—can't and couldn't if it were a question of winning the Queen of Madagascar for my bride. Oh, Manon! . . . "far in the east over Madagascar the morning breaks"—yes, that's where I shall have to go, that's how it will end, it must. For I shall never call Flora my own (that's how some people like to put it) if it depends on writing the family history. And besides—and this is the worst of it because it's so humiliating—I have considerably overestimated Esther's passion for me. Or perhaps a rival has turned up overnight, a more favored suitor. In that case I should be forced to hate Esther. And so as to hide nothing from you: that Quitzow evening which promised so much or at least ended so promisingly—almost nothing of that is left at the end of the week. What a dismal life, and it's thawing outside. I could recite Hamlet's soliloquy, but I will settle for "Nymph, pray for me"; it's shorter. I've probably got it wrong. Most quotations are wrong.

*Your Leo*

# 12

The correspondence between the younger brother and sister continued into February, to the disgust of Therese, who occasionally read one of Leo's letters and then bewailed the fact "that a Poggenpuhl could go so far astray," though she cast the blame chiefly upon her sister. "In my opinon," she regularly remarked when the subject came under discussion, "the whole correspondence is superfluous; but if it is to be carried on, then I should prefer it to have a different content. You will end up by dragging him right over to your side, into that social sphere which you unfortunately seem to enjoy—and to enjoy increasingly. You will not acknowledge that the world which in your flippancy and arrogance, and simply in order to sneer, you refer to as the Germano-Christian world—that this world is worth more than half a dozen Gersons (I assume that there must be that many of them by now). What matters is the inner life, not the outer; the prettiest apple usually has a worm inside."

"Whereas gray russets keep the whole winter through."

Therese shrugged her shoulders and broke off; nor did she seek to return to the subject, especially as the prophecy that her mother had uttered to pacify her was soon fulfilled: "Never mind those two," was more or less what the major's widow had said. "You ought to know Leo and realize how little it all means. Today he wants one thing and tomorrow another. Three weeks from now they will have stopped scribbling of their own accord." And that was how it turned out. Before the end of January, Leo had taken up with a Catholic priest, who cheerfully combined strictness in matters of dogma with

242

games of skat and a merry nature, and this new acquaintance immediately proved fatal to the continuation of the correspondence, which promptly died down.

Yes, the correspondence with Thorn soon came to an end, but Sophie and Manon continued to write to one another, and hardly a week passed without a letter from Adamsdorf, usually accompanied by a carefully packed box. Every time she unpacked it, Friederike greeted its arrival with the same speech, "Fresh eggs again, and all wrapped up and packed in chaff too! Well, I've no objection to *that*, ma'am. Because first of all you can't buy them fresh, even if it says so, and secondly eggs are always better than fresh-killed meat. Ducks aren't too bad, because ducks are fat; but it starts with chicken, and when it comes to veal, that's always a bit off. . . . And I'll boil one for you right away, ma'am; it's time you gave yourself a treat. It's true you've got your pastilles, but there's not goodness in them, and they're only on account of your cough."

Sophie's letters could be divided, according to the period they were written, into those dealing with her recovery and those which, when that was complete, dealt with her painting activities. It was always a pleasure to read them, and sometimes Manon took one to the Bartensteins in order to read it aloud, though usually only when the old gentleman was present; he liked hearing that kind of thing, while the ladies really only listened from politeness. Flora—possibly because she was learning modern Greek in preparation for a trip to Olympia—was inclined to find everything "insignificant"; which finally caused Manon, enamored as she was of her friend, to be a little more reticient in her communications.

One of the letters went:

I have just got to the Flood, which, if one likes to look at it that way, is a landscape subject. For water is nature, and nature is landscape. And can you imagine what my Flood looks like? Quite different from any other; and I can say that without immodesty, because it wasn't my idea but Uncle Eberhard's. And not really his either, as you will hear. Last week, when I announced at tea one day that I was going to start on the Flood, Uncle said, "Well, Fiechen, and how do you imagine it looked? Or rather, I don't want to know, I'd rather tell you how *I* imagine it was and how I'd like you to do it. When I was still in Berlin with the Alexander,[1] I once went to a village church nearby where there were a lot of paintings, including a Flood. And there, sticking up out of the water, was not just the usual Mount Ararat with the Ark, but a bit further back there was another mountain, and on this second mountain there was a church. And this church was the spit and image of the little church in the Mark in which we were standing, with its lantern tower and even with a lightning conductor. And that made a great impression on me at the time, and I want you to do the same thing and put in two mountain tops with the Adamsdorf church on the second one. The Protestant church, that is. And if the Catholics don't like it, they can have their own church painted too. I believe in Martin Luther and the pure doctrine. In that I think I'm an unshakable Poggenpuhl." At first I was a bit taken aback when Uncle said that, because I'd imagined it all quite differently; but as there was no getting out of it, I fell in with his idea, and now that it's nearly finished I have quite fallen in love with it. At first it struck me as childish, and it still does, but at the same time it has a deep meaning. When the old sinful world had gone down and a new and better world was emerging, the first new thing to appear (because the animals belonged to the old world) was the church of that little village in the Mark, and now the Adamsdorf church as well. It was as though the first thing God did was to put them there. Of course you can laugh at the idea, but it can make you rejoice too. And you, my dear Mama, who, thank God, comes from a devout clerical family, you will see the beauty of it and be fonder than ever of Uncle Eberhard. He really is a splendid man. That's all about the idea for the painting. And now you will wonder how and where, never having seen the sea, I got the idea of what it should look like for my Flood. Now listen. You must remember our expedition with the Bartensteins last autumn, when we all went third class, which amused them so much. Third class on the Ring Line we went, as far as Stralow station. And when we got out, the station was high up like Mount Ararat over the Rummelsburg Lake and the Spree, and both together they looked like a mighty expanse of water. That's the panorama I used for my picture. The station is Mount Ararat, and the Rummelsburg Lake is the Flood. As I was only doing the end of the Flood, I thought I could manage without any kind of stormy movement of the water without being unfaithful to the text.

Similar letters arrived frequently; the one describing Sophie's "End of Sodom and Gomorrah" found special favor with Herr Bartenstein. "It's a warning," he said to Manon, without indicating, incidentally, to whom he wished the warning to be addressed.

Fiechen settled in more and more, and the longer she spent with her relatives, the more lively an interest she took—when she was not painting—in the domestic affairs of Schloss Adamsdorf and particularly in the character of her aunt. The conversations they had together as they walked around the great lawn in the park would be reported in great detail in Sophie's letters home, whenever the occasion arose.

Yesterday we went for our walk round the big lawn again; there is an enclosure in the middle with a few young deer, charming creatures—I hope to make use of them one day. Then suddenly, I can't remember in what connection, Aunt said, "Yes, your sister Therese. She can't have been very pleased with me, and perhaps she complained of me to you, because when we were in Pyrmont that time I wasn't very keen on being presented to the Princess of Wied, which she was always urging me to do. Once when there was a carriage parade I wouldn't take part, let alone decorate the harness with rose garlands. It all seemed unfitting to me, and I told her so quite frankly. Therese, as so often happens, had a false idea of my financial position; it was once very brilliant, but is so no longer. I particularly want you to understand these rather complicated matters. I come from a simple, middle-class family which started small and poor and only later acquired wealth. Then my first husband married me; he had nothing at the time, but afterward he bought Schloss Adamsdorf. It had been in the family once before after it had ceased to be a monastery, but then they lost it. He was a perfect gentleman, and our marriage was a very happy one; as to our respective wealth, we soon changed places. My money was lost, and we should have been forced to give up Adamsdorf, if it had not been for a number of deaths through which my husband unexpectedly inherited a considerable fortune. That is how we were able to stay on here. But everything we own therefore became Leysewitz property again, and must pass to the Leysewitzes; your uncle knew that from the start and approved of it. I have had the rare good fortune to have made two marriages with two equally excellent men. Everything has turned out well for me, but I must not forget how it came about, and must live accordingly. This is how things stand; we have only the use of everything you see here. The house, the estate, the money, everything is entailed, and because that is so I have learned to economize. And you—you are a good and intelligent child and you can follow all this. Therese used to listen with only half an ear when I touched on these matters, and she didn't want to believe them. That's how it always is; nobody wants to believe what they don't like to hear."

Yes, dear Mama, that is what Aunt wanted me to know. It will be quite a good thing if Therese finds out too. All the same: even though I think I was told all this in order to pass it on to you, please don't mention it in your reply. I always read aloud my letters from you and my sisters at breakfast, and if you made a reference to this I should feel embarrassed.

By the way, I haven't heard anything from the boys for many weeks. In Wendelin's case that doesn't matter much; he only writes from duty. But Leo? Sometimes I feel anxious and think his next letter will be from the Cameroons or Namaqualand. Until his affairs are in order he'll never settle down. But where is order to come from?

It was the end of May when Sophie wrote this letter, and she wisely refrained from mentioning the subject again. She was content for the letter to take its effect and to change her elder sister's unfair carping for a more just appreciation.

Meanwhile the quiet life of Schloss Adamsdorf continued and only changed with the arrival of summer. Sophie's aunt was a passionate lover of her native Silesia, and she insisted on weekly expeditions into the mountains. They would drive either to Schreiberhau or to Hermsdorf or to Krummhübel, and from there they would climb on foot higher into the mountains, to Kirche Wang or the Mittagsstein or even to the Schneegruben. Sophie would sketch some scene or other for her Old Testament pictures and say, "This is Abraham's tomb, this is Mount Sinai, this is the Brook Kidron." But her greatest pleasure always came on the way home when they halted for a final rest at the place where they had left their conveyance, and watched the doings of the "trippers" from Berlin.

These always gave scope for amusement on the drive home, and Uncle Eberhard never tired of declaring, "Yes, those Berliners, you may love them or hate them; but they *are* entertaining, and watching them like that is just like going to the theater. And actually it *is* something of the kind, because they always look round to see if they've got an audience worth raising the curtain for."

Sophie worked hard all summer at her pictures for the church. By the end of August she had already got to "Saul in the Cave" (she had discovered a suitable cave near the Kräbersteine), and Saul himself was partly Uncle Eberhard and partly the proprietor of the dram shop, who wore a long beard and had the evil eye. David, on the other hand, was the assistant judge. Uncle Eberhard was genuinely delighted with the progress of the work, and every day he would declare that he would never have thought that such a thing could give him so much pleasure. He would then indulge in well-meaning remarks about the artistic life in general, and take back what he had said about it in his earlier days. "You may laugh, but all the same, it's a small act of creation of a sort. And creating is fun. At least, I can't imagine that God created the world in a bad temper."

"Some people look as though He had, Uncle."

"Yes, Fiechen, you're right there. Some people do look like that. But just think of all the things that happen! A single instance proves nothing. People nowadays are terribly inclined to make the exception the rule. And if they'd only choose nice exceptions! But no, it has to be something really nasty. True, thirty years ago it was not much better. I can still remember when that ape business came up, and some orangutan or other was supposed to be our grandfather. You should have seen how delighted everybody was! When we were descended from God, we weren't up to much, but when that ape business came into fashion, they all danced as if it were the Ark of the Covenant."

It was the second of September when Uncle Eberhard and Sophie held this conversation in the attic room that the owners of Adamsdorf had furnished as a studio for their niece. An hour later Uncle Eberhard set off for Hirschberg, where the anniversary of Sedan was to be celebrated in the customary manner. Naturally there had to be a speech about Bismarck, and naturally this had to be made by old General von Poggenpuhl, although the thought of it made him feel worse than he had at the very damnedest moment at Saint Privat. At other times when he drove through the lovely valley, the fields would smile at him in all their bounty, but today he did not notice how the oats were doing; he said nothing at all, and just kept memorizing and saying to himself with increasing anxiety, "It's one o'clock now. In another three hours I shall start living again, and even my appetite may come back. But until then I'm just no good." And he had a headache too, and a slight ticking sensation in two places, which naturally got worse as he kept repeating the question to himself, "What if I dry up?" But finally he came to terms with the idea, or at least resigned himself to it. "And if I really do dry up, what does it matter after all? In my day nobody knew how to make a speech, and all the sensible people there will know that. Besides, I've really got the introduction pat, and if I notice I'm getting in a muddle I shall simply say, '. . . and so I ask you, all you who are assembled here today: are we Prussians? I know what your answer will be. And in that spirit I call upon you. . .' And then we'll have three cheers."

This more or less restored his composure, but he remained somewhat feverish, and the feverishness continued even after the dreadful moment had come and gone. Perhaps it was because, right after the cheers, he had downed a large glass of dry Hungarian wine. After coffee he felt dizzy. But the feeling passed, and he finally set off for home in the best of spirits. The stars sparkled in the sky; and the air had an autumn freshness in it, and he shivered. "Listen, Johann," he said, "haven't you got a rug?"

"No, sir, but I'll take off my coat."

But that was not at all well received. "Nonsense, man; take off your coat! Me, a Poggenpuhl!" And for a while he muttered on in the same manner.

It was one o'clock when they drove into the village street. An old servant was still up at the Schloss, and Sophie too. As soon as he entered the hall, she could see how changed he was. "Uncle, you're so cold, shall I make you some tea or a hot water bottle?"

"Nonsense. General Poggenpuhl. . ."

He sounded so strange that Johann said to Sophie, "Oh Lord, miss, he keeps saying that. I'm afraid he's very ill."

He was very ill. Next morning they called Doctor Nitsche, who said to Frau von Poggenpuhl, "We must hang up damp sheets, shade the light, and give him complete rest." But to Sophie he said, "It's typhus."

"Will he get better?"

The doctor shrugged his shoulders.

# 13

Their fears were soon confirmed. In spite of the doctor's objections, Sophie took charge of nursing her uncle. Every evening she wrote a postcard home, always emphasizing that there was no danger yet—largely because their aunt might read what she had written. But the danger was all too great, and on the seventh day after the onset of the illness Sophie's mother received a letter which read:

Uncle Eberhard died at noon today. He was very restless during the night, then in the course of the morning he fell into a state of apathy, and just before twelve he fell asleep. There was very little hope from the beginning, less than I cared to tell you. I have lost a great deal in him. But not only I—we shall all miss him a lot, except for Wendelin perhaps, who will make his way anyhow. I will tell you more when I see you about some of the things that happened in the last few days. I look forward to seeing you all, you especially, my dear, sweet Mama. I am assuming that you will come. Aunt wishes it very much, and I think we should respect her wishes. First for our own sake, and then because she deserves it so much. She asks you kindly to accept the enclosed from her, and hopes it will be enough for the journey and everything else. What I need will be sent from Breslau. It would be best if you left the day after tomorrow in the evening. Then you would arrive early in the morning on the twelfth. The funeral is at noon.

*Your Sophie*

When Manon finished reading out this letter, all three ladies were more than a little affected, but their feelings were of very different kinds. The mother was filled with heartfelt grief, which would have been even purer if it had not been mixed with many an anxious thought about the future; Manon, in spite of her love and reverence for her uncle, was sadly stricken at having to miss a soirée that the Bartensteins were giving on that very twelfth; while Therese was dominated by the idea of the funeral, which to her was a function of immense public importance. She not only immediately saw herself in the front row of mourners; she was animated by the proud sense that she, and she alone, would be the chief representative of the Poggenpuhl family—the two old ladies who had only married into it scarcely counted. Her pride was mitigated for a moment or two by the thousand-mark note that accompanied the letter, but on the other hand the advantages of this were so obvious that any sense of oppression was soon dispelled, especially when it was agreed that Therese should go into town and buy their mourning attire. Apart from the burial itself they all felt that this visit to the funeral outfitters was the most significant event of all, and the expression with which Therese set out on her mission was so emphatically distinguished that even Manon was moved by it and succumbed to a feeling of reverence for her sister.

The feeling rapidly gave way to the opposite when Therese returned from her expedition. The dresses, she reported, would be delivered by the following morning: they could easily make any small alterations that might be needed. All the rest she had bought on the spot and brought back in a large box. It contained three crepe hats, long black veils, and three mourning caps with a widow's peak in front.

"Are you proceeding on the assumption," said Manon, "that we are actually going to wear these peaked caps?"

"What a strange question."

"That means yes."

Therese nodded.

"Well then, permit me to say that I shall refrain from joining you."

"That you will not. On such a day as this at least you will remember the duty you owe your name."

"I know the duty I owe my name."

"And what is that?"

"To refrain, as far as possible, from making myself an object of ridicule."

"And what, in your opinion, would constitute that?"

"To insist on getting ourselves up as royal widows. We are simply the nieces of an old general."

"Of General von Poggenpuhl! I, at least, will follow the good old tradition."

"But not the dictates of good taste."

They grew more and more heated; at last they wanted their mother to decide. But she refused. "I am not sufficiently experienced in such matters, and I don't know whether it would be suitable or not. I think we should take the box with us and let Aunt decide."

To this they agreed. Next morning the dresses arrived. They "fitted like a glove." The sisters stood before the tall, narrow looking glass, studying their own appearance and approving one another's, and it was here that peace was concluded once more between them.

"What a marvelous man he was," said Manon.

"He was, and may his memory be blessed. His picture will always have a place in my heart."

The night train left at ten o'clock from the Friedrichsstrasse Station. It was not yet nine when they stood ready in their traveling clothes, and Manon, who looked very good, found it hard to resist the temptation to complete her costume with a pair of binoculars that happened to be lying about. But she said it would show "lack of style" (this was one of Flora's favorite expressions), and, once this redeeming phrase had occurred to her, she found it easier to renounce the binoculars. Friederike was in the front room with them to help when the moment came for putting on their coats; but it was still much too early, and they began to wonder what to do to pass the time. The major's widow used it to deliver an urgent speech.

"All I can say to you, Friederike, is: be careful and remember all the things that happen every day. Only yesterday there was something in the papers again."

"Yes, I know, ma'am. But it's not as if I was a child."

"And if the bell rings, don't open the door at once. You'd better get a footstool and climb up and look through the fanlight, so that you can see who it is. . ."

"Yes, ma'am."

"And when you open the door, keep the chain on and only speak through the crack. . . . Only the other day they killed another widow, and if you fling the door open like that, it could happen to you too, or they'll throw snuff in your eyes, or they'll gag you so you won't even be able to scream. And then they'll clear off with everything. . ."

"Lord, ma'am, they always know where to go, they'd never come here."

"Don't say that. *They* know every mickle makes a muckle. Better safe than sorry."

Friederike promised to do everything she said, and then they left.

A cab was already waiting at the door—the porter's wife had condescended to fetch one. They all said good-bye to Friederike once more, and then they were on their way to the Potsdamer Strasse.

Next morning, just after five, the train arrived at Schmiedeberg, and from there it was barely an hour's drive to Adamsdorf. Johann was waiting at the station with an open carriage. The big trunk was put on the box; the major's widow sat on the back seat, with Therese beside her. Manon, across from them, sat facing backward and enjoying the scenery. The sun had not yet risen, but the mountains all around were turning pink, and a fresh breeze was blowing. Everything promised a beautiful autumn day.

Therese too was quite carried away, and as the contours of the mountains grew sharper and clearer she pointed to them and, rising in her seat, she said. "So that is the Riesengebirge?"

The question was addressed to Johann, but he could not immediately adjust to the unfamiliar words and therefore said, "Yes, over there on the left, that's the Koppe."

"The Schneekoppe?"

"Yes, the Koppe."

Manon was amused by the fact that the coachman was reluctant to follow her elder sister's educated speech, while Therese happily indulged in her favorite train of thought about the inferior intelligence of the common people.

It was just six o'clock when the carriage stopped before Schloss Adamsdorf. A manservant helped the ladies to alight, and right after him came Sophie, visibly pleased to see all three—including Therese, although the latter appeared rather reserved. This was because their reception had not turned out as she had expected, and she particularly missed the presence of her aunt.

"Where is Aunt?" she asked. "Not ill, is she?"

"No, she's not ill," said Sophie, immediately guessing what was going on in Therese's mind. "The last few days have been very hard for her. So she wants to rest as long as she can. She asked me to make her excuses."

"Poor relations," Therese murmured half audibly.

After that they climbed the wide stairs to the first floor, where two communicating guest rooms had been prepared, one large and one smaller, with the door between them open and covered only by a heavy curtain. The large room was for Manon and her mother, the smaller for Therese, who was half mollified by the distinction inherent in this arrangement.

"And now you have two whole hours to rest," said Sophie. "Or would you like me to send breakfast up to your rooms right away? Then you can walk in the park until Aunt comes. It's at its best in the morning."

Manon and her mother seemed to hesitate, especially Manon, who had an exalted conception of "morning walks in the park." But Therese thought it unwise to make too much of such things and to behave as though one had never seen anything of the kind before. After all, the Pomeranian estates with which she was familiar also had their parks, and so she said the best thing would be to follow their aunt's example and to gather their strength for what still lay ahead.

# 14

At half past eight the ladies made their appearance downstairs in the great hall, where a fire was burning although the air outside was almost summery. The general's widow greeted them warmly and at the same time with so much breeding in her manner that Therese was somewhat surprised. At Pyrmont her aunt had struck her as very middle-class, and that had been the cause of all their disagreements and little tiffs. And now she was so different. Was it the feeling of being on her own home ground here at Adamsdorf? Or was it simply that grief had ennobled her? Therese decided in favor of grief.

They did not spend long together over breakfast; only a few hours remained before the funeral, and the local nobility would probably appear a good deal earlier. Frau von Poggenpuhl asked whether she might see her brother-in-law once more; her request was refused because the coffin had already been nailed down. Manon and Therese expressed their regret, but actually they were relieved and consoled themselves with the phrase, "We will remember him as he was in happier times."

By ten o'clock the courtyard in front of the castle began to fill with villagers. The old, men and women alike, were solemn and much affected because they had loved and revered the general; but the young people regarded the occasion more or less in the nature of a fair; they giggled and whispered very unotherworldly remarks to one another. At eleven the coaches arrived, and half an hour later the two village clergymen, the Catholic as well as the Protestant; and at twelve the procession set off for the church, singing hymns as they went. The parson gave an address; and after him the old Catholic priest spoke in his private capacity "just to express his thanks for the fine sense of justice which had always distinguished the deceased." After that came the blessing, and then the coffin was lowered into the crypt. Therese was grieved to think that a Poggenpuhl should be fated to lie among the coffins of a strange family, and she expressed her sorrow by a severity of bearing which was noticed by all those present. Some of them approved, but others—members of the Silesian nobility—thought it ridiculous and whispered to one another, "Typical Pomeranian Junker pride." For the Silesians have no Junkers. Or at least no authentic ones.

Everyone, incidentally, was pleased with the ceremony, except for a church elder who could not get over the fact that "the ole Cath'lic" had spoken. If that kind of thing were allowed to take hold, they would soon be in trouble and simony would raise its ugly head. What he meant by this was never fully ascertained.

Refreshments were served immediately after the church service. There was no luncheon as such, and when the visitors had gone, the two old ladies, the general's widow and the major's widow, retired to their rooms. They needed rest and wanted to be alone. Sophie still had things to do in the household, and so Manon and Therese were left to themselves. They soon decided on a walk around the outer edge of the park, which was bordered by a little stream. It must have been about four o'clock; the sun was already sinking and shone through the tall Lombardy poplars. Not a breeze stirred, everything lay quiet; the only sounds to be heard were the hammering and clinking from a nearby smithy and, later, when they had almost reached the fields, the tinkle of a scythe being sharpened. Small white birchwood bridges crossed the stream, and every now and then the wooded path widened into little openings and embrasures with seats in them. The birds had stopped singing, but a squirrel ran across their path. Therese abandoned her critical mood and condescended to sprinkle her conversation with approving remarks about the Silesian nobility. "Everything here is richer," she said. "You can feel it; nobody thinks about saving money. With us everyone does, even people who can afford not to. Look at this seat—granite, and faced with sandstone. At home it would be made of wood."

Manon really agreed with this. But the chief form of conversation among the Poggenpuhl sisters consisted of one contradicting the other. And so she said, "You always overdo things, Therese. When we arrived there was nothing you didn't dislike, and now everything is beautiful and rich and superior to what we have. I can't agree. I much prefer the Tiergarten."

"How can you say such a thing, and all for the sake of contradicting! All right, the Tiergarten is not too bad but it's public, and anything public is always vulgar. And some of the things you see in the Tiergarten are positively cynical."

"Cynical?"

"Yes. You see statues and reliefs that are shamelessly cynical. I choose the expression deliberately. It's this predilection for the natural that modern art thinks it has a right to. I, on the other hand, believe that art should throw a veil. However, be that as it may, I don't want to discuss it. When I deliberately used the word 'cynical' just now, I was thinking more of the living pictures and scenes—of the people you come across there. On every bench there is a couple whose attitude is offensive. And when you finally feel like sitting down somewhere where there doesn't happen to be a couple, it's still impossible, because you never know who has been sitting there before. The Tiergarten especially is supposed to be full of dreadful people."

"I always sit where there are children playing."

"You shouldn't do that, Manon. You can't be sure even there— there least of all, sometimes. And anyway, the magic of the un-polluted is totally absent. Here I know the air I breathe is pure. Look how the water flows; at home it's all murky puddles."

Therese went on talking in this vein and was so far carried away as to speak with the highest esteem of their aunt. "Sophie did not exaggerate in her letters. A woman whose past has been totally eradicated. Not everyone can claim as much. Now, when I think of Mama. . ."

"You shouldn't speak ill of Mama. Mama is good and has had much to bear, and has borne it. Not everyone can claim to have done that either."

It was not until tea that they were all reunited. Manon talked about the guests, about various incidents, and finally about the address. The vicar had said a lot about the Resurrection, and the general's widow asked Sophie whether the Resurrection could not also be illustrated by some incident from the Old Testament. She would be glad to know that it could.

"Yes," said Sophie. "There is a story in the Old Testament which is thought to signify the Resurrection."

"And which is it?"

"It's when the whale spews up Jonah. You must admit it's full of significance. But I don't feel I could do it justice."

"Thank goodness," said Manon with a sudden attack of mischief.

"Don't say that, child," said her aunt. "It sounds funny to you. But what has been regarded with solemn reverence for centuries has always seemed to me something we should respect."

Manon blushed; then she rose and kissed her aunt's hand.

They retired early, assuring one another that they would all be down to breakfast next morning by seven at the latest. There were still a number of things to discuss. And they agreed that after all this time in semi-isolation, Sophie should accompany her family to Berlin, though only for a short stay. Sophie, said her aunt, was so good and wise and unassuming that her presence had become a necessity to her. Of course she must go and have a vacation in the city, but the sooner she returned the better she—her aunt—would be pleased. She decided that Sophie was to be back in Adamsdorf by the middle of November. There would probably be no more painting at that dark and foggy time of year, but that did not matter; if Sophie would only sit beside her looking into the fire and thinking of the dear departed, that would be better than any painting. As she said this, she reached for Sophie's hand, and they were all glad that such a warm relationship had grown up between these two. Even Therese was pleased; her family feeling was stronger than her personal pride, and she regarded the whole thing as a victory for the Poggenpuhl spirit—with which Sophie too was imbued, albeit in a manner different from the others, especially from Therese herself. Sophie had the loving, friendly, humble characteristics that dear Uncle, after all, had also possessed.

After these arrangements had been made, the girls retired to call on the vicar and his young wife, who was supposed to be a beauty— and was. Only the two old ladies who bore the name of Poggenpuhl without being Poggenpuhls remained behind on the veranda. The servant came to clear the breakfast table. "Wait awhile, Joseph," said the general's widow; and when they were alone once more they both looked across the center bed of the garden, and then across the ivy-covered wall to the place where the green copper roof of the church stood out among the other roofs in the village street. The thoughts of both went in the same direction: they thought of him who now lay in the silent crypt over there.

A few minutes went by without a word being spoken; then the general's widow took the major's widow by the hand and said: "Dear sister-in-law, I have to make something clear between us, a business matter; and I think you will agree with what I am about to propose."

"I am sure I shall. I think I can say that without knowing what it's about. I know only too well how kind you are."

"All right then, I won't beat about the bush. You know from Sophie—she confessed to me afterward that she had told you—how I am situated as regards the property. Adamsdorf is mine as long as I live, and then it reverts to my first husband's family. The fortune I brought him has been lost. You will know about that too. But I was able later to make good this loss, at least up to a point. Poggenpuhl paid for his little hobbies out of his pension, we lived economically, and so I am in the happy position—in spite of bad harvests—of having collected another modest private fortune. I am free to do as I like with that, and before you leave Adamsdorf I want you to know how I have decided to dispose of it. At the moment the sum itself does not amount to more than seventeen thousand talers—I still reckon in talers—twelve thousand of which are deposited in five percent shares with my banker in Breslau. From the first of October onward you will receive the quarterly interest on those, so that your annual income will increase by about six hundred talers. The capital is not redeemable. Only in the event of one of your daughters marrying, her share will be paid to her. If all three get married, you, sister-in-law, would not have much left, but you would then get the whole of the pension I have from the state; and I know how modestly you manage to arrange your life."

Frau von Poggenpuhl was so touched the she sat in silence looking straight ahead, while the general's widow continued, "Then of course there are your sons, and they are not to be forgotten. But that is a private matter, nothing to do with the other; they will have to be content with just one small outright gift each. I intend to send a thousand talers to Wendelin, who is a good manager and understands the value of money. Leo will get five hundred. He will blow it; he's a harum-scarum, but I don't mean that as a moral judgment. I like harum-scarums, as long as they preserve their decency and their convictions in spite of their way of life. As for my beloved Sophie, I shall make some special decisions about her later. That was what I wanted to tell you before you leave, my dear sister-in-law."

The sun's rays shone muted through the trees, which were still thick with leaves; but its full light fell on the center bed and on the borders along the veranda, where it made the few verbena and balsamine still flowering glow more intensely red or white. Pigeons rose from the farm buildings and flew high above the garden to the church steeple, where they circled before alighting on its copper helmet or on the ridge of the roof.

Frau von Poggenpuhl tried to kiss her sister-in-law's hand, but the latter embraced her and kissed her on the forehead.

"I am happier than you," said the general's widow.

"You are, indeed. To make others happy is the greatest happiness. It has not been my lot. But to know how to receive with gratitude is happiness too."

# 15

On the day the Poggenpuhls were expected back, not only Friederike but also the porter's family were in a state of
considerable excitement. In the case of the Nebelungs this was due
to a fortuitous circumstance: a Free Conservative privy councillor
on the second floor happened to be away, but his newspapers
continued to be delivered to the porter's apartment; and Nebelung,
who was both inquisitive and lazy (his wife had to make up for it by
working her fingers to the bone) studied them carefully or just
glanced through as the mood took him. Among these papers was
the *Post*, and on this particular day the morning edition carried a
mention of the death of Major General von Poggenpuhl, accompanied by the words, "See also Deaths." Nebelung immediately
pounced upon the deaths column, and, when he had found the
black-rimmed announcement, he read it carefully. A strange grin
spread across his face as he pushed the paper toward his fourteen-
year-old daughter Agnes, who was just having her afternoon coffee
with her two brothers. "There, Agnes," he said, "read that. The bit
with the thick black border." And Agnes, who was not only anemic
but also destined for the stage on account of her figure and her
passion for *The Maid of Orleans*, read out loud while the rest
listened:

Today our dear husband, brother-in-law, and uncle,
  *Major General (retired) Eberhard Pogge von Poggenpuhl*,
Knight of the Iron Cross (1st Class), Knight of the Order of

Albrecht the Bear, passed away, aged sixty-seven, at Schloss Adamsdorf, Silesia. No individual announcements will be sent by the sorrowing relatives:

Josephine Pogge von Poggenpuhl, née Bienengräber, widow of Freiherr von Leysewitz, widow

Albertine Pogge von Poggenpuhl, née Pütter, widow of Major von Poggenpuhl, sister-in-law

Wendelin Pogge von Poggenpuhl, First Lieutenant in the Trzebiatowski Grenadiers

Leo Pogge von Poggenpuhl, Second Lieutenant in the Trzebiatowski Grenadiers

Therese Pogge von Poggenpuhl

Sophie Pogge von Poggenpuhl

Manon Pogge von Poggenpuhl

Nieces
and
Nephews

Agnes's somewhat sallow complexion had turned quite red with the effort of getting out all these names—the only one she could not quite manage was the Polish name of the regiment. As she put down the paper, the old man said, with most obvious relish, "What a lot of Pogges.[1] I can positively hear them croaking." This joke was greeted with howls of gleeful applause by his sons, true Nebelungs both, but his daughter had expected quite another response to her dramatic rendering; she rose and left the room. As she passed her mother, who was sitting a little apart, she said, "*I* don't know, but Father is being so common again today." Her mother, a sickly and perpetually bad-tempered woman, corroborated this remark with several nods. But Nebelung himself called after his daughter as she disappeared through the door, "Don't be so impudent, toad; you're not on the stage yet."

In one sense Agnes had been unjust to her father. In the depths of his soul Nebelung was not completely unmoved by all these things; but being a true Berliner he had tried to joke away the impression made upon him by the enumeration of so many glorious names. On the other hand he was genuinely annoyed because "those paupers up there" were now being forced on his attention as being something very special. Ridiculous; all rubbish. All the same, even as he protested, he was willing to put a good face on it, and the occasion soon arose.

It was about half past four (the boys had just returned from school) when the quarrel took place between father and daughter; barely an hour later a cab loaded with luggage came up the Grossgörschenstrasse. The whole house was waiting. Like Friederike, the Nebelungs had planted themselves outside, albeit adopting very different attitudes and occupations. The two boys were leaning against the wall, half-curious and half-lolling because they did not want to compromise their status as free German citizens; Nebelung himself, a sort of fez on his forehead, was patrolling the sidewalk while Agnes stood slender and upright in the open doorway as though she were impersonating Mondecar or some other lady of the Spanish court. When the major's widow walked past her, she dropped a well-rehearsed court curtsy, which she repeated even more emphatically when Therese appeared a moment later. For Therese was the only member of the family still wearing the long mourning veil: together with her funereal bearing it had already earned her a measure of homage on the journey. She had been taken for the young widow of an officer who had died in a Silesian spa.

The cab was still standing by the pavement, and Manon and Sophie were arguing with the driver—a sly-looking man—about carrying up the luggage. He couldn't leave his horse, he kept saying, otherwise he would be fined. At this awkward movement, Nebelung, usually so aloof, approached the young ladies, lifted his fez with an obliging air, and declared himself willing to carry the big trunk up to the flat. "Oh, Herr Nebelung . . ." said Sophie. But he had already grasped the trunk and skillfully hoisted it onto his shoulder; he was not deflected by the car driver, who, his diplomatic maneuver having miscarried, now sneered after him, "Look out, or you'll do yourself an injury!"

But no injury befell him, because the trunk, though large, was not heavy, and Nebelung seemed scarcely out of breath when he reached the top of the stairs. Friederike relieved him of the trunk, and at the same moment Sophie said, "Please, Herr Nebelung, . . . I want to thank you." And when he returned to his lodge, Nebelung threw a bright new mark piece on the table and said, "There, Mother. We must put that in the money box. Pogge von Poggenpuhl. . . . And from little Sophie too. . . . Virgin money. That breeds."

Agnes caught only the last words, and she turned contemptuously aside.

Upstairs half a sheet of paper with the word *Welcome* in Friederike's own hand hung over the door. Perhaps because she was uncertain of her spelling, or possibly from economy, the letters were barely filled in with ink and consisted only of double lines. The flower bowl under the Sohr major held red and white asters from the market. Some of them had been intended for the Hochkirch major: Friederike was going to stick them under the frame. But she abandoned the idea with the observation, "I know that one. Just touch him and he falls down."

"Well, you're still alive," said the major's widow as Friederike dutifully took her coat. "Are you sure you haven't been stinting too much? You mustn't do that. I know you always boil up the old coffee grounds. You'll never get fat like that."

"Oh, I'll get fat all right, ma'am."

"Well, I hope it's true. But now bring us some coffee. The cups are out already, I see. I must say, I'm half-frozen. There was a lady who kept opening all the windows."

"Yes, Mama, that's what everyone does nowadays."

"I know it's what everyone does. And it may be a good idea. But not for everyone. When you suffer from rheumatism . . ."

Meanwhile Sophie too had made herself comfortable. She threw herself into the corner of the sofa with a certain relish, and studied first the room and then all the little objects scattered about that she had held in her hands so many times.

"Come, Mama, you must sit beside me. Or I'll move up a bit— this is your corner. Goodness, when I look at it all! It's really very nice here in your apartment."

"You might say 'in our apartment,' " said Therese.

"Of course, of course. Of course I belong to you and I always shall. But it's been such a long time. Nine months or very nearly. And then I'm supposed to be going back."

"And do you want to? Do you really want to?"

"Of course. And it's settled. And even if it weren't settled, I like being at Adamsdorf and I like being with Aunt."

"Who wouldn't?" said Therese. "The park and the crypt where our uncle the general now sleeps. Everyone must feel the draw of that. And that woman has much to forgive me; I thought her enslaved to her middle-class origins, but she has quite the manners of society. It's a pity that such metamorphoses are so rare."

Sophie and Manon glanced at their sister with the obvious purpose of diverting her from this delicate topic. But though they meant well, it was quite unnecessary, for their mother felt no bitterness on the subject. She merely smiled sadly with the quiet assurance that comes from having lived and from knowing that one has fought life's battles honestly through to the end. "Ah, my dear distinguished daughter," she said, "there you go again."

"I didn't mean to hurt you, Mama."

"I know. And I'm not hurt. Once I had my self-esteem too and my own pride, but life has eroded all that and worn me down. . . . What you said about Aunt—yes, there you were right. An excellent woman, and—if that's how you want it—a *noble* woman too. I've always known that, and since this last visit I know it even better. But—and it's hard that I should have to keep proclaiming it to my own daughter, who ought to realize it without any assurance from me—I too could have turned out like her if life had given me the opportunity; but it didn't. To live in a castle and to be able to make hundreds of people happy—and then to be able to punish them by withholding their happiness—that's a different school of life from having to watch Herr Nebelung's expression and to beg favors from him. All I have been taught is care and want. That has been *my* school. It hasn't made me very distinguished, but it has taught me humility. God forgive me if what I say is wrong, but real, genuine humility is a virtue that need not be ashamed of itself even among the nobility."

Sophie slid softly from the sofa to her knees and covered the old lady's hands with tears and kisses. "You have much to answer for, Therese," said Manon and went to stand by the window.

But Therese herself calmly cast an eye over the "gallery of ancestors" above the sofa, and that eye seemed to say, "You are witnesses that I said no more than I had a right to say." But then another, better feeling overcame her, and that too she put into words. "Forgive me, Mama," she said, "perhaps I was wrong."

It was not in the nature of the family to allow such a scene to disturb their good humor for long. The mother had learned to bear harder trials and was always ready to pardon and give way, whereas Therese, although fundamentally she persisted in her views, was not really obstinate and felt an urge to mitigate what she had said. A conversation with Manon seemed the best way to do that. So she took her sister's hand and led her back from the window to the coffee table. She drew her down beside her on a footstool and said, "Many things will have to change for us now—and for you too. You my dear little scamp, are farthest from the right path. What do you think about your future now?"

"Future?. . . Oh, you mean marriage?"

"Yes, that too, perhaps. But first of all I mean the company you keep, the society you move in. What do you think about that?"

"Well—exactly as before. I shall keep the company I've always kept."

"You ought to think it over all the same."

"Think it over? I ask you . . . I'd like to see old Bartenstein's face if I suddenly remembered my ancient lineage just because I've got an income of two hundred talers. If it was more he might forgive me. But . . ."

"So everything is to go on as before?"

"Yes. And as for marriage! We mustn't start having silly ideas like that; we shall still be poor girls. Mama will eat better and Leo won't have to go to the equator. Because I imagine he'll be able to pay his debts now, without the Blumenthals and even without Flora. But Flora herself will still be my friend. That's what *I* want. And so we shall live happily ever after until Wendelin and Leo have really got somewhere and we have a few more celebrities in the family like the Sohr and Hochkirch majors."

"You forget the third—your father," said the major's widow, who felt the Poggenpuhl spirit rising in her for the first time at this omission.

"Yes, my father—I'd forgotten about him. Funny, fathers are nearly always forgotten. I must talk to Flora about it. She was saying something of the sort the other day."

*Translated by Gabriele Annan*

# Translator's Notes to
# Delusions, Confusions

In translating a work such as *Delusions, Confusions,* a variety of considerations had to be kept in mind. Steering a middle course between slavish fidelity on one side and a translation that re-creates the work almost completely, on the other, even to the point of embellishing beyond the implications of the source, is not always easy. Similarly, the attempt to find the right tone, the literary melos of the writer, is all the more vital in the case of Theodor Fontane inasmuch as we are dealing with an author famous in his native land for the casual and often lightly skeptical voice with which events are narrated. Moreover, Fontane wrote in an age and culture whose values are to a great extent contrary to our own. The sentimentality and melodramatic posing of his era make much of its literature unpalatable today. Yet, one of the most winning facets of Fontane's genius was his ability to portray the moral, social, and historical conflicts of the era without sentimentalizing them. Nevertheless no reader will forget that this author was very much a child of the declining nineteenth century, the era of Bismarck and Nietzsche, and also of Wagner and Wilhelm II.

By and large, an effort has been made to preserve the ebb and flow of the German original wherever possible without doing injury to the demands of English. German sentence structure permits the accumulation of subordinate clauses, however, which often defies the syntactical logic of English. For this reason overly complex sentences have sometimes been divided and German paragraphs, sometimes several pages long, have been broken for the English reader at what seemed to be appropriate places. Thus the opening of chapter 2, which consists of a single paragraph describing the Dörr's living quarters, its history, the background of the Dörr's marriage, his living arrangement, as well as comments on Dörr's personality and physical appearance, is rendered in six English paragraphs devoted to each of these topics.

Far more complex than organizational aspects in attempting a translation of *Delusions, Confusions* were questions of language level and dialect.

Although the writers of the naturalist generation in the 1880s admired Theodor Fontane and considered him one of their own, Fontane was no naturalist. His use of realistic description and dialect in no way approaches the naturalist norm of grimly scientific exactitude in rendering speech as a means of showing the baleful effect of heredity and environment on the individual. For the older writer, who looked askance at dogmatism of any sort, dialect, was primarily a means of characterization, and especially in this novel, of social delineation. Moreover, in a letter concerning *Delusions, Confusions* of February 1888, Fontane argued that he was not comfortable in attempting to reproduce genuine Berlin dialect in his novel. "Everything," he asserted, "had such a dead or clumsy effect that in many cases I reinstated my incorrect forms. They were still always better than what was 'authentic.'. . . Here too one just has to stick with a suggestion of things, according to the well-known children's caption, 'This is supposed to be a tree.' "

In following this principle, Fontane limited his use of dialect to relatively rudimentary forms connoting the argot of Berlin without actually deviating significantly from standard German. Employing relatively modest means he was able to suggest *Berlinisch* to his readers and with it the images and types associated with that city, especially its lower classes.

In English, of course, the matter is not so simple; no speech can convey the particular associations of the Prussian capital and any attempt to render Fontane's forms with a British or American metropolitan dialect would fail. Yet, because of its significance in the social structure of the novel, some effort had to be made to present class characterization through language. In keeping with Fontane's own tenet, "This is supposed to be a tree," wherever dialect is employed in the original, a neutral but substandard English, characteristic of uneducated classes, is used in the translation. In some cases this occurs to a greater extent than in the German text; it is obviously impossible to establish perfect balance between both languages and it is English tone that must be the final determinant.

Any translation is, of course, an effort to mediate between two languages and their cultures. As with every compromise, complete justice can never be done to the merits of either side. Moreover in a book as rich as this, of which its author despaired that readers would have "desire or ability to take note of the hundred or . . . thousand nuances imparted to this especially beloved work," one can scarcely presume that a rendering in another language, no matter how carefully wrought, will do them justice either. No doubt inadequacies of every magnitude can be discovered throughout. Here too one can only refer to the author for justification. Continuing in his letter of February 1888, Fontane defended the inconsistencies of his novel, asserting, "I am convinced that something erroneous is to be found on every page.

And yet I honestly strove to describe real life. It just doesn't work out that easily. One simply has to be satisfied if at least the total impression is, 'Yes, that's life.' " In the case of a translation one must more or less hope for the same thing.

This translation and notes are based upon Theodor Fontane, *Romane und Erzählungen,* Vol. 5, *Irrungen, Wirrungen,* edited by Jürgen Jahn (Berlin, Aufbau Verlag, 1984). Also consulted were editions of *Irrungen, Wirrungen* edited by Dirk Mende (Munich, Goldmann Verlag, 1983) and G. W. Field (New York, St. Martin's Press, 1967).

The translation of the title is drawn from Henry Garland, *The Berlin Novels of Theodor Fontane* (Oxford, Clarendon Press, 1980).

W. L. Z.

# Notes

## Chapter One

1. The location specified by Fontane was in the 1870s on the outskirts of the city. Today it marks the very heart of West Berlin. Except where specifically stated, all sites in the novel are parts of greater Berlin.

2. Civil Court: A veiled reference to the institution of civil marriage that was introduced in the Reich in 1875 under vehement protest by representatives of the Catholic Church during the famous anti-Catholic *Kulturkampf.*

## Chapter Two

1. *Berliner Weiße:* A wheat beer that is a specialty in Berlin. It is drunk in large wide-mouthed goblets with a *Schuß* of raspberry or wintergreen flavoring.

*Gilka:* a liqueur made from caraway seeds.

2. *Bosdorfer:* An apple that wrinkles considerably but that retains its quality in storage for a long period.

## Chapter Three

1. Gendarmenmarkt: One of old Berlin's most famous and imposing squares.

## Chapter Four

1. Botho refers to the poem *Die alte Waschfrau (The Old Washerwoman)* by the romantic poet Adelbert von Chamisso (1781–1838).

2. Saxon Switzerland *(die Sächsische Schweiz):* a popular resort area not far from Dresden, containing the fortress Königstein and a famous overlook of the Elbe, the Bastei.

3. *Großer Garten, Zwinger, Grünes Gewölbe:* Sights of Dresden, one of the most popular cultural centers of Germany before its destruction during the Second World War. The *Großer Garten,* originally laid out as a preserve for peacocks in the latter part of the seventeenth century, was by the time of the story a public nature preserve. The *Zwinger,* considered one of the masterworks of German baroque architecture, and one of Dresden's most famous sights, was a palace built in 1701. In 1874 a gallery of famous paintings and artifacts was installed there. In the Royal Castle, where the *Grünes Gewölbe* (the Green Vaulted Chamber) was located, a collection of handworker's treasures of the sort mentioned by Botho was to be found.

## Chapter Five

1. Slanderers' Boulevard: The main promenade of the Zoological Garden, so named because onlookers sitting on the benches took stock of passersby.

## Chapter Six

1. Brandenburg Gate: Monumental arch built by Friedrich Wilhelm II between 1789–93. Today, standing just inside the Berlin Wall, it is the symbol of the divided city.

Tiergarten: A large park, formerly a royal hunting preserve, stretching west of the Brandenburg Gate.

## Chapter Seven

1. Unter den Linden: Berlin's most famous boulevard, extending from the Brandenburg Gate eastwards towards the palace and the center of Imperial Berlin.

2. Neumark blood: The March (German, *Mark*) refers essentially to the province of Brandenburg. The *Neumark* is the area east of the Oder River.

*Mensch:* A pun based on the names of these villages that rhyme with the word *Mensch,* meaning *human being.*

3. Dobeneck: Freiherr Ferdinand Dobeneck (1791–1867), Prussian officer who rose to the rank of lieutenant general and who served in the Wars of Liberation (1813–15).

4. *Rittmeister:* Commander of a cavalry troop equal to the rank of captain.

5. Manteuffel: Edwin Hans Karl Freiherr von Manteuffel (1809–85), Prussian field marshal and reorganizer of the army.

6. Halberstadt Cuirassier: Bismarck, although not in active service, was fond of wearing the blue uniform with yellow trim of the Halberstadt Cuirassiers. Von Osten takes the position of many conservative members of the Prussian landed gentry who resented Bismarck's rapid ascent to power and his high-handed dealings with members of the aristocracy, once his power base had been secured through victory in the Franco-Prussian War (1870). The bloody final assault on St. Privat (18 August 1870) cut off the French retreat and led to their encirclement at the decisive Battle of Sedan (1 September 1870).

7. Dispatches: The famous Ems Telegram that led to the Franco-Prussian War. The French ambassador, Benedetti, had requested the assurance of King William of Prussia, who was taking the waters at Ems, that Prussia would never again support the candidacy of Prince Leopold of Hohenzollern for the throne of Spain. The king relayed the note to Berlin in a telegram from Ems. Bismarck, then Prussian chancellor, edited the text for publication. By making certain omissions without, however, altering the meaning, he made the French demand and the Prussian refusal appear more provocative than they were, thereby exacerbating the strain between both countries. Once the document was made public, both nations felt themselves affronted and Bismarck's goal was achieved; the French declared war, leading the majority of German states to unite with Prussia in defense of German honor. The outcome was the defeat of the French Second Empire and the establishment of the German Empire under the domination of Prussia. With Bismarck as Imperial Chancellor, King William of Prussia was exalted to the rank of William I, German Emperor.

8. Fehrbellin, Leuthen, Blücher, Yorck: all famous names of Prussian military history. At Fehrbellin, not far from Berlin, the Great Elector won a significant battle over the Swedes in 1675. Frederick the Great, Prussia's most famous king, defeated the Austrians in 1757 at Leuthen. Blücher and Yorck played major roles leading to the defeat of Napoleon during the Wars of Liberation (1813). Blücher also commanded the Prussian forces whose appearance late in the day turned the tide at Waterloo.

9. The *Kreuzzeitung:* named after its symbol, the Iron Cross, was the leading conservative newspaper in Prussia.

10. Von Osten's tirade refers to the celebrated case of Count Harry von Arnim, Prussian ambassador in Paris, who was recalled by Bismarck in 1874 and indicted for the presumed theft of official documents. He fled to Switzerland and from there published documents in the press against Bismarck. He was condemned in absentia for high treason for using such

material in a foreign country. His brother-in-law, Count Friedrich Adolph von Arnim-Boitzenburg, governor of the Prussian province of Silesia, and leader of the conservative opposition to Bismarck, also resigned his office as a result of the affair.

## Chapter Eight

1. Gichtelians: disciples of Johann George Gichtel (1638–1710), whose religious teachings espoused purity and perfection of the soul even to the point of living according to the commandmant of absolute chastity.

2. Moltke: Helmuth Karl Bernhard Count von Moltke (1800–91), chief of staff of the Prussian and later Imperial German Army.

3. Humboldt: Either Alexander von Humboldt (1769–1859), famous naturalist, explorer, and author of numerous books on natural science, or his brother, Wilhelm von Humboldt (1767–1835), famous diplomat, scholar, and educator, whose reorganization of the Prussian school system became the model for most modern universities.

Ranke: Leopold von Ranke (1795–1886), one of the most significant German historians of the nineteenth century and founder of the modern school of historical study.

4. Prince Pückler: Hermann Ludwig Heinrich, Prince of Pückler-Muskau (1785–1871), a famous German world traveler and writer, who was also the designer of parks.

5. Lady in White, Castle Avenel: allusions to the then-popular opera *La Dame blanche* by François-Adrien Boieldieu (1775–1834), based on Sir Walter Scott's novel *The Monastery,* in which the stepdaughter of the castellan, dressed as the ghostly "Lady in White," saves the count's properties for him.

## Chapter Nine

1. *Vielliebchen:* A custom originating in France, according to which lovers ate either from an almond with two kernels or twin fruits. Whoever surprised the other next day with the greeting *"Guten Morgen, Vielliebchen"* had the right to demand a present, usually a kiss. The implication is that Botho would spend the night with Lene.

2. Morning's glow: The German song, *"Reiters Morgenlied"* *(Cavalryman's Morning Song")* by Wilhelm Hauff (1802–27), which includes the lines, "Yesterday, still on my proud steed, / Today, shot through the breast, I bleed, / Tomorrow in the cool, cool grave."

3. Lene's first choice is the third stanza of the famous folk song, *Muβ i denn, muβ i denn,"* which roughly translates as follows: "In a year, in a

year, when the wine is harvested, / I'll return, my dear, to you. / In a year my time is over, / My life is mine and yours, / If then I'm still your sweetheart, / Our marriage will take place." The reference to a year's time away from the beloved, is obviously to military service. *"If You Remember"* was a sentimental popular song derived from the popular operetta, *Der alte Feldherr (The Old General)* by Karl von Holtei (1798–1880).

### Chapter Eleven

1. Hankel's Depot: in German, *Hankels Ablage,* a landing and excursion spot on the Spree, some six miles east of Berlin. In May of 1884 Fontane spent some time there and wrote eight chapters of this novel.

### Chapter Twelve

1. Old Fritz: King Frederick II (1712–86), Frederick the Great, Prussia's most famous monarch. His father, Frederick William I (1688–1740), the "Soldier King," created the efficient Prussian Army, with which Frederick II later established Prussia as one of the leading European powers in the latter half of the eighteenth century.

2. Heidelberg Keg: A gigantic wine barrel that still can be seen in the cellar of Heidelberg Castle, capable of holding 56,091 gallons of wine.

3. Schwedt Dragoons, Fürstenwald Uhlans, Potsdam Hussars: Cavalry regiments of the Prussian Army.

4. *Washington Crossing the Delaware:* an engraving after the famous painting by the German-American painter Emanuel Leutze (1816–68).

*The Last Hour at Trafalgar,* by the American-English painter Benjamin West (1738–1820), depicts the death of Admiral Nelson on the deck of the flagship *Victory* in the famous battle against Napoleon's fleet in 1811. Significantly, both paintings depict turning points in great battles.

### Chapter Thirteen

1. Queen Isabeau, Mistress Joan, Mistress Margot: The names applied to the questionable "ladies," are drawn from Schiller's drama *Die Jungfrau von Orleans (The Maid of Orleans)*. Joan and Margot are the daughters of Thibaut d'Arc. Queen Isabeau is the mother of the French Dauphin.

2. Agnes Sorel: In Schiller's play the mistress of the Dauphin Charles.

### Chapter Fourteen

1. Sibylline Books: According to Roman legend, the Sibyl of Cumae offered to sell King Tarquin Priscus nine books of oracles. Finding the price

too high, the king refused. The Sibyl then burned three of the books and doubled the price. Once again the king refused, whereupon the Sibyl again burned three of the books and again doubled the price. The king then bought the books.

2. Daughter of the Regiment: Botho ironically refers to Gaetano Donizetti's comic opera, *La Fille du régiment* (1840), in which the heroine, a canteen girl, is dressed as he imagines Lene.

3. Ludwig von Hinckeldey: Chief of Police in Berlin during the reactionary period following the unsuccessful Revolution of 1848. Because of his harsh and uncompromising measures in the pursuit of public order, Hinckeldey fell afoul of his aristocratic peers. When he attempted to close an exclusive gambling club, he was challenged to a duel by one of its members, Hans von Rochow. Although dueling was forbidden by that time and it was his duty as police superintendent to uphold the law, Hinckeldey's sense of class honor compelled him to accept the challenge. He was shot to death on the Jungfernheide. Von Rochow was pardoned by the king.

## Chapter Sixteen

1. *Monsieur Herkules:* A popular farce of the day by Georg Belly (1836–75).

Wilhelm Knaack (1824–94): a well-known Viennese comedian.

*Bacchus on the He Goat, The Dog Scratching Himself:* artifacts contained in the *Green Chamber* of the Royal Palace at Dresden.

Peter Vischer: a Nuremburg sculptor of the fifteenth century.

## Chapter Eighteen

1. Schlangenbad: Schlangenbad and Schwalbach are two mineral spas in the Taunus Mountains of Western Germany, considered especially useful in the treatment of gynecological problems.

2. The German word *Schlange* means serpent or viper.

3. In the Prussian army the so-called heavy cavalry including the cuirassiers of which Botho is a member, enjoyed a higher standing than the "lighter" cavalry, which included hussars. The difference was based upon the type and size of their horses as well as their arms.

## Chapter Twenty

1. The original offers an exaggerated rendering of Viennese dialect, obviously to suggest Käthe's snobbish sense of superiority at what she considers the bumpkinish speech of her traveling companion.

Like English, German forms the comparative of most adjectives and adverbs by adding -er.

2. The Kingdom of Hanover was annexed to Prussia by Bismarck in 1866. As can be seen by Käthe's comments, this did not occur with the enthusiastic support of much of the local population. The term *Guelphic* refers to the medieval controversy between the Guelphs and the Ghibellines concerning the domination of the pope or the Holy Roman Emperor over German affairs. Supporters of the House of Hanover, historically a Guelph dynasty, maintained their claim to the throne of Hanover until 1884 and formed an anti-Prussian opposition.

3. Oppenheims: A wealthy Jewish banking firm that, similar to the Rothschilds, acquired dominance in European finance in the nineteenth century.

### Chapter Twenty-one

1. Silesia: An eastern province conquered for Prussia by Frederick the Great. Since the Second World War, part of Poland.

2. Luck and glass: German saying, *Glück und Glas, wie leicht bricht das:* "Luck and glass, how easily smashed."

### Chapter Twenty-three

1. Vandals: Botho pokes fun at the German university fraternities, often little more than patriotic beer-drinking societies named after Germanic tribes or mythological figures. Such fraternities often retained a hold on their members, who frequently participated in reunions. Even obituaries bore the insignia of the 'corps' to which the deceased belonged. *Hofbräu* and *Spatenbräu* are popular Munich beers. The latter implies a pun as well, since the German word *Spaten* means spade, with obvious allusions to the grave.

### Chapter Twenty-four

1. Beer garden: According to a letter by Fontane, the reference is to a beer garden whose owner's name was Bubenritz. The Berliners, known for their mocking and often scatological humor, colloquially altered the sound *b* to *p* when pronouncing the name. The vowel *u* in the name would be the equivalent of a long *o* in English, as in *boot,* and the effect would be the same in both languages. The second syllable suggests rip or hole.

### Chapter Twenty-five

1. Königgrätz: The battle in which Prussia defeated Austria on 3 July 1866, establishing Prussia as the dominant German-speaking power in nineteenth-century Europe.

2. Seven Years War (1756–63): Frederick the Great's victory against all odds in the war against the combined powers of Austria, France, Russia, and Sweden, thrust Prussia into the ranks of the great powers, leading to its geographical and political expansion.

3. The mausoleum: Located in the park of the Charlottenburg Palace, the burial place of a number of Hohenzollerns, including Frederick William III and Queen Louise. Subsequent to the action of the novel, it became the burial place of Emperor Wilhelm I and Empress Augusta.

4. General von Bischofswerder (1741–1803): A member of the Rosicrucians and a mystic, who had an influence on King Frederick William II of Prussia due to his occult inclinations.

5. Queen Louise (1776–1810): Wife of Frederick William III of Prussia, who, despite the vacillation of her husband, furthered many of the reforms of the Freiherr vom Stein, Gneisenau, and Scharnhorst, which led to the rebirth of Prussia and contributed to its role in the defeat of Napoleon.

6. Tree frog: Such animals were kept in glass jars with a small ladder and were supposed to ascend or descend according to the weather.

### Chapter Twenty-six

1. Madame Pompadour (1721–64): Mistress of Louis XV of France, after whom a type of ladies' evening bag was named.

2. *Réticules, Ridicules:* The *reticule* was a small net bag whose name in folk etymology was altered to *ridicules*.

# Translator's Notes to
## *The Poggenpuhl Family*

Germans, however well-born or educated, speak with a regional accent. Sometimes it is so slight as to be hardly detectable, and it gets broader as you go down the social scale until in some parts of the country the local dialect is almost a separate language. Educated persons speaking to uneducated ones often use a broader accent and more dialect words than they would when speaking to their equals. Fontane was brilliant at rendering these nuances, and much of the charm of his novels lies in the way he does it. But there seems to be no way of producing English equivalents that do not sound phony, so I have reluctantly abandoned the attempt to do so. My editor has also persuaded me not to use the German forms of address such as "Herr General" or "Gnädige Frau" (gracious lady), which punctuate the text, but either to leave them out or to replace them with more general expressions such as "sir" or "ma'am."

G. A.

# Notes

### Chapter Two

1. Gerson Bleichröder (1822–79) was a Jewish banker generally re-

garded as the richest man in Berlin. He was banker and financial adviser to Bismarck.

### Chapter Three

1. A popular amusement place.
2. "Canoness" is the nearest English word for *Stiftsdame*. A *Stift* is a foundation for unmarried daughters of the Protestant aristocracy. It retains the structure of a pre-Reformation convent, but the inhabitants are not bound by vows.

### Chapter Four

1. *Schloss* is untranslatable: It can mean a castle, but more often, as here, it means an unfortified building of any size between a large country house and a palace.

### Chapter Six

1. Litfass columns are still found in Berlin. Their purpose is to carry advertising, and they are pasted all over with public notices, theater programs, and advertisements.
2. A public entertainment palace founded in 1844 by Joseph Kroll. It contained a theater and concert hall.
3. Patriotic play by Ernst von Wildenbruch (1845–1909).
4. Officers received their discharge from the War Office in blue envelopes.

### Chapter Eight

1. Serious offenders in the army were put into punishment cells with nothing to sit or lie on and sharp slates nailed all over the floor.
2. Quotation from Schiller's poem *"Hoffnung"* ("Hope").

### Chapter Ten

1. Medieval family of Polish rulers.
2. Unusual, affectionate diminutive of Sophie. It is pronounced exactly like "Viehchen," which would mean "little animal."

### Chapter Eleven

1. Home for delinquent girls.
2. Ernst von Drysander was the court preacher.

### Chapter Twelve

1. After the Napoleonic wars the first regiment of Prussian Grenadiers was named after Czar Alexander I.

### Chapter Fifteen

1. Pogge is a dialect word for "frog."

# ACKNOWLEDGMENTS

Every reasonable effort has been made to locate the owners of rights to previously published translations printed here. We gratefully acknowledge permission to reprint the following material:

*The Poggenpuhl Family* (including Translator's Notes), translated by Gabriele Annan, from Theodor Fontane, *The Woman Taken in Adultery* and *The Poggenpuhl Family,* with an Introduction by Erich Heller. Reprinted by kind permission of The University of Chicago Press: Chicago and London, 1979. Copyright © 1979 by the Chicago University Press.

# THE GERMAN LIBRARY
## in 100 Volumes

Gottfried von Strassburg
*Tristan and Isolde*
Edited and Revised by Francis G. Gentry
Foreword by C. Stephen Jaeger

*German Medieval Tales*
Edited by Francis G. Gentry
Foreword by Thomas Berger

*German Humanism and Reformation*
Edited by Reinhard P. Becker
Foreword by Roland Bainton

Immanuel Kant
*Philosophical Writings*
Edited by Ernst Behler
Foreword by René Wellek

Friederich Schiller
*Plays: Intrigue and Love* and *Don Carlos*
Edited by Walter Hinderer
Foreword by Gordon Craig

*German Romantic Criticism*
Edited by A. Leslie Willson
Foreword by Ernst Behler

Heinrich von Kleist
*Plays*
Edited by Walter Hinderer
Foreword by E. L. Doctorow

E.T.A. Hoffman
*Tales*
Edited by Victor Lange

*German Literary Fairy Tales*
Edited by Frank G. Ryder and Robert M. Browning
Introduction by Gordon Birrell
Foreword by John Gardiner

Heinrich Heine
*Poetry and Prose*
Edited by Jost Hermand and Robert C. Holub
Foreword by Alfred Kazin

Heinrich von Kleist and Jean Paul
*German Romantic Novellas*
Edited by Frank G. Ryder and Robert M. Browning
Foreword by John Simon

*German Poetry from 1750 to 1900*
Edited by Robert M. Browning
Foreword by Michael Hamburger

Gottfried Keller
*Stories*
Edited by Frank G. Ryder
Foreword by Max Frisch

Wilhelm Raabe
*Novels*
Edited by Volkmar Sander
Foreword by Joel Agee

Theodor Fontane
*Short Novels and Other Writings*
Edited by Peter Demetz
Foreword by Peter Gay

Wilhelm Busch and Others
*German Satirical Writings*
Edited by Deiter P. Lotze and Volkmar Sander
Foreword by John Simon

*Writings of German Composers*
Edited by Jost Hermand and James Steakley

Arthur Schnitzler
*Plays and Stories*
Edited by Egon Schwarz
Foreword by Stanley Elkin

Rainer Maria Rilke
*Prose and Poetry*
Edited by Egon Schwarz
Foreword by Howard Nemerov

*Essays on German Theater*
Edited by Margaret Herzfeld-Sander
Foreword by Martin Esslin

Friedrich Dürrenmatt
*Plays and Essays*
Edited by Volkmar Sander
Foreword by Martin Esslin

Hans Magnus Enzensberger
*Critical Essays*
Edited by Reinhold Grimm and Bruce Armstrong
Foreword by John Simon

Georg Büchner
*Complete Works and Letters*
Edited by Walter Hinderer and Henry J. Schmidt

Gottfried Benn
*Prose, Essays, Poems*
Edited by Volkmar Sander
Foreword by E. B. Ashton
Introduction by Reinhard Paul Becker

*German Essays on Art History*
Edited by Gert Schiff

*German Novellas of Realism I and II*
Edited by Jeffrey L. Sammons

Max Frisch
*Novels, Plays, Essays*
Edited by Rolf Kieser
Foreword by Peter Demetz